CW00690353

Hunters over Arabia

Hunters over Arabia

Hawker Hunter Operations in the Middle East

Ray Deacon

Pen & Sword
AVIATION

First published in Great Britain in 2019 by
PEN & SWORD AVIATION
An imprint of
Pen & Sword Books Ltd
Yorkshire - Philadelphia

ISBN 978 1 52672 150 1

Printed and bound in India by Replika Press Pvt. Ltd.
Typeset in Ehrhardt MT Std 11.5/14 by
Aura Technology and Software Services, India

Pen & Sword Books Ltd incorporates the imprints of
Pen & Sword Aviation, Pen & Sword Maritime, Pen & Sword Military,
Wharncliffe Local History, Pen & Sword Select,
Pen & Sword Military Classics and Leo Cooper.

For a complete list of Pen & Sword titles please contact
Pen & Sword Books Limited
47 Church Street, Barnsley, South Yorkshire, S70 2AS, England
E-Mail: enquiries@pen-and-sword.co.uk * Website: www.pen-and-sword.co.uk

Or

PEN AND SWORD BOOKS
1950 Lawrence Rd, Havertown, PA 19083, USA
e-mail: Uspen-and-sword@casematepublishers.com
website: www.penandswordbooks.com

Contents

This book is dedicated to the servicemen and women from all three armed services who served in the Middle East and especially to those who never returned.

Foreword: Group Captain John Jennings DFC

When Colonel Nasser came to power in Egypt in 1954 at the age of 34, he stated that he would do everything in his power to drive the British out of Arabia. Following the Suez Crisis he achieved his aim in respect of Egypt and turned his attention to the wider Arab world. The airwaves were soon filled with anti-British rhetoric and, in the age of the transistor radio, reached the furthest corners of the region. Tribal members were encouraged to rise against those rulers who had friendly or had treaty associations with the British. In the particular case of the Yemen, which had a common border with the Aden Protectorates, Egyptian influence and supply of arms led to the overthrow of the ruling family followed by the presence in 1962 of Egyptian military land and air elements stationed within the country. The direct threat to Aden was starkly apparent.

The tribes on the Aden Protectorate side of the border, which was loosely embraced by the term Radfan, had resorted to banditry and hostage-taking for centuries. Indeed they considered this as their birthright and, when not involved in disputes with each other, resorted to their primary banditry mode. They were easily persuaded by offers of modern rifles and other weapons to take on the Protectorate forces.

The British had recognised the growing threat and had steadily improved the facilities, infrastructure and military units in Aden and, by April 1963, RAF Khormaksar hosted nine squadrons and several flights. It was described as the largest air base in the RAF.

Three of those squadrons were composed of Hunter FGA.Mk.9 fighter ground attack aircraft and they were supported by a reconnaissance flight of Hunter FR.Mk.10s. In short, a very potent force indeed. It is an accepted fact that vehicles of any kind that move at speed in close proximity to the ground will suffer accidents and although the Hunter was a very fine aircraft it suffered mishaps and losses. These are recorded in the appendices and contain the names of twelve fine young men who flew their last flights in this model.

The detail contained in this book is quite remarkable and reflects great credit to the author. A selection of operational missions are listed together with the names of the pilots, identity numbers of the aircraft and, where appropriate, the success or otherwise of the mission. I have no doubt that this book will be a point of reference for future historians researching RAF activity in the years in question.

OC TacWing, Wg Cdr John Jennings (with left foot on his helmet), standing alongside OC 208 Squadron, Sqn Ldr Gordon Lewis and the pilots who flew various formations at a number of locations during the celebrations marking the independence of Zanzibar and Kenya in December 1963.

The photograph was taken at Embakasi Airport and the remaining seven pilots were; (seated on the wing) l to r; Flt Lt A Mumford, Fg Off 'Pud' Slade, Flt Lt Jerry Lee, Flt Lt Dickie Dicken, Fg Off Tim Webb, plus Flt Lt Les Dawson (astride the drop tank) and Fg Off Dave Pack (John Jennings).

Preface

Designed specifically for the role of defending the skies above United Kingdom, the story of the Hawker Hunter, its development, service history and life after retirement has been extensively explored by various authors over the years and it is not the intention of this narrative to replicate in any great detail information that currently exists in the public domain. Up until now, however, very little has been produced on the period in which the Hunter operated with great distinction over the desert plains and high mountains that proliferate in the South Arabian landscape. For it was here in this hot, dusty, hostile environment that this beautifully engineered aircraft established its credentials as a potent ground-attack and reconnaissance fighter. A summary of the Hunter's evolution from the role of air defence fighter to one of counter-insurgency is included and will, hopefully, prove of value to those less familiar with the aircraft's background.

Aden had been a well known hotbed of dissident revolt for many years, inter-tribal feuding dating back to the Middle ages being a major reason for the troubles. Warring factions were continually being separated by locally-sourced Arab armies, supported by the British Army and an air force equipped with obsolescent fighters and bombers. By the late 1950s, egged-on by a jubilant post-Suez Egyptian general called Nasser, the perpetrators began to turn their focus on the British garrison, taking every opportunity to attack Army convoys, patrols and guard posts. Such a situation could not be allowed to fester too long.

One of the biggest challenges facing the British government during that period was to ensure that its military forces were supplied with the right equipment with which to manage an ever deteriorating security situation in Aden State, while maintaining law and order across a swathe of Southern Arabia. A bigger stick was needed to contain rebellious tribesmen!

The Hawker Hunter, re-incarnated in the role of ground attack, was that stick and it could not have arrived at a more opportune time. It was to quickly establish its credentials as the most potent weapon in the Middle East armoury. As the Fighter Ground Attack (FGA) Mark 9, the new variant first entered service as a Venom replacement with 8 Squadron at RAF Khormaksar in January 1960. Six months later 208 Squadron became the second Middle East Venom unit to convert to type when it received the Mark 9 at RAF Eastleigh in Kenya. The progression continued in the summer of 1961 when the Fighter Reconnaissance version of the Hunter, the Mark 10, displaced the Meteor FR.Mk.9s still in service with 8 Squadron. The Hunter force reached peak strength in March 1963, following the redeployment of 43 Squadron and its FGA.Mk.9s from Cyprus to Khormaksar.

A high percentage of operations in the Middle East required close co-operation between various other RAF squadrons and units of the Army and Royal Navy. You will, therefore, find that at relevant points throughout the narrative, references to squadrons that flew a diversity of aircraft types, ranging from the Shackleton, Beverley, Argosy, Valetta, Twin-Pioneer and Belvedere, to the Auster, Beaver and Scout of the Army Air Corps operating from isolated up-country airstrips, and Royal Navy Sea Vixens, Scimitars and Buccaneers flying off carriers in the waters around Aden.

My objective when writing this book was to produce a factual account that encompasses many of the hundreds of operations performed by the Middle East Hunter squadrons between 1960 and 1971. This was a campaign that has, sadly, become known by veterans from all three elements of the armed forces as 'The Forgotten War'; hopefully, the narrative within these pages will in some way compensate for the lack of recognition. It is based mainly on reports contained in squadron and station operations record books (ORBs – Form 540), which are held at the National Archives in Kew.

A companion volume to *Hunters over Arabia* called *Tales from the Front Line: Middle East Hunters* is in the course of preparation and will concentrate on anecdotes and other material contributed by former members of the Middle East Hunter and associated squadrons.

Ray Deacon, June 2018.

Acknowledgements

It is impossible to adequately thank all those whose generous co-operation has made this book possible. In sending my appreciation to everyone who submitted photographs and material for the project, I recognise that this book would have been far less comprehensive without your enthusiastic support.

The acquisition of suitable illustrations and compilation of the narrative and research involved has taken a decade to reach a stage where it is ready for publication. I wish to register the guidance through the maze of documentation received from National Archive staff at Kew. Similarly, I wish to record the value of Colin Cummings' superb set of publications which enabled me to extract details of the accidents incurred by the Hunter units in Middle East Command.

I would also like to offer my sincere thanks to John Jennings for writing the Foreword, to Ben Bennett, Vic Cozens and Barry Potter for edit-checking the manuscript, while making suggestions for its improvement, to Alan Pollock, Ken Simpson and David Watkins for their enduring encouragement and support, to Nick Adamson and Mal Grosse for allowing me to use their images on the covers, and to Simon Watson and Justin Sawyer at the Aviation Bookshop for providing access to their extensive photographic archive.

Lastly, and by no means least, to the following people who contributed their treasured photographs and were always happy to respond to my persistent questions: David Ainge, Chris Bain, Tom Banks, David Barnes, David Baron, John Batty, Derek Bell, Pete Biddiscombe, Sandy Burns, Ralph Chambers, Phil Champniss, Paul Constable, Ian Dick, Les Dunnett, Tony Gannon, Richard Grevatte-Ball, Dave Griffin, Mike Halpin, Roy Hollow, Bill Horspole, Roy Humphreyson, Ronnie Hush, Bryan John, Martin Johnson, Ted Lambe, Peter Lewis, Alan Lowe, Gordon Macadie, Doug Marr, Willie Marr, Anthony McLauchlan, Peter McLeland, Sandy McMillan, Des Meek, Robin Morrell, Simon Morrison, Tim Notley, George Nute, Ken Parry, Graham Pitchfork, Roger Pyrah, Ken Rochester, John Severne, Barry Shaw, Peter Sturt, Tam Syme, Tim Thorn, Fred Trowern, Ron Turrell, Nigel Walpole, Tim Webb, Keith Webster, Roger Wilkins and Graham Williams.

Without the enthusiastic encouragement and co-operation of the staff at Pen & Sword Books this work would certainly have been a much slimmer volume.

While every endeavour has been made by the author to acknowledge the correct ownership of the photographs reproduced in this book, I offer my sincere apologies for any mistaken accreditations that may appear. The author and publisher would welcome any information in this regard.

Finally, a special thank you to my dear wife Rose for her encouragement and understanding during my long periods hidden away at the keyboard.

Hunter sunrise! 8 Squadron Hunter FGA.9s on the line at Bahrain stand ready for an early morning exercise during the early period of the aircraft's operation in the Middle East (author).

Chapter 1

Aden: A Historical Perspective

Legends link Aden with Eden in a time when Arabia was much more fertile than it is today. Rumour has it that Cain, the son of Adam, who murdered his brother Abel and then 'dwelt in the land of Nod, on the east of Eden', is buried in the cemetery beside Crater Pass. Noah's Ark is believed to have been built in the shipyards of Ma'alla and there are claims that this was also Queen of Sheba territory.

Following the discovery of the Cape route to India by Portuguese voyagers in the sixteenth century, Aden lost its importance as a port. At the time of the British occupation in 1839, Aden was little more than a fishing village and home to some 500 inhabitants. A coaling station was soon established and, with the opening of the Suez Canal in 1869, it regained its importance as a refuelling stop for ships sailing on routes from Europe in the west to Asia and the Antipodes in the east. Aden's strategic importance militarily was acknowledged following the discovery of oil in the Persian Gulf and its proximity to the oil fields. In 1954 an oil refinery and harbour capable of handling 32,000-ton tankers was opened at Little Aden.

At 1,800ft, the rugged heights of Mount Shamsan dominate this view of the Ma'alla district of Aden, taken from Hunter T.7 XL613 on 14 February 1964 (author).

The core of Mount Shamsan, a long extinct volcano, is home to the town of Crater. Access from Khormaksar at the bottom of the picture is via a coastal road or through a high pass from Ma'alla on the right. Another view from Hunter T.7 XL613 taken on 14 February 1964 (author).

At first glance the fortress and port – the celebrated 'Barren Rocks of Aden' – present a forbidding aspect.

Stark, black crags with no hint of grass, rise from flat desert sands and jut out into the Indian Ocean. They once sheltered a harbour that became one of the busiest in the world, one where an average of seventeen ships a day replenished their fuel tanks and food stores. A few miles to the north the former RAF airfield and current civil airport at Khormaksar straddle the neck of land connecting the harbour district and townships with the Western and Eastern Protectorates that extend as far as the border with Yemen.

Aden Colony

The rugged rocks of an extinct volcano called Mount Shamsan rise more than 1,800 feet and dominate the landscape. In 1960 the Colony covered an area of just seventy-five square miles, had less than seventy-five miles of paved roadway, and was home to 140,000 inhabitants who relied heavily on the vibrant harbour and adjacent commercial district, together with the various military establishments, for employment opportunities. The current population is around 800,000.

The oldest settlement, Crater, is located deep within the heart of the volcano from which it takes its name and was Aden's main harbour and principal business centre in earlier times. Access from Crater to the present-day harbour at Tawahi, more commonly known as Steamer Point, is via a high gorge known as Main Pass and down to a coastal road in the district of Ma'alla. The other important districts consist of the former RAF airfield at Khormaksar and nearby Army barracks, and Sheikh Othman, a township located a few miles north-west of the airfield.

The volcanic peninsula of Little Aden, which forms a near-mirror image on the western side of Aden Harbour, became the site of a large oil refinery and tanker port in the 1950s. Both were established and operated by British Petroleum until they were taken over by the Yemeni government in 1978. Situated on the road to Little Aden, the town of Al Ittihad dates from more recent times and was built specifically to accommodate the South Arabian Federal Government.

Population

While the people of the Protectorates were almost entirely of Arabic origin, the Colony was more cosmopolitan. The 1955 census, for example, gave the following composition;

- 36,910 Aden Arabs
- 18,991 Protectorate Arabs
- 48,088 Yemenis
- 15,817 Indians
- 10,611 Somalis
- 3,763 Britons
- 2,608 Palestinians, Syrians, Lebanese and Americans
- 831 Jews
- 721 other Europeans

Religion in the Colony, as in the Protectorates, was predominantly Muslim and fasts and festivals were carefully observed. The custom of purdah was rigidly preserved, Arab women seldom being seen in public without black cloaks and veils. Many resorted to stylish Western fashion once in the privacy of their own homes or in all-female social gatherings.

Climate

Due to its position in the great belt of tropical deserts stretching from the Sahara in Africa to the Gobi in Asia, Aden has low precipitation, resulting in a hot desert climate with no large differences in temperature between the seasons. Temperatures during the summer months often exceed 40 degrees C for days on end, while those in the winter are reasonably warm with an average a little below 30 C. Rainfall is a

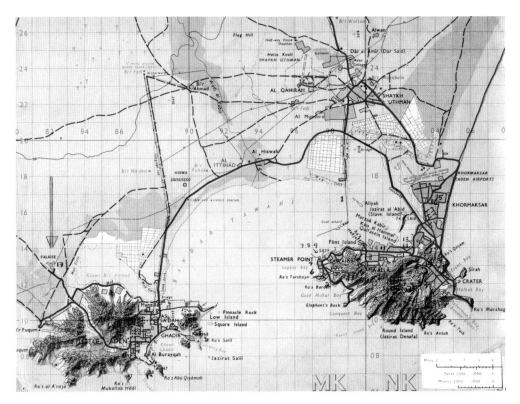

Map of Aden Colony supplied to Army Air Corps pilots in the mid-1960s. The RAF airfield at Khormaksar straddled the neck of the peninsula linking the Aden townships to the south to south Arabia continent (Richard Grevatte-Ball).

rare occurrence making it susceptible to dust and sandstorms. Living and working in such conditions was extremely uncomfortable, especially for those exposed to the sun for lengthy periods. This was especially so for airmen working on the aircraft pans, where the standard dress was a pair of shorts, bondu boots and rolled-down socks, with a sweat towel tucked into the shorts. Pilots climbing into cockpits in which temperatures could soar to 50 C needed to beware of touching metal objects with bare skin to avoid being burnt. Standard dress comprised much the same as for airmen plus a flying suit.

Shops and Bazaars
Agriculture was the principal activity in the Protectorates north of Aden with cotton being the main export of importance. Vegetables, fruit, poultry and eggs were also traded with the Colony. The Colony thrived on its commerce, the trade in transhipment and distribution of goods for neighbouring territories in particular. There was also a thriving trade in the bazaars lining the back streets of Steamer Point and in luxury items sold to passengers visiting the port from ocean liners and cruise ships.

Two views taken in 1960 depicting the back streets of Ma'alla above (Des Meek) and deep in the bowels of Mount Shamsan, the Crater Palace Hotel below (Barry Shaw).

The streets and shops presented a colourful scene for the tourist, the bazaars in particular. Most were narrow with open fronts, their goods semi-screened by blinds and hanging merchandise. Venture inside and there lay an Aladdin's cave of jumbled wares ranging from cameras, transistor radios, thermos flasks, perfume, cheap Hong Kong silk blouses, tape-recorders, wax flowers, men's shirts, shoes, watches, electric razors and cosmetics to quality knitwear. Many pedlars plied their wares in the street – from the water seller with buckets and tatty tumblers hanging from a donkey-hauled cart, to the hawker of nuts and lentils. Perfume merchants would mix their fine fragrances of Arabia to a buyer's instructions from cases containing bottles, phials and sandalwood. Toy stalls for the children were tucked away behind corners of doorways. A letter-writer would be camped on the pavement with chair, table and portable typewriter, proffering a service to those unable to write.

The Protectorates

With the signing of a treaty between Britain and rulers of the states surrounding Aden in the nineteententury, the area was partitioned into two protectorates; the Eastern Aden Protectorate (EAP) and a Western Aden Protectorate (WAP). As part of the agreement, the rulers promised not to enter into relations with any other foreign power, so anxious were they to preserve their independence from Yemen. Under the terms of the treaty, Britain agreed to defend the Protectorates from external attack. In the 1930s agreement was reached for the Governor of Aden to have advisory powers in matters of welfare and development, but no direct British administration. Each protectorate retained a ruler who governed with the aid of British advisory staff.

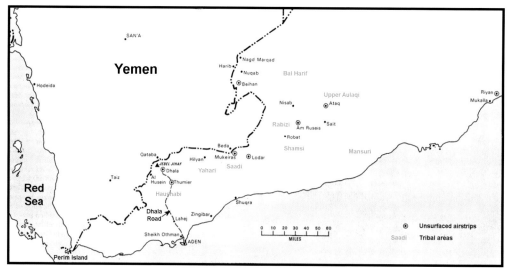

Map depicting the position of Aden relative to the Protectorates, the Yemen, and some of the unsurfaced airfields and airstrips serving the main tribal areas.

The Protectorates covered a much wider area than that of the Colony, stretching from the Straits of Bab-el-Mandeb, 100 miles to the west, to the border with Muscat and Oman in the east. Over 650,000 inhabitants lived in towns and villages scattered across the 112,000 square miles of rock, sand and fertile valleys. Using water extracted from shallow wells, large areas were given over to the cultivation of wheat and barley. Apricots, which grew naturally, plums, apples, peaches and walnuts were also cultivated in the lush green valleys. In areas where water was more plentiful, such as in Lahej and the Hadramaut, date palm and banana plantations proliferated alongside those dedicated to the growth of melons.

Federal agreement

In 1959 six states in the Western Protectorate joined a newly-formed Federation of Arab Emirates of the South with the objective of furthering their political and economic progress. With financial and technical assistance from Britain, the Federal Government took over many of the services formerly provided by the Protectorate.

A locally recruited military force, known as the Aden Protectorate Levies (APL), under the command of British and Arab officers, was not capable of defending the whole Protectorate area, while Government and Tribal Guards were intended for

A low-level photograph of one of the up-country townships that proliferated the wadis of the Western Aden Protectorate, captured on a hand-held camera by 43 Squadron Hunter pilot Roger Wilkins in 1965 (Roger Wilkins).

The sheer cliffs aligning the valley in this photograph, taken by 'Mac' McLauchlan from his Hunter FGA.9 in 1962, was typical of the terrain encountered by pilots flying in the extremities of the Eastern Aden Protectorate (Mac McLauchlan).

internal security only. Although Turkey had relinquished the Yemen after the First World War, the threat from the north remained, an independent Yemen still laying claim to the Aden states. They succumbed to Yemeni rule in the seventeenth century but a rebellion in the early eighteenth century enabled them to regain their independence. The rulers of the Yemen are Zeidis, a Shiah sect, while Protectorate Arabs are Shafeis, a Sunni faction of Islam.

Yemeni attacks and incursions into the southern states were common until 1934 when an Anglo-Yemeni treaty stabilised the situation at the frontier as it existed at the time. Nevertheless, border infringements became more frequent after the Second World War and such blatant interference with the internal affairs of the Aden states could not be tolerated. Under the terms of its treaty, Britain was obliged to counter these intrusions. The airfield at Khormaksar and nearby army barracks were expanded and garrisoned by increasing numbers of British military personnel.

Chapter 2

Middle East Command and its airfields

It is not the intention of this narrative to present the various command and sub-command structures in force at the end of the Second World War, but a brief outline of the organisation of the RAF in the Middle East during Britain's final decade of occupation should prove beneficial to the reader.

British Forces, Arabian Peninsula

Ever since the end of the Second World War, the presence of British forces in the Suez Canal area had been a source of irritation for the Egyptian authorities and, with pressure mounting, Middle East Air Force Command (MEAF) relocated its headquarters to RAF Nicosia in Cyprus on 1 December 1954.

Following the nationalisation of the Canal in 1956 the Command found itself effectively divided into northern and southern sectors. As communications between the two sectors became increasing disjointed, the decision was taken to create a separate southern command and British Forces, Arabian Peninsula (BFAP) was established at RAF Steamer Point later that year. Thereafter, British forces based in South Arabia, the Persian Gulf and East Africa reported to the new command, although the three service elements, RN, Army and RAF, maintained separate organisational structures with headquarters in different locations. The Middle East Air Force (MEAF) formed the RAF element with an HQ at RAF Steamer Point.

Middle East Command

On 1 March 1961 the three service elements were fully integrated within (BFAP) and the title changed to Middle East Command (MEC). Staff officers from the three services were brought under the same roof in a new headquarters at Steamer Point, in close proximity to the Commander-in-Chief. As control of British forces in South Arabia had been headed by an RAF officer since 1928, the first C.-in-C. of the new command was Air Chief Marshal Sir Hubert Patch KBE CBE. The RAF element was renamed Air Forces, Middle East (AFME) with Air Vice Marshal D.J.P. Lee CB CBE as its first AOC.

The Middle East Command territory encompassed an extensive area of Arabia, from Bahrain Island in the north, through the Trucial States and Muscat and Oman on the east coast, to Aden Colony and the Protectorates in the south. Four RAF route stations, namely Sharjah, Masirah, Salalah and Riyan, were positioned at strategic locations in between to provide refuelling facilities for aircraft in transit and others on short duration detachments. The majority of operations were initiated from the main airfield at RAF Khormaksar, located on the neck of the Aden Peninsula. Across the Horn of Africa to the south, lay Ethiopia, Somalia and the lush green hills of Kenya. There, close to the capital, Nairobi, RAF Eastleigh provided airfield facilities for the Command's East Africa sector.

The flying distance from Eastleigh to Khormaksar is around 1,000 miles (1600 km) and from the latter to Bahrain between 1,300 and 1,500 miles (2,100 and 2,400 km), depending on the route taken. Aircraft flying from one end to the other would encounter considerable variations in topography, from 7.000-foot high mountains to mile upon mile of flat featureless desert. Climatic changes between the north and south of the area were important factors to consider when flying from one to the other; from 49 C (120 F) in the shade and 90 percent-plus humidity in Bahrain to more congenial, European-like, temperatures experienced in Kenya.

RAF airfields

A brief description of the eight MEC stations is included here, beginning with Bahrain in the north and working down to the southern tip in Kenya.

RAF Bahrain

The Kingdom of Bahrain consists of a group of thirty- three small islands covering an area of 300 square miles (770 sq km) and is located in the Persian Gulf off the north-east coast of Saudi Arabia. The kingdom takes its name from the largest island, Bahrain, and is linked by causeway to Muharraq Island, the current home of the international airport and one-time operational base for the RAF.

Until 1960 RAF Bahrain functioned mainly as a peaceful staging post between the UK and the Far East, and home for the Twin Pioneers and Pembrokes of 152 Communications Squadron. Then suddenly, in the summer of 1961 and within the space of a few days, the airfield was transformed into one of strategic importance. To deter Iraq from invading the tiny oil-rich protectorate of Kuwait, large numbers of RAF fighter and transport aircraft were flown in, together with a large force of ground troops. Even when the crisis was over, Bahrain never returned to the idyllic peace of earlier times, the airfield playing permanent host to rotating detachments of Hunters from Khormaksar, Canberras from Akrotiri and Beverleys from Khormaksar and Eastleigh. On 1 December, 1963 the name was changed to RAF Muharraq.

The status quo continued until 1964 when 208 Squadron relocated its Hunters to Muharraq on a permanent basis and further expansion occurred in 1967 with the arrival of aircraft evacuated from Aden in line with the closure of Khormaksar.

The dark shaded areas depict the amount of territory covered by Middle East Command through much of the 1960s. The distance from RAF Bahrain in the north to RAF Eastleigh in the south was approximately 2,500 miles (4,000 kilometres).

Muharraq Island is part of Bahrain and home to the main civil airport. The RAF section was located at the extreme centre-right of this photograph, taken in 1971 from the oblique facing camera of David Ainge's FR.10 (David Ainge).

Muharraq remained an operational airfield until British forces pulled out in December 1971.

RAF Sharjah

Located in the Trucial States (now part of the United Arab Emirates), some 200 miles (320 km) east of Bahrain and twelve miles east of Doha, RAF Sharjah played an increasingly important role during the final decade of RAF tenure in the Persian Gulf.

In addition to performing a primary role as a major routing station for MEC and other RAF aircraft in transit to and from the Far East, the close proximity of the Jeb-a-Jib range offered the Hunter squadrons an ideal base from which to hold their armament practice camps. With its closure in December 1971, transit aircraft were rerouted via Masirah.

RAF Masirah

Located in the Indian Ocean some nineteen kilometres off the coast of Oman, RAF Masirah was an important refuelling station for aircraft flying between Khormaksar and Bahrain throughout the fifties and sixties. Until then, most fuel and food ration provisions were delivered by sea and transported via a unique RAF narrow-gauge railway from the quay to the airfield from November to

The Hunter pan at Sharjah on 23 November 1963, the day following the assassination of President Kennedy. A heavy deluge left the sand too soggy for the Kuwait Airways Viscount to use its normal parking area (author).

The 30 Squadron Beverley bringing 8 Squadron spare pilots and groundcrew back from detachment in Bahrain in 1962 makes a refuelling stop at Salalah before continuing on to Khormaksar (Alan Lowe).

February; it was too difficult for ships to dock during the south-west monsoon period (March to October).

However, following the construction of a concrete runway in 1963/4, stores were delivered by air. Having a close proximity to Oman, and being better suited for training exercises, Masirah became a regular destination for MEC Hunter detachments. After the closure of Muharraq and Sharjah in 1971, Masirah became the sole route station for aircraft flying between Cyprus and Gan. When the RAF withdrew in March 1977, Masirah became an Omani Air Force base.

RAF Salalah

RAF Salalah, was a route station located in the fertile coastal plain of Dhofar in the Sultanate of Muscat and Oman, some 650 miles (1,050 km) north of Aden. The airfield dated back to 1928, having been built as a military and civilian staging post. Throughout the 1960s Salalah provided refueling and replenishment facilities for Valetta, Beverley, Argosy, Dakota and other transport aircraft operating on the Aden-Masirah-Sharjah-Bahrain route, and offered accommodation for a limited number of personnel should an overnight stop be necessary.

The climate could be a problem, especially between May and September when the normally arid Arabian Waste is subjected to the south-west monsoon. The broad strip of land 100 miles (160 km) either side of Salalah endures lengthy periods of continuous light rain and low cloud cover for the much of that period, requiring pilots using that corridor to ensure they have adequate reserves of fuel should they need to divert.

RAF Riyan

Situated in the Quaiti State, within the Eastern Aden Protectorate, some 273 miles (440 km) along the coast to the north-east of Aden, RAF Riyan was the smallest of the route stations. In the 1960s the local ruler was the Sultan of Quaiti and he lived in the nearby city of Mukalla.

The station itself was a collection of white, flat- topped buildings, with a compacted sand airstrip laid in the centre of shallow, scrub-covered desert, surrounded on three sides by high mountains. The station was built in 1945 and most of the buildings were those erected at the time. They were, however, in good condition, providing an airy and cool home for the two officers and thirty airmen who were based there.

As a route station, Riyan was primarily concerned with the refuelling of short-range RAF and AAC aircraft operating in the South Arabian area, although much of the traffic was civilian. Aden Airways operated a scheduled service almost every day and was popular with those travelling between Aden and the Hadhramaut. For a small airfield the volume of civilian traffic made Riyan a very busy stop. The local population consisted of a mixture of Bedouins, Somalis, Malays and Arabs. Deemed to be friendly and honest, a number of them were employed on ancillary tasks on the station.

RAF Khormaksar

The primary role of the RAF in Aden was to support British and Arabian Army units in the defence of the Colony and Protectorates from external attack, and maintaining law and order within the territory.

Approximately 75 percent of Middle East Command aircraft were allocated to the main operational base at RAF Khormaksar, a joint-user airfield straddling the neck of a peninsula at the southernmost tip of Arabia. In addition to providing facilities for the wide range of aircraft types allocated to Tactical/Strike and Transport Wings, the RAF was responsible for providing airfield, navigational, meteorological and communications facilities for military and civil aircraft transiting through Aden.

A huge building programme instituted in the early 1960s saw Khormaksar expand into the largest staging-post between the UK and the Far East. In providing a home for nine squadrons and three flights, it became the busiest airfield in the RAF. As such it was equipped to handle the multiplicity of tasks unique to the Middle East theatre. Most of the flying units were maintained on semi-permanent alert in readiness for redeployment at a moment's notice to locations anywhere within the Command's territory.

In January 1960, 8 Squadron replaced its venerable Venom FB 4s with the Hunter FGA.9, the first squadron in the RAF to receive the latest mark, followed six

A crystal clear photograph of Aden with Khormaksar airfield in the foreground, taken from a 1417 Flight FR.10 nose camera on 20 August 1965 (Richard Johns via Roger Wilkins).

months later by 208 Squadron which re-equipped with the Hunter at its Eastleigh base. In co-operation with Shackleton MR.2s of 37 Squadron, the two ground attack squadrons were soon using their aircraft to great effect when operating up-country. The strike capability was augmented in 1963 when 43 Squadron moved its FGA.9s from Cyprus to Khormaksar leaving a re-formed 1417 Flight, equipped with Hunter FR.10s, to concentrate on the fighter-reconnaissance role. The Hunter allocation now totalled forty-six aircraft, a formidable force with which to defend and police the vast area.

RAF Steamer Point
The second of two stations located in Aden Colony, RAF Steamer Point was built on the hillside site of the original garrison and, many years later, became the Headquarters of Middle East Command and an RAF hospital. Overlooking Aden Harbour, Steamer Point had no airfield facilities apart from a helicopter pad and was financially independent of its neighbour, Khormaksar.

RAF Steamer Point provided administrative services for most of the units in the base area which roughly consisted of the 'boot' of the Aden peninsula. It was responsible for a diverse group of units that included the RAF Aden Communications Centre, No. 114 Maintenance Unit, the Aden Supplies Depot, 50 Movement Unit, the HQ Provost and Security Services (responsible for enforcing service discipline and keeping down crime throughout the Colony), the staff at Command HQ, RAF Hospital, Aden Protectorate Levies Hospital, No. 7 Anti-Malarial Unit and a single Army unit, No. 222 Signals Squadron, which manned the telephone exchange and had responsibility for maintaining up-country land lines.

One of its most challenging tasks was the management of all hirings occupied by the RAF and Army. These comprised houses and flats rented by the Air Ministry to supplement married quarters.

RAF Eastleigh
RAF Eastleigh was located on the eastern fringe of Nairobi and was the principal RAF station in East Africa. Eastleigh also provided civil airport facilities for airlines such as BOAC, EAA and SAA, until a new airport was opened at Embakasi in 1958.

At an altitude of 5,300 feet, however, and with short, red murram-surfaced runways, Eastleigh was not a suitable airfield from which to operate fully-armed and fuelled Hawker Hunters, requiring 208 Squadron to locate its front-line aircraft at Embakasi Airport. Second-line servicing continued to be undertaken at Eastleigh, the aircraft being flown in and out with light fuel loads.

Other squadrons located at the base in the early sixties were 21 Squadron equipped with Twin Pioneers, 30 Squadron with Beverleys and the East African Communications Flight operating Pembrokes.

Hunter squadrons on detachment to Kenya operated from Embakasi Airport. In this view, five 8 Squadron FGA.9s face a trio of 120 Squadron Shackleton MR.3s and a Victor B.1 during a detachment undertaken in July/August 1963 (Tom Banks).

Chapter 3

Wings and Squadrons

This chapter takes a more in-depth look at the squadrons and flights that comprised Middle East Command.

RAF Khormaksar

For most of the period covered in this narrative, nine squadrons and three flights were based at Khormaksar, operating an allocation of about 100 aircraft of various types. The units were allocated to one of the two flying wings – Tactical or Transport – according to aircraft type and purpose.

The first year of Hunter operations in Aden was carried out from the confined apron at the western end of the airfield. When a new purpose-built apron, office and hangar complex was opened between Aden Civil Airport and the Shackleton pan, 8 Squadron relocated to the new facility. It was joined by 208 Squadron, following its redeployment from Kenya following the Kuwait crisis of 1961. Under the command of Wing Commander C.R.G. Neville, the organisation worked very well initially but, as the operational commitment became more complex, it was clear that a new structure was needed.

Tactical Wing

Tactical Wing (TacWing) was formed on 1 March 1963 and comprised a Headquarters and Operations Staff under the command of Wing Commander J. Jennings.

A third Hunter squadron, number 43, which had redeployed from Cyprus was incorporated into the new wing alongside 8 and 208, and a newly formed 1417 (FR) Flight. The Belvedere heavy-lift helicopters of 26 Squadron, recent arrivals from the UK, maritime Shackletons of 37 Squadron and Sycamore SAR Flight helicopters completed the wing's line-up.

A dedicated TacWing Operations HQ was tasked with controlling and co-ordinating all operational flying activities authorised by HQ MEC. Briefings for pilots and groundcrews within the command, and crews of visiting aircraft from other commands, the Army Air Corps and Royal Navy were just a few of the Ops Room staff duties.

The Hunters were regularly detached to other airfields within MEC territory, from Bahrain in the north to Nairobi in the south. Each squadron was charged with providing a minimum of eight aircraft for detachments of two-months' duration to Bahrain with the objective of deterring General Kassim from attempting a second annexation of Kuwait. The detachments were organised on a rota basis.

At Khormaksar one squadron was held on a constant state of alert throughout daylight hours in readiness to react quickly to requests for air support from ground forces and incursions by Yemeni aircraft. The duty alternated between the squadrons on a 24-hour rota, the changeover taking place at midday.

Under the command of a British Army major, a small army ground liaison section (225 GLS) was established within TacWing to maintain close liaison with the Federal Government, Federal Regular Army and political advisers. In providing a direct interface with army units operating up-country, assisting with the identification of targets for Hunter strikes and unravelling many of the complexities involved with inter-tribal feuding, the unit was a vital intelligence source for pilot briefings.

New organisational structure
On 14 December 1964 the flying unit reporting lines at Khormaksar were re-organised under a more logical wing structure – Strike and Transport.

Strike Wing
The formation of Strike Wing brought together all the offensive elements under the command of the current OC Tactical Wing, Wing Commander J. Jennings and comprised:

- 8 Squadron   Hunter FGA.9
- 43 Squadron   Hunter FGA.9
- 1417 Flight   Hunter FR.10
- 37 Squadron   Shackleton MR.2

Number 208 Squadron had redeployed to Muharraq in June 1964 but could be recalled at a moment's notice should the need arise. To ensure that the best possible use was made of the Shackleton's capability to bomb and strafe the same targets as the Hunters, especially at night, 37 Squadron was brought into the Strike Wing fold. The Belvedere and Whirlwind helicopters of 26 Squadron and SAR Flight respectively, were re-allocated to Transport Wing.

8 Squadron
Apart from a brief interlude immediately after the Second World War, 8 Squadron had maintained close links with Khormaksar since 1928. Commonly cited as 'Aden's own', the squadron formed at Brooklands in January 1915 as part of the Royal Flying Corps and undertook an active role in the campaign in France. Disbanded in 1920, it reformed in Egypt before relocating to Iraq a few months later. The move to Aden took place in 1928 and there it remained throughout the inter-war period.

Although coastal reconnaissance and anti–submarine patrols were its primary concern during the war years, it endured a lengthy period of action during the East African campaign of 1940-41. The small number of Allied ships lost in the Red Sea and Gulf of Aden was probably due to low number of u-boats that operated in the area. The squadron was disbanded in May 1945 and its unit number transferred to 200 Squadron (Liberators) based at Minneriya in Ceylon. Operating as a special duties unit, the squadron was employed on supply drops to clandestine agents in Malaya and Sumatra until a further disbandment occurred in November 1945.

The squadron renewed its acquaintance with Aden on 1 September 1946, when 114 Squadron was re-numbered as 8. Equipped with Mosquito FB.6s, it reverted to policing the Protectorates in the light-bomber role and securing their borders with the Yemen. Hawker Tempests took over in 1947 but they were found to be unsuited to the task and were replaced by Bristol Brigand B.1s two years later. The question of which aircraft type most suited the policing role, bomber or fighter, was finally settled when DH Vampire FB.5s arrived in 1952. As with the Brigand, the Vampire was equipped with rocket rails and proved a more effective deterrent when facing hostile tribesmen.

The squadron standard was presented by the Governor of Aden in April 1954 and, later that month, was paraded for the first time when the squadron provided the Guard of Honour when the Queen and Duke of Edinburgh visited the Colony.

The Vampire succumbed to the Venom in 1956 and the squadron soon found itself detached to Cyprus to strengthen forces employed in the Suez conflict. As soon as operations ceased, the Venoms returned to Khormaksar to continue with the task of defending and policing the Protectorates.

The Venoms had a relatively low fatigue life and were replaced by the fighter ground attack (FGA) variant of Hawker Hunter, the Mark 9, in January 1960. Following a period working up on the new type, the squadron was declared operational on 8 March.

In August 1960 the Aden Peninsular Reconnaissance Flight (APRF) Meteors were transferred to the 8 Squadron inventory as its B Flight, extending the scope of operations that could be undertaken. The obsolescent Meteors were replaced by Hunter FR.10s in April 1961. When 1417 Flight was reformed two years later, the FR.10s were transferred to the new flight along with the unit's Hunter trainers.

In June 1964 a major re-organisation saw the introduction of centralised servicing and pooling of aircraft. Individual squadron markings were replaced with a combination of 8 and 43 Squadron markings.

The status quo continued until 8 August 1967 when, after nearly forty years of almost unbroken service in Aden, 8 Squadron departed for the final time and headed north to a temporary home at Masirah. With the disbandment of 1417 Flight on 9 September, the FR.10s returned to the squadron fold and the whole moved north to Muharraq where it remained until September 1971. After three further months at Sharjah, disbandment beckoned and the Hunters were flown back to the UK in

The pilots and groundcrew of 8 Squadron (above) pose in front of an FGA.9 and FR.10 at Khormaksar on 23 June 1962 (via author), while (below) a pair of FGA.9s form the backdrop to the 43 Squadron photograph from 1965 (via Roger Wilkins).

December that year. Number 8 Squadron thus became the last unit in the RAF to fly the legendary Hunter in a front-line role.

The squadron badge is a sheathed Arabian dagger known as a *Jambiya*, its motto 'Uspiam et Passim' – 'Everywhere Unbounded' and the squadron colours are yellow, blue and red to represent the sand, sea and blood of South Arabia.

43 Squadron

Number 43 (F) Squadron was formed in April 1916 at Stirling, Scotland, by Major Douglas (who later became Marshal of the Royal Air Force Lord Douglas of Kirtleside). From a humble beginning of one officer, one senior NCO and no aeroplanes, the squadron soon expanded and was to gain impressive records in two world wars.

Initially equipped with 100 mph Sopwith Strutters, 43 Squadron introduced 'ground strafing' to the Royal Flying Corps in 1917. Re-equipped with Sopwith Camels by early 1918, the squadron was credited with shooting down twelve enemy aircraft in a single day, a First World War record, and went on to claim 110 enemy aircraft destroyed and forty-nine others forced down.

Disbanded in 1919 the squadron re-formed in July 1925 with Gamecocks at Henlow where it gained the nickname 'Fighting Cocks'. Two years later, it began performing formation aerobatics with its aircraft tethered together, a performance that captivated large crowds at the Hendon Air Displays.

Having re-equipped with Hawker Hurricanes before the outbreak of the Second World War, 43 Squadron gained the distinction of claiming the first German aircraft to be destroyed over Britain and was heavily involved in the Battle of Britain. While operating from Tangmere, the squadron was credited with shooting down forty-five Luftwaffe aircraft. However, it was declared non-operational for a short period beginning on 8 September 1940 after sustaining heavy losses. Over the course of the war, 43 Squadron went on to serve in France, North Africa, and Italy where it added the Anzio and Salerno landings to its battle honours.

Disbanded in 1947, the squadron re-formed with Meteors at Tangmere in 1949 and moved north to Leuchars in the following year. It was there, in July 1954, that 43 became the first squadron in the RAF to receive he Hunter F.1 and it went on to fly the F.4, F.6 and FGA.9 variants. Nominated as the official RAF aerobatic team in 1955, it displayed at events across Britain and Europe. Their precision flying was rewarded when they won the prestigious international formation aerobatics competition in Italy, beating teams from eight countries. The 'Fighting Cocks' were in demand again in 1956 and, in April, the team was selected to perform in front of Bulganin and Khruschev during their visit to Britain. The squadron received its Standard from HM Queen Elizabeth II during a ceremony at RAF Leuchars on 5 June 1957.

Having replaced the Hunter F.6 with the FGA.9 in 1960, the squadron moved to Nicosia, Cyprus, on 20 June 1961. Eighteen months later, in March 1963, it was on the move again, this time to Khormaksar to augment the Hunter force. Although officially disbanded on 14 October 1967, 43 Squadron remained at Khormaksar until the end of the British occupation of Aden in November 1967, before flying its aircraft off to Masirah.

The squadron badge is a Gamecock, hence the nickname 'Fighting Cocks', its motto 'Gloria Finis' – 'Glory is the End' and squadron colours are black and white chequers.

208 Squadron

Formed out of 8 Squadron RNAS in France at the time of the formation of the RAF in April 1918, 208 Squadron moved to Netheravon in September 1919, only to be disbanded a short while later. The squadron's links with the Near East began with its re-formation at Ismailia, Egypt, in February 1920, and it went on to serve in North Africa, Greece, Palestine and Italy. Its nomadic existence continued during the early post-war period, during which it operated out of bases in Egypt, Turkey, Palestine, Cyprus, Jordan and Malta.

On 18 November 1955 Air Vice-Marshal Sir Geoffrey Bromet KBE CB DSO presented the squadron Standard during its period at Abu Sueir in Egypt. The squadron was the last RAF fighter unit to leave the Canal Zone in 1956.

Disbanded in early 1957, the squadron re-formed at Tangmere in January 1958, equipped with the Hunter F.6 and its ties with the Near East were re-established

208 Squadron pilots and airmen assemble for a photograph at their Muharraq base in the late 1960s. The large servicing hangar was constructed on the site of premises previously used by Gulf Aviation (via Graham Pitchfork).

following a move to Cyprus. In March 1960, 208 Squadron disbanded in order to release its pilots for ground attack training on the Hunter FGA.9 at Stradishall. On 1 April, the number 208 re-appeared with the re-numbering of 142 Squadron, a Venom-equipped squadron based at Eastleigh in Kenya, some 5,300 feet above sea level. The thirteen FGA.9s, plus a T.7, allocated to the squadron were flown out to Kenya by the newly-qualified pilots in June 1960. As tests with an 8 Squadron T.7 proved that the Hunter could not operate safely from the relatively short, murram-surfaced runway at that altitude, the decision was taken to use the nearby civil airport at Embakasi for operational flying while retaining the facilities at Eastleigh for second-line servicing.

After a year spent flying in support of 24 Brigade, 208 Squadron was swiftly despatched to Bahrain in July 1961 to bolster 8 Squadron in attempting to dissuade General Kassim from invading Kuwait. As soon as the alert level eased, the squadron moved south to its new base at Khormaksar. Some two-and-a-half years later, in May 1964, the squadron departed Aden and headed for the relative sanctity of Muharraq (the new name for RAF Bahrain), where it remained until September 1971.

The long association with the Near and Middle East led to the squadron adopting an image of the Sphinx at the centre of its crest. The motto is 'Vigilant' and squadron colours are pale blue and yellow – blue for the sky and yellow for the desert sands.

Aden Peninsular Reconnaissance Flight

When 208 Squadron withdrew from the Canal Zone in 1956, its Meteor FR.9s were redeployed to Aden to add a photographic capability for operations against insurgents. Operating initially as C Flight 208 Squadron, it was re-designated as the Aden Protectorate Reconnaissance Flight on 1 August 1959.

Meteor FR.9 WH546, last of the breed to see front-line service with the RAF, was pictured outside the 131 MU hangar in 1960 (author's collection).

Two months later, on 1 October 1959, the flight was renamed the Arabian Peninsular Reconnaissance Flight (APRF). It continued to fly tactical reconnaissance missions from Khormaksar with the Meteor FR.9 until disbandment beckoned in August 1960, when its aircraft were absorbed into 8 Squadron as its B Flight. The Meteors went on to serve with the Squadron until finally replaced by Hunter FR.10s in July 1961.

1417 Flight

First formed from 417 (General Reconnaissance) Flight at RAF St. Athan on 1 March 1941, 1417 (General Reconnaissance) Flight was issued with Avro Anson Mk.1s for use on maritime patrols. It had hardly begun working-up on the task when it was disbanded on 18 March 1941.

Reformed at RAF Chivenor on 8 January 1942, 1417 Flight was tasked with carrying out trials on ASV radar and Leigh Light equipped Wellington GR.Mk.VIII aircraft operating as maritime reconnaissance-bombers and to develop tactics for their use. Three months later, the flight was reformed as 172 Squadron.

More than a decade later, on 1 November 1953, 1417 Flight was reconstituted as a communications unit at Bahrain, equipped with the Avro Anson Mk.XIX and Percival Pembroke C.Mk.1. The flight continued to operate in the communications role until 1 October 1958 when it was absorbed into the newly-reformed 152 Squadron at Bahrain.

Number 1417 Flight's next reincarnation occurred on 1 May 1963 when five pilots were transferred from 8 Squadron, together with its four Hunter FR.10s and the four T.7s from the ground attack squadrons.

The flight's peak operational activity occurred during the Radfan campaign between May and July 1964, when a total of 205 sorties was flown. Otherwise a high proportion of the unit's activities were devoted to Operation RANJI. This required a thrice-weekly reconnaissance of the South Arabian coast line to locate and photograph suspicious-looking vessels, particularly dhows, to find and discourage arms smugglers from supplying guns and ammunition to dissident tribesmen.

The flight was heavily involved with a classified operation called THESIGER which took place during August and September 1965 and again in March 1966. Sorties were flown in support of the Sultan of Oman, reaching far into the wastes of the Empty Quarter in search of dissident tribesmen. During those periods, some of the flight's aircraft operated from Salalah and Masirah respectively.

Such operations kept the Flight busy and were scheduled so as not to conflict with its primary mission – visual and photographic intelligence gathering over the whole of Southern Arabia. Sorties varied in scope from identification and location marking of tiny, pinpoint targets, such as small houses, to the production of photographic 'line-overlaps' covering an area of perhaps four or five miles through deep, uncharted wadis.

Although reconnaissance predominated, the flight's aircraft, including the T.7s, were often called in to fire their guns in support of ground-attack operations. Results from

Bearing the initials of its pilot, 1417 Flight FR.10 XE589 awaits a post-refurbishment air test at Khormaksar on 20 January 1965 (Ralph Chambers).

the range indicated that most of its pilots achieved above average scores with their air-to-ground firing.

No. 1417 Flight disbanded on 8 September 1967 when personnel and aircraft were reassigned to 8 Squadron to form a fighter-reconnaissance element for operations in the Gulf. By the end of the four-and-a-year period in which it flew the Hunter, the flight had flown 765 operational sorties across a wide area of Arabian desert.

37 Squadron
Number 37 Squadron was formed as an RFC experimental squadron at Orfordness, Suffolk, on 15 April 1916. Six months later, it was re-assigned as a Home Defence squadron with headquarters at Woodham Mortimer in Essex. As part of a line of defence intended to repel enemy aircraft and airships heading for London, the squadron was split into three flights spread across three locations, Rochford, Stow Maries and Goldhanger. On the night of 16/17 June 1917, Lieutenant L.P. Watkins, a Canadian Army officer attached to the squadron, destroyed Zeppelin L48 over Suffolk when flying his BE 12. After peace was declared, the three flights assembled at Stow Maries in preparation for a move to Biggin Hill. This occurred in March 1919, five months before being re-numbered 39 Squadron.

Number 37 Squadron was reformed in April 1937 from a nucleus of 214 Squadron, as part of the military build-up prior to the Second World War. Equipped initially with Handley Page Harrows, Vickers Wellingtons had arrived by the time of the onset of war. Within hours of the declaration, six 37 Squadron Wellingtons undertook a mission to attack German warships near Heligoland but were forced to return due to adverse weather conditions.

The loss of five aircraft to Bf109s and Bf110s while carrying out a bombing raid over Germany on 18 December 1939 was a bleak day for the squadron. The high loss rate suffered by the Wellington was deemed unacceptable and the aircraft was banished from flying over enemy territory during daylight hours, although it was cleared to continue night bombing.

In November 1940, 37 Squadron moved to Egypt to bolster allied operations in the desert and there it remained until the end of the war. After a short period in Palestine, the squadron disbanded on 31 March 1946. Two weeks later, it re-formed as a Lancaster unit but disbanded again on 1 April 1947. The worsening situation in Palestine, however, saw it re-form with Lancasters once again but this time in the maritime reconnaissance role. In May 1948 it moved to Malta where, in August 1953, it re-equipped with the Shackleton.

In August 1957, 37 Squadron began its long association with Khormaksar. Its mission was extended from maritime reconnaissance to include locating missing aircraft in the mountains and deserts of the Middle East and the support of up-country

Number 37 Squadron Officers and airmen line-up in front of one of the unit's four Shackleton MR.2s during rehearsals for a forthcoming AOC's inspection at Khormaksar in 1960 (Ray Jones).

operations, making full use of the Shackleton's bombing and strafing capabilities. Along with the Hunter units, the helicopter SAR Flight, Marine Craft Unit and other rescue elements, 37 Squadron performed a prominent role in maintaining internal security.

In an attempt to reduce excessive temperatures inside the aircraft, special dispensation was given for a greater area of white to be applied to the upper fuselage surfaces, but as this had little effect, the livery was returned to standard Maritime Command dark sea grey and white in 1963. After a decade of service in Aden, 37 Squadron disbanded on 5 September 1967, shortly before the final pullout of British forces from Aden.

The squadron badge is a hooded hawk, belled and fessed with elevated wings, indicative of the duties of blind flying. The squadron motto is 'Wise without Eyes'.

Transport Wing

Transport Wing squadrons provided pivotal roles in ensuring a successful execution of the MEC mission. The wing's main objectives were: to provide regular passenger services for military personnel within the command's territory; maintaining supplies to route stations between Aden and Bahrain; and re-supplying Army forces based at up-country garrisons. A number of unsurfaced airstrips were located at strategic points around the Protectorates for use by the smaller transport and Army Air Corps aircraft.

The five squadrons allocated to Transport Wing were formed into two smaller wings and assigned the aprons located in the centre and western end of the airfield.

Medium Range Transport (MRT) Wing:
- 105 Squadron   Argosy
- 84 Squadron   Beverley
- MRT Servicing Squadron, under the command of the then OC 105 Squadron.

Short Range Transport (SRT) Wing:
- 26 Squadron   Belvedere
- 78 Squadron   Twin Pioneer
- Middle East Communications Squadron
          Valetta, Andover, Dakota
- Search and Rescue Flight
          Whirlwind
- SRT Servicing Squadron, under the command of the then OC Transport Wing.

26 Squadron
Formed at Netheravon on 8 October 1915, the first 26 Squadron intake consisted of airmen drafted in from the South African Air Corps. Equipped with BEs and Farmans,

the squadron moved to Mombasa in Kenya in January 1916. Two years later it returned to the UK and was disbanded six months later.

On 11 October 1927, 26 Squadron reformed at Catterick as a flight of Armstrong Whitworth Atlas Army co-operation aircraft, which were retained until the arrival of the Hawker Audax in July 1933. After four years service, these were exchanged for Hawker Hectors.

By the time of the outbreak of the Second World War, the squadron had re-equipped with Westland Lysanders, and moved to France in October 1939. The pullout following the German invasion of Belgium in May 1940 saw 26 Squadron move across the Channel to Lympne from where it could continue to fly reconnaissance, re-supply and coastal patrols over northern France. In February 1941 replacement of the Lysander with the Curtiss Tomahawk signalled a change of role to one of tactical strike and reconnaissance. Due to their limited endurance when flying at low level over France, however, the Tomahawks were replaced by Mustangs in January 1942.

As final preparations for the Normandy landings were taking shape, the squadron was briefed to destroy enemy gun positions along the coastal belt and continued with this mission until some time after D Day. By the end of 1944, it had moved north, flying low-level reconnaissance missions over the Netherlands, seeking out pockets of German resistance for Royal Navy warships to bombard.

One of two camouflaged 26 Squadron Belvederes, XG467 is seen on the helicopter pan at Khormaksar in March 1964 (author).

The return to peace in Europe brought a move to Germany in August 1945 where, on 1 April the following year, the squadron was disbanded. On the same date, 41 Squadron at Wunstorf was renumbered 26 Squadron. It was equipped with a mix of Spitfires and Tempests which it flew for the next three years. The squadron's introduction to the jet age came in 1949 with the arrival of the de Havilland Vampire. These were retained until November 1953 when their replacement by the Canadair Sabre coincided with a move to Oldenburg.

The Sabre was only intended as a stop-gap measure and following conversion to the Hawker Hunter F.4 in July 1955, the unit retained its day-fighter commitment until disbandment on 10 September 1957, a casualty of the infamous Sandys defence cuts. That was not the end of the squadron's association with the Hunter, however, as it re-formed with the more powerful F.6 version at Gütersloh on 7 June 1958. This reincarnation continued until 30 December 1960, when it was disbanded once again.

A complete change of role awaited 26 Squadron on its re-formation at Odiham on 1 June 1962. Equipped with Bristol Belvedere HC 1 helicopters, its rotary-wing service began in earnest with a move to Khormaksar in March 1963, its six aircraft being flown out in pairs over a ten-month period. During its service in Aden, the squadron performed an invaluable role, lifting troops, heavy equipment and artillery pieces to locations and mountain tops that hitherto had been inaccessible by road or on foot. The Army made full use of the potential available, enabling it to take the fight to dissident tribesmen when the situation demanded. Without the Belvedere, the Radfan campaign would undoubtedly have lasted longer and incurred higher casualty rates.

Following the re-equipment of 78 Squadron with Wessex helicopters, 26 Squadron disbanded on 30 November 1965 and its aircraft were flown onto HMS *Albion* for transfer to 66 Squadron in Singapore.

The squadron badge is a springbok's head couped. The squadron motto is 'N Wagter in der Lug' (Afrikaans) – 'A guard in the Sky'.

78 Squadron

The history of 78 Squadron dates back to 1916 when it was formed as a Home Defence unit. Like many other units at the end of the First World War, it was disbanded in 1919. Reformed as a bomber unit in 1936, the squadron entered the early years of the Second World War flying the Whitley Mk.V on bombing raids over Germany and ports in occupied territory. Re-equipped with Halifax Vs in 1942, its efforts were concentrated on night-time raids over Germany, Italy and the occupied countries. As the war drew on, its mission changed to targeting V1 'doodle-bug' sites during daylight hours.

With the return to peace, the squadron was re-allocated to the newly-formed Transport Command, and based at Almaza in the Middle East. A year later it moved to Kabrit and, in 1951, to Fayid, where it disbanded three years later.

Scottish Aviation twin-pioneer XM284 on the 78 Squadron pan at Khormaksar in 1961 (Simon Morrison).

Equipped with the Scottish Aviation Single Pioneer, 78 Squadron re-formed at Khormaksar on 24 April 1956. By 1958 the squadron had received the twin-engined version of the Pioneer, its short take-off and landing capability offering much improved short-range re-supply of up-country Army units using short unsurfaced airstrips. In the casevac role, the 'Twin-Pin' was frequently called in to repatriate sick and injured servicemen who needed treatment at Steamer Point hospital.

Flying slow and at low level, the aircraft was vulnerable to ground fire and it was felt that a defensive capability should be added. A machine gun could be mounted in the entrance and missiles fitted under the wings. In 1962 the unit achieved what is believed to be the first firing of a guided missile by the RAF in an up-country attack against rebel forces, quite an achievement for a transport squadron!

In 1965 the Twin Pioneers were transferred to 21 Squadron and 78 Squadron became a helicopter unit, operating the Wessex. One of the last units to leave Aden on the withdrawal of British forces in November 1967, it redeployed to Sharjah and continued to fly in the army support and search and rescue roles until disbandment in 1971.

The squadron badge depicts a rampant tiger, approved by King George VI in November 1939. The theme of the badge was based on the squadron's aircraft at the time, the Whitley, which had Tiger engines and twin tails. The squadron motto is 'Nemo non Paratus' – 'Nobody Unprepared'.

84 Squadron

Formed at Beaulieu in 1917, 84 Squadron first saw service as a fighter squadron in France. After the Armistice it formed part of the Army of Occupation Force and was based at Cologne before returning to the UK and disbandment in 1920. Within three months it had been re-formed in Baghdad as a bomber unit flying the DH 9A. On being re-equipped with Vickers Vincents in 1934, it moved on to Shaibah.

By the onset of the Second World War, the Blenheim had taken over and the next few years saw the squadron participating in campaigns as diverse as the Western Desert, Greece, Iraq, Syria, Persia and the Far East. All of its aircraft were lost, however, during the Japanese attack on Java.

In 1944 a re-formed 84 Squadron took up residence in India, initially flying the Vengeance and later the Mosquito. Beaufighters took over in September 1945 as the squadron returned to the Far East. Eight years later, shortly after re-equipping with Brigands, the squadron disbanded in Singapore in early 1953.

In February 1953, 204 Squadron, a medium-range transport squadron flying Valettas from Fayid, was re-designated 84 Squadron. In January 1956, shortly after being awarded its Standard, the squadron moved to Nicosia where it remained until being redeployed to Khormaksar in January 1957. Its first Beverley arrived in 1958 and the aircraft became a faithful workhorse in Middle East Command during the troubles in Aden and Kuwait.

Supplies from an 84 Squadron Beverley are unloaded by FRA soldiers at an up-country airstrip in 1965 (Charlie Donaldson).

Both types continued to be employed on operations until September 1960 when the Valetta element re-formed as an autonomous unit, 233 Squadron. Although its primary role was the re-supply of up-country garrisons in Aden, 84 Squadron aircraft were regularly operated on routes to Bahrain in the north and as far south as Southern Rhodesia.

As the Aden rundown gathered pace, 84 Squadron began a move to Sharjah in August 1967 to prepare to re-equip with Andover C.1s. In December 1970, the squadron moved to Muharraq where it could offer better support to Army units operating in the Trucial States, and Muscat and Oman. On 30 September 1971, 84 Squadron disbanded at Muharraq.

The squadron badge was a black scorpion and the motto 'Scorpiones Pungunt' – 'Scorpions Sting'.

105 Squadron

Formed as a day bomber unit at Andover on 14 September 1917, 105 Squadron was re-instituted as a reconnaissance unit in April 1918. Equipped with RE 8s it was sent to Ireland to support local security units. Bristol Fighters arrived in December 1918, the squadron remaining in Ireland until disbandment on 1 February 1920.

Reformed at Upper Heyford on 12 April 1937 as an Audax-equipped light-bomber unit, it had moved to Harwell by the end of that month. New equipment in the form of Fairey Battles arrived in August 1937 and these were taken to France as part of the Advanced Air Strike Force in September 1939. With the advance of German forces, however, the squadron was forced to return to England in June 1940.

Back home and re-equipped with Blenheims, the squadron mission changed to one of low-level daylight raids against enemy shipping, ports and airfields. On one particular mission, on 4 July 1941, nine 105 Squadron aircraft together with a further six from 107 Squadron carried out a raid against docks and factories in Bremen. Wing Commander Hughie Edwards, the squadron OC, attacked under fierce retaliatory fire, flying through the barrage balloon defences to strafe targets after releasing his bombs. His aircraft was hit several times and his gunner had his knee shattered, but he managed to escape enemy fire and fly back to England. He was awarded the Victoria Cross.

Following periods in Malta and Horsham St Faith, the squadron was selected to introduce the de Havilland Mosquito into front-line service in a bombing role. After a period dedicated to developing low-level precision attack techniques, the first operation to be flown with the 'Wooden Wonder' took place in May 1942. Its aircraft were later fitted with 'Oboe' and, bearing an all-over matt black paint scheme, formed one of the first Pathfinder squadrons. It remained a night-time target-marking unit in Bomber Command for the rest of the European war and disbandment on 1 February 1946.

Number 105 Squadron Argosy C.1 XN819 on the Khormaksar Transport Wing pan shortly after its arrival in Aden in June 1962 (Keith Webster).

Newly formed with the Armstrong Siddeley Argosy at Benson on 21 February 1962, 105 Squadron moved to Khormaksar in the following June to bolster the expanding requirement for mid-range transport aircraft. The original intention had been to locate the squadron at Embakasi, but the impending independence of Kenya ruled that option out.

As the drawdown of RAF forces at Khormaksar moved into full swing, 105 Squadron began to redeploy to Muharraq in August 1967 and disbanded there on 20 January 1968.

The squadron badge is a battleaxe, signifying a powerful weapon and the motto 'Fortis in Proeliis' – 'Valiant in Battles'.

233 Squadron

Number 233 Squadron was formed on 31 August 1918 through the merging of 407, 471 and 491 Flights at Dover and Walmer. The Dover element operated Short 184s on Channel patrol duties, leaving its Walmer-based Sopwith Camels to provide fighter defence over the coastal area. The squadron disbanded on 15 May 1919.

Re-formed at Tangmere on 18 May 1937 as a general reconnaissance unit equipped with Ansons, it moved to Thornaby in July and to Leuchars in September of the following year. Re-equipped with Hudsons in August 1939, its role was directed

The second Hercules engine on 233 Squadron Valetta C.1 VW837 bursts into life as the aircraft prepares to depart Khormaksar in 1962 (Keith Webster).

to anti-shipping operations along the Norwegian coast following the German invasion of Norway.

In December 1940 the squadron moved to Northern Ireland before moving on to St Eval eight months later. A detachment of one flight to Gibraltar in December 1942 was joined by the rest of the unit the following July. Two years later, in February 1944, the squadron returned to the UK to re-equip with the Dakota which it flew in support of the Normandy landings of June 1944, Operation MARKET GARDEN in September 1944, the Arnhem operation and the crossing of the Rhine in March 1945. A short period in India then ensued before disbandment on 15 December 1945.

Valetta transports had operated as a flight within 84 Squadron since 1958 but on 1 September 1960, the Valetta element became the nucleus of a newly-formed 233 Squadron at Khormaksar. Making full use of a larger allocation of aircraft, the squadron continued with the important up-country support role until disbandment beckoned on 31 January 1964.

The squadron badge was an eight-pointed star In front of a trident and sword in saltire. The squadron motto was 'Fortis et Fidelis' – 'Strong and Faithful'.

Search and Rescue Flight
Helicopters had performed an important role at Khormaksar since 1955. Along with the Shackletons, Sycamore HR.14s formed part of the SAR organisation, maintaining a permanent standby to rescue crews from crashed aircraft and

Backbone of the Khormaksar SAR Flight rescue fleet for nearly a decade, Sycamore HR.14 XG518 lifts off the helicopter pad in 1962 (Keith Webster)

individuals stranded on rocks and beaches. Much of the flight's work was directed to repatriating casualties from up-country garrisons and evacuation centres to Steamer Point hospital.

Occasionally, they were detached for duties elsewhere in the command, supporting operations in the Trucial Oman in 1959, Bahrain in 1960 and for displays at the Royal Agricultural Show in Nairobi. Replaced by Whirlwind HAR.10s in early 1964, the Sycamores were flown on to HMS *Albion* on 28 March 1964 and returned to the UK.

Middle East Communications Squadron

Many RAF stations operated communications flights and Khormaksar was no exception. During the mid-fifties it was equipped with Pembrokes and Sycamores, but these were superseded by a pair of all-white Canberra B.2s, a Hastings C.4, Valetta C.2 and a Dakota C.4 in 1962. The latter was maintained by DC-3 technicians at Aden Airways and was normally parked and operated from the civil airport apron. The Canberras were scrapped in early 1964 and a year later, under the name Middle East Communications Squadron, the unit received a second Dakota C.4 and an Andover CC.2. The second Dakota was subsequently destroyed in a sabotage attack at the airport.

One of three Dakota C.4s still in service with the RAF in the 1960s, KN452 is seen taking off from one of the many remote airstrips (Richard Grevatte-Ball).

RAF Eastleigh

With Kenya being at relative peace following the Mau–Mau troubles of the mid-fifties, a solitary ground attack squadron and two transport squadrons maintained the military commitment at the turn of the sixties.

21 Squadron

Number 21 Squadron was first formed at Netheravon on 23 July 1915 and, following training on the RE 7, was despatched to France as a general duties and reconnaissance unit in January 1916. From 9 March its role was expanded to that of a bomber squadron. On 30 June 1916, the eve of the Somme offensive, six 21 Squadron RE 7s opened the bombing campaign with an attack on the railway station at St Sauveur, where the enemy was known to have stockpiled ammunition. Each RE 7 was armed with a large, heavy-cased, Royal Aircraft Factory 336lb bomb, the first occasion on which bombs were used in France.

In August 1916 the squadron re-equipped with the BE 12 single-seat fighter which it continued to use on offensive and defensive patrols, escort work and bombing raids. In early 1917 these gave way to the RE 8 which the squadron continued to fly until the end of the war, when it received congratulations from General Trenchard for the best artillery squadron in France.

Disbanded in October 1919, 21 Squadron re-formed as a bomber unit at Bircham Newton in December 1935, equipped with Hawker Hind two-seaters. Following successive moves to a number of bases, it found itself at Watton at the outbreak of the Second World War.

Flying Blenheim Mk.IVs, 21 Squadron played a prominent part in the offensive against shipping in the English Channel, the North Sea and coastal targets on the continent. A move to Luqa in Malta in December 1941 saw the squadron continue in this role, attacking shipping in the Mediterranean and land targets in North Africa. Disbanded on 14 March 1942, it re-formed at Methwold on the same day and, on receiving an allocation of Lockheed Ventura aircraft, was involved in the daring low-level raid on the Phillips radio and valve factory at Eindhoven on 6 December.

No. 21 Squadron exchanged the Venturas for Mosquito fighter-bombers in early September 1943. These were employed mainly on night-time bombing raids and daylight precision raids, including the spectacular attacks on the Gestapo Headquarters at Aarhus and Copenhagen on 31 October 1944 and 21 March 1945 respectively. In February 1945 the squadron moved to France in order to fly intruder operations over Germany for the rest of the war and was disbanded on November 1947.

Six years later, on 21 September 1953, 21 Squadron reformed at Scampton as part of the home-based Canberra force. It disbanded again on 30 June 1957, only to

Sporting recently introduced sand and brown markings, Twin Pioneer XM286 taxies in at AAC Falaise airfield in 1967 (Richard Grevatte-Ball).

reform with the re-numbering of 542 Squadron at Upwood on 1 October 1958. This reincarnation lasted for a few months only, the squadron being disbanded again on 15 January 1959. On 1 May 1959, 21 Squadron reformed at Benson in an unfamiliar role, that of medium transport unit equipped with the Twin Pioneer.

In September, the squadron flew its aircraft out to Eastleigh where it remained until June 1965. Kenya had settled down following the troubles experienced during independence, allowing 21 Squadron to be relieved of its duties and move up to Khormaksar. There it remained until two months before the British withdrawal from Aden when, on 15 September 1967, the squadron was disbanded. Some of its aircraft were flown up to Muharraq to reinforce 152 Squadron, leaving the remainder to be flown back to the UK.

The 21 Squadron badge was a hand erased at the wrist, holding a dumb-bell to symbolise strength. Its motto was 'Viribus Vincimus' – 'By Strength We Conquer'.

30 Squadron

Formed at Ismailia on 24 March 1915 from an RFC detachment, 30 Squadron spent its first months in a state of flux but had reached full squadron status by the end of the year. The squadron's first task was to provide a number of detachments to protect key installations in Mesopotamia, critically the oil pipeline at Basra. In April 1916 the squadron carried out the first ever air supply operation, using its BE 2s, Longhorns and Shorthorns to drop food and ammunition to besieged British forces defending Kut Al Amara against the Turks. In total, thirteen tons of supplies were dropped over the two-week operation, but it could not stop the garrison from being overrun. Reconnaissance and bombing missions became the focus of attention until the end of the war, when the squadron was reduced to a cadre.

In February 1920 the squadron returned to full strength, having re-equipped with DH 9s and RE 8s for the day bomber role. For the next twenty years, 30 Squadron was based in Iraq and Egypt where it was re-equipped with Wapitis and Hardys. These were superseded by the Blenheim in January 1938 for use in the bomber escort role over the Western Desert. Shortly after moving to Greece in March 1941, the squadron received its first Hurricanes, which it took back to Egypt in the following May. In February 1942 the squadron embarked on HMS *Indomitable* and headed for Ceylon to defend the island from a Japanese attack. A move to Burma followed in May 1944 and the Hurricanes were replaced by Thunderbolts. By the time of the Japanese surrender in August 1945, 30 Squadron had moved to India and was disbanded in December 1946.

Having reformed with Dakotas at RAF Oakington in late 1947, 30 Squadron became part of the newly-formed Transport Command, one of its first missions being the supply of food and provisions to the citizens of Berlin. Re-equipped with Valettas, its next move was to Abingdon in November 1950. Seven years later, 30 Squadron

Eastleigh-based, 30 Squadron Beverley XH120 undergoing maintenance while on detachment at Bahrain on 19 November 1963 (Gordon Macadie).

was one of the first to receive the Blackburn Beverley. After a short period in the UK, the squadron redeployed to Eastleigh in 1959 where it remained for the next five years. During this period its aircraft were regularly detached to support operations at Khormaksar and Muharraq, before redeploying to the latter on a permanent basis in 1964. As the rundown of British forces in the Middle East gathered pace, 30 Squadron was disbanded in 1967.

The squadron badge depicts a date palm tree to commemorate its long service in the Middle East. The squadron motto is 'Ventre a Terre' – 'All Out'.

RAF Muharraq

Strategically positioned at the heart of the Persian Gulf, the relative tranquillity of the region did not require an establishment of offensive aircraft until the early sixties. Until then, the sole squadron in permanent residence operated five Pembrokes on communications duties and five Twin Pioneers in an Army support role.

152 Squadron

Equipped with Camel night-fighters in readiness for a move to France to defend Allied bases against enemy night bombers, 152 Squadron was formed at Rochford on 1 October 1918. With the end of the war three weeks later, the squadron disbanded.

Twin Pioneer XL996 was the first of its type to appear in grey/green camouflage when delivered to 152 Squadron at Bahrain in April 1963 (author).

On 1 October 1939, 152 Squadron re-formed at RAF Acklington equipped initially with Gladiators but by January 1940 it had converted to the Spitfire. As Luftwaffe attacks from bases in northern France increased, the squadron moved south to Warmwell, from where it could play an integral role defending Portland naval base during the Battle of Britain.

A change of scenery beckoned in 1942 when 152 redeployed to North Africa followed in June 1943 by a move to Malta. To cover the Allied landings in Sicily, the squadron flew regular sweeps in the area before hopping between various captured airstrips on the island. By September it had arrived in Italy.

Its task in this theatre completed, the Squadron moved to Burma on 19 December 1943, where it flew from improvised airstrips in support of the Fourteenth Army during the final conquest of the country. In September 1945 the squadron redeployed to Singapore following the Japanese capitulation and was disbanded there on 10 March 1946.

On 8 May 1946, 136 Squadron was renumbered 152 while in transit to Bombay. Equipped initially with Spitfires, it converted to the Tempest in August, but problems with a lack of spares saw it disband on 15 January 1947.

On 1 June 1954 the squadron re-formed at RAF Wattisham as a Meteor night-fighter unit and continued in this role until disbandment on 31 July 1958. Two months later, on 1 October 1958, 152 Squadron re-formed once again, this time at Bahrain in the role of a communications and transport provider. Equipped with Pembrokes and Twin Pioneers it remained at Bahrain until disbandment on 15 November 1967.

The squadron badge was a head-dress of the Nizam of Hyderabad and its motto 'Faithful Ally'.

AAC Falaise Airfield

The main base for Number 3 Wing of the Army Air Corps (AAC), home to 653 Squadron, was located at Falaise Airfield, near Little Aden. During its tenure in Aden, in addition to its responsibilities and commitments to the Army, the squadron maintained a close relationship with the RAF and many operations were carried out in conjunction with the units based at Khormaksar.

653 Squadron

In 1963 dissident tribesmen in the Radfan rebelled against the Federal Government and 24 Brigade Group was sent into the region with 653 Squadron Army Air Corps (AAC) in support. The squadron was initially equipped with nine fixed-wing aircraft (Austers and Beavers) and a pair of Scout helicopters with which to provide air reconnaissance, re-supply, liaison and artillery fire direction. Many important lessons were learnt during this campaign, including how to land and take off in areas of enemy

653 Squadron Beaver XP819 pictured at Habilayn in 1966 (Richard Grevatte-Ball).

activity, the vulnerability of helicopters to small arms fire and the morale boosting effect of using helicopters to evacuate casualties from locations that were inaccessible by other means.

By 1966, to reflect the growing number of AAC aircraft in theatre, 653 Squadron gained a new title, 3 Wing AAC, but continued to use the official crest of 653 Squadron. It comprised 15 Flight AAC with DHC 2 Beavers, 8 Flight AAC and 13 Flight AAC, with Westland Scout Helicopters and some four or five 'Air Troops' or 'Air Platoons', operating Augusta/Westland Sioux (Bell 47G) helicopters. Whilst these came under command of the wing for servicing and technical matters, they were under the control of individual Army units, such as the Royal Artillery, infantry battalions and cavalry regiments, to ensure greater flexibility in the field.

In the summer of 1967 Falaise Airfield was vacated and the wing's aircraft, helicopters and equipment moved to Khormaksar where they remained until the final withdrawal.

Chapter 4

Middle East Hunters

As with many early post-war jet fighters, the Hawker Hunter never fired its guns at enemy aircraft while in service with the RAF. Indeed, expectations were that the Hunter would be superseded by the English Electric Lightning in the interceptor role by the early 1960s. Had it not been for an urgent need to replace the de Havilland Venom in the Middle and Far East, the Hunter would have been relegated to a secondary role in tactical training.

The most pressing requirement for a Venom replacement was in Aden. To ensure that the best aircraft was selected, a Venom Replacement Evaluation Trial (VRET) was conducted at RAF Stations Khormaksar and Riyan in August 1958. These airfields were chosen as being the best locations to test the operational capabilities of various aircraft types from the tarmac-surfaced runway at Khormaksar and that of compacted sand at Riyan.

VRET trial

Three aircraft types were submitted for the trial by their respective manufacturers; a single-seat Folland Gnat F.Mk.1, the Hunting Jet Provost T.Mk.2 and Hawker Hunter F.Mk.6.

Prototype T.Mk.2 Jet Provost XN117 equipped with four HE rockets on a pre-VRET demonstration flight in 1958 (David Watkins).

Of the three, the Gnat was considered odds-on favourite, the example under test being an Indian Air Force production aircraft, IE1064. Equipped with a special cold air unit for the air-ventilated suit and low pressure mainwheel tyres for operation out of Riyan, it was allocated serial number XN122 and was flown out to Aden in an RAF Beverley together with Folland support staff.

Equipped with rocket rails and a pair of wing-mounted machine guns, the Jet Provost T. 2 trainer, XN117, was given little chance of success.

Lined up against these two was a pair of Hunter F.6s, XK150 and XK151, the last two production single-seat examples delivered to the RAF and allocated to the Central Fighter Establishment (CFE) at West Raynham. Tail-braking parachutes were fitted to prevent their brakes overheating in the extreme temperatures. Hawker Aircraft Ltd (HAL) had not intended to enter the Hunter, thinking it would prove uneconomical but, following fierce internal lobbying, the company made a late entry.

Trial Objectives

Eight objectives were defined in the trial documents:

- Performance
- Ferry range
- Strike radius
- Weapon loads and their effectiveness
- Take-off and landing distances
- Cockpit environment
- Ability to defend when intercepted
- Vulnerability to ground fire

The tests were conducted under high ambient temperatures at varying altitudes and included one-*vs*-one combat between each type and against No. 8 Squadron Venoms. Air-to-ground strikes were carried out on different target types over a combination of flat desert plains and treacherous mountainous terrain. The Hunters and Jet Provosts were flown by pilots from the Air Fighting Development Squadron at CFE and full ammunition loads were carried on all sorties.

The Gnat quickly established its ability to out-climb the Hunter and Venom at altitudes of 40,000 feet and out-turn the Hunter. The aircraft's excellent rate of climb and turn, together with its very small size, made it an impressive adversary in the fighter combat role and, in this respect, it was deemed superior to its competitors. Furthermore, its high speed and small size made it difficult to detect at low level and, thus, less vulnerable to ground fire. In spite of requiring only the most basic ground-support equipment, the Gnat's Achilles heel was the need for an external source of pressurised air to start the engine.

Hunter F.Mk.6 XK151 (above) shortly after its arrival at CFE, West Raynham, in 1958 (Aviation Bookshop). (below) Folland Gnat F.Mk.1 XN122 and Hunter F.Mk.6 XK150 captured during the VRET trial at Riyan on 3 August 1958 (via Peter Amos).

When operating from the unsurfaced runway at Riyan, the Gnat tended to pitch, causing the nose oleo to audibly bottom out and the nosewheel was reluctant to lift off when the stick was held fully back at 130 knots IAS. Other problems were raised concerning damage to the runway surface during its take-off run, due to the low jet efflux, and damage to the braking parachute canopy caused by debris being thrown up by the main wheels. The narrow undercarriage track also made for unsteady landings, especially in cross winds.

This aside, the most significant objective that could not be fulfilled by the Gnat was one of range. In strike configuration, it was capable of flying a radius of action of 188 nautical miles (nm), 52 less than the stipulated 240. In addition, a ferry range of 673 nautical miles was not sufficient to enable it to fly between some MEC airfields without refuelling more than once. Note: One mile is a unit of distance on land, a nautical mile is used to measure distances at sea. 1 nautical mile = 1.151 miles.

The Gnat proved an excellent contender in the air-combat role, but could not meet the crucial criteria required for ground attack, leading to the conclusion that, without major modifications, the Gnat should not be considered for use in the Middle East theatre.

Despite having the lowest operating costs of the three trial aircraft, the Jet Provost could not meet either the performance or firepower criteria and was quickly eliminated.

Although outclassed by the Gnat in air combat, the Hunter was found to excel in the crucial role of a ground attack and was thus selected as the replacement for the Venom.

Fighter Ground Attack

Work on a prototype conversion of a Mark 6 airframe to full ground-attack standard began in 1959. Equipped with a fully tropicalised refrigeration and ventilation system, increased oxygen supply, strengthened wings, tail-braking parachute and a surge-free Rolls Royce (RR) Avon 207 engine rated at 10,150lb thrust, the prototype FGA.Mk.9 (XG135) made its maiden flight on 3 July 1959. Contracts were issued for the conversion of a further thirty-six F.6 airframes, many of which had only flown between 300 and 600 hours. Fitted with RR Avon 203 engines delivering 9,700lb thrust, this batch was only partially equipped to Mark 9 standards and became known as 'Interim Mark 9s'. The conversions were carried out by RAF and HAL working parties at RAF Horsham St Faith. Five follow-on contracts brought the total number of conversions to 128, culminating with a batch of nine from 5 MU at Kemble in 1965.

The devastating firepower of the four 30mm nose-mounted cannon was retained and the strengthened wing enabled the carriage of a choice of pylon-mounted

Looking in pristine condition following refurbishment in the UK, the last single-seat Hunter delivered to the RAF, FGA.Mk.9 XK151 pictured in 208 Squadron markings on the Khormaksar pan in March 1964 (author).

ordnance and additional fuel. Although 500lb or 1,000lb bombs could be carried on the inner pylons, the standard fit for Middle East Command Hunters was three Mark 12 rocket rails under each wing. The ferry range and radius of operation was substantially increased when 230-gallon underwing tanks were fitted to the inner pylons, the outer corners of the flaps having been cut away to facilitate their carriage. The subsequent attachment of a bracing strut between the 230-gallon tank and wing enabled the FGA.9 to be flown in normal combat conditions.

The RAF now possessed a potent ground-attack aircraft and initial deliveries were made to 8 Squadron at Khormaksar in January 1960. Among the twelve FGA.9s were VRET participants XK150 and XK151 and the prototype Mark 9, XG135. Another aircraft worthy of note was XE600 which, having been used for nosewheel braking trials by HAL, was converted to F.Mk.56 standard and delivered to the Indian Air Force (IAF). Having discovered its trials background, however, the aircraft was rejected by the IAF and it was returned to HAL. It was then converted to FGA.9 standard and issued to 8 Squadron.

During the next two years, the Mark 9 would be allocated to a further seven squadrons, Nos. 1, 20, 28, 43, 54, 66 and 208. Numbers 1 and 54 Squadrons were based in the UK and were integrated into the newly-formed 38 Group. Number 20 Squadron was stationed in Singapore, 28 in Hong Kong, 43 in Scotland and 208 in Kenya. Number 66 Squadron disbanded in September 1960, having operated a handful of Mark 9s for a period of six months only.

Except for overseas detachments, the 38 Group squadrons remained on home soil and were seldom called upon to discharge their ordnance over enemy territory. A similar situation existed in Hong Kong, where 28 Squadron concentrated much of its time seeking out seagoing arms smugglers, while 20 Squadron regularly employed its Hunters on attacking targets in support of ground forces operating in dense Malay and Borneo jungles.

By far the busiest RAF theatre of operations was in Aden where 8 Squadron flew the FGA.9 in support of Army units operating up-country, helping to maintain a fragile peace between warring factions, while deterring errant aircraft from crossing the Yemen border on hit-and-run attacks on local villages. As the intensity of operations increased, 208 and 43 Squadrons were relocated to Khormaksar in 1961 and 1963 respectively. Following the British withdrawal in 1967, the FGA.9 continued to operate in a front-line role with 8 and 208 Squadrons at Muharraq (Bahrain) until 1971.

Fighter Reconnaissance

The fighter-reconnaissance version of the Hunter was a development of the F.Mk.6 by HAL to fulfil a requirement to replace the Swift FR.5s in service in Germany. A trial installation of five cameras was fitted to the nose of F.Mk.4 WT780, followed by a revised installation comprising three F.95 Vinten cameras in F.6 XF429. In this configuration, and equipped with a tail brake-chute, the aircraft was air tested for the first time on 7 November 1959 and christened the prototype FR.Mk.10.

Apart from the camera installation, the FR.10 was outwardly similar to the Mark 9 with subtle differences. The radar-ranging equipment was dispensed with and the gunsight offset to the right of centre to give the pilot a clear view forward when seeking a target at extremely low levels over uneven terrain. To counter a reduction in weight forward of the centre of gravity, armour plating was built into the cockpit floor and the port and starboard instrument console side panels, to offer protection from small arms fire. UHF radio replaced that of the VHF-equipped Mark 9 and a Wirek voice recorder and sub-miniature radio compass were further additions. Other modifications entailed the repositioning of equipment, such as the compass, radio control unit, stopwatch holder, fuel warning lights and camera controls so that they could be seen at a glance without the need for the pilot to look down into the cockpit. A fully tropicalised refrigeration and ventilation system and an increased oxygen supply were also incorporated.

External provision included the carriage of two 230-gallon underwing tanks on inner pylons and two 100-gallon tanks on outer pylons. There was no provision for

Hunter FR.Mk.10 XF460 on detachment to Masirah in 1965 (above) together with a close-up of the Mark 10 camera fit in the forward fuselage (below). Of interest is the eyelid that protected the forward facing camera (via Aviation Bookshop).

the attachment of rocket rails. In operational guise, the Mark 10 was configured for maximum endurance, both 230– and 100-gallon drop tanks being the standard fit. From the outset, the FR.10 was powered by a non-surge RR Avon 207 engine rated at 10,150lb thrust.

A contract for the conversion of a further thirty-two Mark 6s to FR.10 standard was signed in 1959 and the first production aircraft, XE585, was delivered to 19 MU at St Athan on 28 November 1960. Initial deliveries were made to 4 Squadron at RAF Gütersloh in the following month and to 2 Squadron at RAF Jever in March 1961. The FR.10 quickly gained a reputation as the consummate low-level, high-speed visual reconnaissance aircraft. 'Royal Flush', the annual NATO competition for this class of aircraft, saw the two squadrons frequently beating their American, French and German counterparts by virtue of the Hunter's superior flexibility and manoeuvrability under operational conditions.

B Flight 8 Squadron received four FR.10s in April/May 1961 as replacements for its obsolescent Meteor FR.9s. A fifth FR.10 was placed in local storage with 131 MU as command reserve. On 1 May 1963 B Flight was separated from 8 Squadron to provide the nucleus of a reformed 1417 Flight. Over the ensuing years many thousands of photographs were taken by the FR.10s to supplement the poor quality maps of the operational area in the quest to reduce the time required to locate targets. Another 1417 Flight mission was to keep HQ MEC informed of smuggling activities in and around the Protectorates and to provide pre- and post-engagement photographs for assessment by photographic interpreters.

The FR.10 continued to serve with 1417 Flight until its disbandment on 8 September 1967. Its aircraft were re-allocated to 8 Squadron, two joining the squadron at Masirah in late August, leaving the remaining two on detachment at Khormaksar until the final withdrawal in November. The Mark 10 remained in service with 8 Squadron until September 1971.

Range

Concerns regarding the Hunter's range and radius of operation were of particular significance for Middle East Command due to the long distances between the route stations and limited options to divert in an emergency. The problem of endurance with the early Hunters was partially resolved by fitting a pair of 100-gallon underwing tanks. These could be released in an emergency, but were too expensive to discard without reason.

The first production tanks were of 100-gallon capacity. Normal configuration for practice combat sorties with the Hunter F.4 was for two tanks to be mounted on inboard pylons but the aircraft could carry a second pair on outboard pylons to increase its radius of operation. That was fine for the UK Air Defence role but squadrons equipped with the thirstier Mark 6 were expected to make regular detachments to bases in Cyprus, requiring three refuelling stops en route. The notion that four 100-gallon tanks would be adequate for quick reaction, long-range deployments was no longer acceptable.

Long-range underwing fuel tanks

Hawker Aircraft Ltd was, therefore, encouraged to develop a much larger 230-gallon tank that could be fitted to the inboard pylons for long-range ferry flights. Former 8 Squadron pilot Ken Parry summarises the three-phase development of the 230-gallon tank:

Phase 1   Comprising a single chamber; intended for use on ferry flights only.

Phase 2   Single chamber but fitted with a strengthening strut; could be used over the full flight envelope.

Phase 3   Two chambers and strengthening strut; this resolved the problem of tanks coming off under high g loadings. A bulkhead separated the rear section from which fuel was used first. This tank could be identified by a horizontal blue stripe across the joint at the front and centre section.

With these and a pair of 100-gallon tanks on the outboard pylons, the Hunter could reach Cyprus with a solitary stop at Malta. By the time Roger Wilkins joined 43 Squadron in Aden in July 1963, the 230-gallon tank was well established.

These huge tanks were fitted to the inboard pylons only and had originally been intended purely for ferrying purposes, their being removed at the destination. However, pilots never have enough fuel and the distances involved from Khormaksar-Masirah-Sharjah-Bahrain were too great for the little 100s. Initially the ferry fit was 2 x 230s inboard and 2 x 100s outboard, giving an external 660 gallons; the 230s were removed on arrival. But soon squadron pilots were asking for the 230s to be permanently fitted, requiring the manufacturer to strengthen the attachment points and further stabilise the big tank for high g-forces encountered in the ground-attack and day-fighter combat roles. When I arrived in Aden all of the aircraft and tanks had been modified and so the 230-gallon tank became the standard fit.

Although the 230s could be jettisoned with the stabilising struts fitted, it was done only as a last resort such as in an emergency. Even with big tanks fitted we treated the Hunter as though it was clean and carried out practice dog-fighting, ground attack manoeuvres and pulling g regardless of how much fuel remained in them. However, with all four drop tanks attached it was a different ball game and although gentle ground attack manoeuvres and gun firing were permissible, this configuration was used only for ferry purposes.

Former Hunter armourer David Griffin describes the design features built into the strut:

> Phase 2 and 3 tanks could be jettisoned should the need arise. The strut on these tanks was attached by a ball and socket joint with a pin on a tensioner thread. The whole was lock-nutted in place and then lock-wired to the strut and tank attachment point. A sleeve covered the attachment point and was screwed in position. The top portion of the strut had a similar sleeve arrangement. The upper attachment had a similar ball and threaded tensioner but it was seated in a tapered socket built into the underside of the wing leading edge. As the tank was jettisoned the strut fell away from the wing at the upper attachment point, leaving the tank and strut to fall away cleanly.

Training

Developed as a private venture by HAL, the first of fifty-five production Hunter T.Mk.7s, XL563, flew for the first time on 11 October 1957 and deliveries to 229 OCU at Chivenor commenced in May 1958. With the exception of a longer and broader front fuselage section to accommodate side-by-side seating, the airframe

The last Hunter to operate in RAF service when withdrawn in August 2001, T.Mk.7 XL612 awaits its next training mission during earlier times while on an 8 Squadron detachment to Masirah in 1967 (Aviation Bookshop).

was identical to the F.4. A single 30mm cannon was fitted to the forward fuselage, offset to the starboard side, sawtooth extensions adorned the wing leading edges and a braking parachute was housed in a fairing above the jet pipe. Power was provided by a 7,500lb thrust RR Avon 122 which retained the cartridge starter system from the Mark 4. Despite its lower power rating, the area rule principle generated by the bulbous front fuselage enabled the trainer to attain a maximum speed just 20mph short of its more powerful cousin.

To prepare 8 Squadron pilots for conversion to the Hunter, two T.7s, XL613 and XL615, were flown out to Khormaksar in September 1959. Number 208 Squadron received a solitary trainer, XL597, in 1960 as did 43 Squadron – XL566.

In the main the T.7s were used for instrument rating checks and area familiarisation rides over the hostile terrain above which new pilots would eventually fly. Even so, equipped with four rocket rails and a solitary cannon, they were often used on operations during periods of high FGA.9 utilisation. The single cannon was just as capable of keeping heads down, particularly when HE ammunition was used.

Firepower

The advent of high-speed aircraft such as the Hunter required the development of a gun capable of greater firepower than available on earlier aircraft.

The Aden cannon

The Armament Development establishment at the Enfield Royal Small Arms Factory in London had recently completed the development of such a gun: the Aden 30mm cannon. To meet the Hunter specification, which required it to deliver a lethal blow in a very short space of time, the gun was required to fire approximately 1,200 rounds per minute. The Aden 30mm cannon met this requirement and had been adopted by the British authorities in May 1949.

The gun was capable of firing various types of ammunition but in the Middle East two types of shell were commonly used on Hunter operations, one with an inert filling (Ball) and a high explosive (HE) version packed with TNT.

The Hunter was equipped with four 30mm cannon contained in an interchangeable gunpack that formed an integral part of the aircraft's fuselage. Each magazine could hold up to 150 rounds of belt-fed ammunition giving a total of 600 rounds or 7.5 seconds of firing per gun. An empty gun pack could be removed and replaced with one fully-armed in very quick time, enabling 'operational turn-rounds' to be achieved well within the stipulated 10-minute window during periods of intense activity.

All four guns could be fired at once when required but, depending on the type of target under attack, pilots had the option of selecting the inner or outer pairs at the

Colour-tipped 30mm cannon shells stacked on a trailer ready for loading into 8 Squadron Hunter gunpacks at Akrotiri during an APC in 1961. The paint left a trace on the target to identify hits from individual pilots (Mike Halpin).

The ingeniously designed gunpack enabled the Hunter to be rearmed in as little as eight minutes. Here we see, Bob Scales and Jock Harman lowering an empty pack onto the trolley as Baz, a trusted Arab, collects the links for re-use (author).

flick of a switch. The two-gun mode gave about fourteen seconds of fire and this was generally employed on armed recces to spread the rounds. The four-gun mode was usually reserved for strikes on specific targets and scrambles.

'The drain pipe'

Development of the Hunter from interceptor to ground attack fighter included an option to mount up to four Mark 12 rocket rails under each wing, each rail capable of carrying up to three 60lb 3-inch rockets. The default configuration in Aden was three rails per wing and a maximum of two rockets per rail.

Dating from the Second World War and nicknamed the 'drain pipe', the 3-inch rocket was difficult to aim at the best of times, particularly when fired at targets in the difficult terrain and high wind-sheer conditions encountered in the Radfan. The concrete-headed rocket was used for practice firings on the ranges and, on occasions, knocking down stone-built structures, whereas the HE GP Hollow Charge and the HE SAP heads were used for various targets – in operations against armour, vehicles, forts, buildings and insurgents, for example.

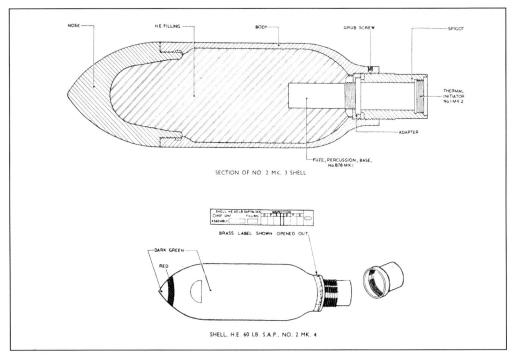

Cut-away drawings depicting the two main types of head fitted to the rockets used by the Middle East Hunter squadrons. The HE SAP version (above) was used to demolish solid targets such as stone-built houses and forts, whereas the pointed-nose on the HE Hollow Charge type (opposite above) was designed to penetrate armour (Mike Halpin).

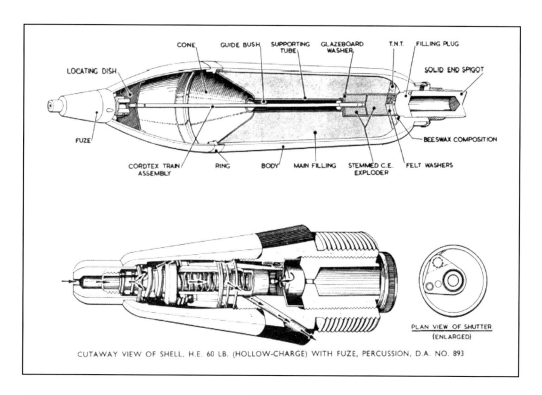

CUTAWAY VIEW OF SHELL, H.E. 60 LB. (HOLLOW-CHARGE) WITH FUZE, PERCUSSION, D.A. NO. 893

43 Squadron armourers attach a 60lb HE SAP rocket to an FGA.9 at Khormaksar in 1965 (Willie Marr).

8 Squadron armourers, Fred Lawson and Larry Forster, attach a concrete-headed practice rocket to an FGA.9 at Khormaksar in 1963 (author).

SNEB

The French-made SNEB 68mm armour-piercing folding-fin rocket was a far more effective weapon than the 3-inch rocket but was never used in Aden. Designed for use against armoured vehicles, bunkers and soft targets, SNEB had been in service with

The SNEB rocket system broadened the scope of Middle East Hunter operations in the late 1960s. As illustrated in the image above, the pod was mounted on the outer pylons on the FGA.9 (via Mark Taylor).

Royal Navy Sea Vixen and Hunter GA.11 squadrons, and RAF Canberra units based in Near East Command for a number of years, but the RAF had to wait until 1964 before it was considered as a weapon of choice for its Hunters. The task of easing the system into RAF service was undertaken by 208 Squadron at Muharraq in 1966 but the establishment of a support structure in the UK was slow to materialise.

The SNEB pod housed up to nineteen rockets, fired in a single rippled salvo of 0.5 seconds with a time interval of 33 milliseconds between each rocket firing. It was capable of achieving Mach 1.53 at 1,000 yards and had a shaped charge warhead capable of penetrating fifteen inches of armour. It was accurate and could be delivered in a shallow dive which was a distinct advantage for the pilot.

Keeping them flying

The extremely hot conditions and blowing sands were major factors affecting aircraft availability levels and the RAF's ability to undertake its operational commitments in the Middle East. Without the dedication of the ground crews and their desire to keep as many aircraft in serviceable condition as possible, often working in painfully uncomfortable conditions, some operations would have had to be scaled back.

Groundcrew structure

As on many stations throughout the RAF, tradesmen on MEC squadrons were organised into two servicing teams, First Line and Second Line, with airmen of all trades assigned to each team. In general, the first-line crew was responsible for undertaking all tasks relating to activities on the aircraft pan – strapping pilots in, aircraft starting and marshalling, refuelling, re-arming and turning-round the aircraft between flights. Second-line teams, in the case of the Hunter Wing, performed their duties out of the glare of the sun inside the hangar. They were responsible for carrying out the more lengthy, intricate activities such as, engine changes, fuel tank changes, serious defect rectification, primary star servicing and aircraft modifications.

Line activities

In this section we take a look at some of these activities in more detail, beginning with the starting procedure. Having helped the pilot strap himself in, handed him his helmet and plugged the R/T lead into the radio socket, the ejection safety pin is removed, shown to the pilot and stowed in the storage holder on the side of the seat. The steps are then released from the fuselage side and the starter waits for the pilot to complete his pre-start checks. A twirl of the fore-finger indicates that he is ready and the starter reciprocates the signal, having first checked the area behind the aircraft is clear. As the start button is pressed, a 'weee-futt' sound signals the ignition sequence of the Avpin starter and automatic lighting up of the Avon 207 engine. Despite the toxic fumes from the Avpin starter stinging the eyes, the airman then ducks under the

Pete Wootton uses an asbestos glove to douse the Avpin exhaust flame. The large screwdriver is carried just in case the Avpin fails to ignite. A solid thump is then applied to the starter relay box mounted on the hanging door and a second attempt to start the engine would be made (author).

Dave Waring assists Pete Loveday with the strapping in process (author).

It may be a single-seater but three Armourers have found sufficient space to cram in the cockpit and remove the ejection seat (Alan Lowe).

As Taff John marshalls a stray 208 Squadron FGA.9 onto an 8 Squadron bay, the turnround team assemble to carry out their checks. As soon as the aircraft comes to a halt, Taff will place the chock behind the nosewheel and clip the access ladder to the Hunter fuselage (author).

fuselage to extinguish any flames that emit from the starter's exhaust, using an asbestos glove. The starter-bay door is then closed and the airman stands by for the signal to remove chocks and marshall the aircraft out.

During the period when the aircraft are away from the airfield on operations or training, the groundcrew would make the most of the opportunity to take a break or get to work on minor defects reported on other Hunters remaining on the line. Typically, these would range from performing turn-rounds, wheel changes and brake checks, instrumentation and electrical faults, to radio and radar failures.

Hunter operations in Aden were usually carried out by two or four aircraft, although eight would often be flown on those requiring the attention of heavy firepower. A run in and break would prelude their return to the airfield, a signal for airmen assigned to marshalling duties to ensure the pan was clear of obstacles in readiness to guide their aircraft onto their individual parking bays.

Away from home
Although detachments away from Khormaksar were regular, they were rarely the same, either in destination or content. On occasions it was necessary to change from one transport aircraft at another at one of the route stations and as these were not blessed with air movements sections, it was down to the squadron groundcrew to unload the

Accidents will happen! An 8 Squadron FGA.9 has wandered off the peritrack at Sharjah requiring the heavy-lift capability of the groundcrew to extract it (Barry Potter).

On the same 8 Squadron detachment to Sharjah, a fully-laden 3-ton Bedford truck has backed up to the Beverley's ramp, enabling the groundcrew to unload the packup kits and auxiliary equipment (Barry Potter).

packups and associated equipment from one aircraft and load it into another. As heavy lifting equipment was also not available at these remote airfields, any mishaps with the Hunters had to be handled manually by the groundcrew.

Chapter 5

1960 – Steep learning curve

This chapter, together with Chapters 6 to 13, describe the events and operations undertaken by Middle East Command strike aircraft during the period 1960 to 1971. They are based on information gleaned from the unit and station Operations Record Books (ORBs, also known as F540) held at the National Archives in Kew.

Venom swansong

As the de Havilland Venoms that had replaced the Vampires on 8 Squadron in 1956 had relatively short fatigue lives, approximately 500 hours, they were replaced with refurbished machines from stocks held in the UK on a regular basis. As noted in Chapter 4, the requirement for a suitable replacement aircraft type was acknowledged in early 1958 and culminated with the Venom Replacement Evaluation Trial held at Khormaksar in August of that year. Having outclassed

A rare colour photograph depicting an airborne 8 Squadron Venom FB.4 (Peter Goodwin).

The dramatic sight of 8 Squadron Venom FB.4 WR405 starting-up at Khormaksar in 1959 (Bill Horspole).

the Gnat and Jet Provost in the ground attack role, the primary requirement, the Hawker Hunter, was selected as the Venom's successor.

Hunter conversion

The initial stage in the re-equipment programme commenced in the late summer of 1959 when seven pilots were despatched to the UK for conversion training on the Hunter. Once this had been accomplished, two T.7s (XL613 and XL615), painted in camouflage markings with yellow training bands, were flown out to Khormaksar where they arrived at 17:30 on 22 September. Two civilian engineering representatives, Mr Dale of Rolls Royce and Mr Mackay of Hawker Aircraft Ltd (HAL), were seconded to the squadron for a three-month period to help smooth the transition to the new aircraft. They were soon at work instructing groundcrew personnel on acceptance check procedures on the T.7s.

The first post-check air test was undertaken on 13 October, followed by that of the second aircraft three days later. By the end of the month, the seven pilots had gained their Instrument Ratings on type and thirty-seven hours flying time had been accrued. The remaining pilots were converted to the Hunter as and when they could be spared from operational flying on the Venoms.

A cloud of black smoke indicates that the starter cartridges have ignited on three 8 Squadron Venom FB.4s, WR400, WR431 and WR420, during a detachment to Sharjah in 1959 (author's collection).

The two aircraft were initially fitted with four rocket rails under each wing (the standard fit for the trainer was subsequently reduced to a pair on each side between the drop-tank pylons) and test flights flown on the Khormaksar range to establish the requisite range settings for rocket projectiles (RPs).

New year – New era

Towards the end of 1959, a large group of dissidents from the Bubakr tribe had moved into a proscribed area of Wadi Aadz, to the south of Said. Nearby water holes and sangars were strafed with rockets and cannon by 8 Squadron Venoms on 4, 5 and 6 January 1960. When a sizeable number of Marazaqi tribesmen were detected in the area to the west of Said, flagwaves were flown over them on the 5th in an attempt to persuade them to disperse. This was a busy period for the squadron. On the 6th of the month, a pair of Venoms was scrambled when a Dhala military convoy was attacked three miles north of Nobat Dakim. Despite a thorough search of the area by the pilots, none of the perpetrators was spotted.

Despite their imminent withdrawal, individual flight markings were added to the tip-tanks of the Venoms in readiness for an AOC's inspection, yellow flashes for A Flight, red flashes for B Flight.

(above) Lying down on the job! All part of a 208 Squadron armourers lot when rearming a Venom as depicted in this scene at Eastleigh in 1959. (below) The ungainly pose adopted by 208 Squadron Venom WR400 was the result of the pilot taxiing the aircraft into a ditch during a night flying session at Eastleigh on 6 August 1959 (both Pete McLeland).

Welcome the FGA.9

With long-range 230-gallon underwing tanks fitted to the inner pylons and 100-gallon tanks on the outer pylons, the first of 8 Squadron's allocation of twelve Hunter FGA.9s were flown out from the UK in the middle of January 1960, the remainder following at the beginning of February. All were fitted with 203-series Avon engines, bar one (XG135, the prototype) which was equipped with a more powerful, surge-free Avon 207. The other eleven aircraft were gradually fitted with the uprated engine over the next few months.

As each aircraft passed through its acceptance check, the four drop tanks were removed and 100-gallon tanks fitted to the inboard pylons only. The intention was to remove the outboard pylons and fit four rocket rails under each wing but, in the event, the decision was taken to retain the outboard pylons and fit two rocket rails between the pylons as with the trainers.

The final operational sorties flown by the Venoms occurred during the late afternoon of 18 January and comprised flagwaves over Wadi Farah, close to Said. The pilots and aircraft allocated for this sombre occasion were Flight Lieutenants Brown (WR419) and Merret (WR532), and Flying Officers Dowling (WR473) and Webb (WR546).

To mark the AOC's annual inspection, on 21 January, a flypast consisting of a single Hunter, five Venoms and four Meteors from the Aden Protectorate Reconnaissance Flight, was flown over the station. Ten Venoms and a Vampire T.11 then departed Khormaksar and headed south to Kenya, there to provide a reserve for 208 Squadron at Eastleigh. No. 8 Squadron was declared non-operational on 23 January while it continued to work-up on the Hunter, its operational commitments being covered by APRF Meteor FR.9s and 37 Squadron Shackleton MR.2s.

The pilot work up comprised a period of ground training and eighteen sorties concentrating on aircraft handling techniques, up-country recces, gunfiring on the local range and long-range, route-staging exercises to Bahrain.

To ensure that the *Pilots' Notes* correctly reflected those needed for operations in the Middle East, a team of pilots from the Handling Squadron at Boscombe Down arrived at Khormaksar to review and refine them. Several inaccuracies were uncovered and corrections incorporated into an updated set.

As 208 Squadron would soon be embarking on its conversion to the Hunter, an 8 Squadron T.7 was flown to Eastleigh (5,300 feet asl) via Mogadishu in Italian Somaliland, to determine the suitability of the 1,500-yard runway for operations by the Hunter during the dry season, June to October. This was the first occasion on which a Hunter had visited either country and the flight south was reported by the crew, Wing Commander Hegerty from HQ British Forces Arabian Peninsula (BFAP) and Flight Lieutenant Merret (8 Squadron) as, 'Challenging; the short runway at Mogadishu providing a degree of excitement on take-off'.

By early February, 8 Squadron's complement of Hunters had risen to sixteen aircraft, comprising FGA.9s XE581, XE600, XE620, XE649, XE651, XE654, XF424, XF455, XG128, XG135, XG136, XG169, XK150 and XK151, plus the two T.7s.

The squadron work up was completed at the end of February with an evaluation of the Hunter's long-range capability under hot conditions. Three Mark 9s were fitted with two 230-gallon and two 100-gallon drop tanks and flown nonstop to Sharjah in the early hours of the 29th. The 1,140nm flight was uneventful, the aircraft returning to Khormaksar in the afternoon.

Squadron declared operational

The first operation involving the Hunter was carried out on 4 March when Flight Lieutenants Leach (XE620) and Lydiate (XE600) performed cannon and RP strikes on a target at Khureiba. This was the first occasion on which RAF Hunters had fired their ordnance at an enemy target. No. 8 Squadron was declared operational following an inspection by the AOC, Air-Vice Marshal D.J.P. Lee CB CBE on 7 March.

To gain experience of operating away from Khormaksar, the squadron undertook a short detachment to Sharjah, two Mark 9s preparing the way on 9 March followed by a further four aircraft on the 14th. Ground support was provided by two SNCOs and

Pilots and airmen parade in front of their newly acquired Hunter T.7s and FGA.9s at Khormaksar to await the AOC's inspection and affirmation that 8 Squadron was now operational on the aircraft, 8 March 1960 (Ronnie Hush).

thirty-six corporals and airmen who flew up in a Beverley. During the detachment, the Hunters were used in support of military operations and exercises in Oman and to provide logistical and technical guidance for future mobility operations in the area. The highlight of the detachment was a firepower demonstration by four aircraft using 30mm HE cannon at Bait-Al-Falaj for the Sultan of Muscat and Oman. Also in attendance were members of his family, local sheikhs and members of the Sultan of Oman's Air Force (SOAF), approximately 3,000 people in total. The SAS and 208 Squadron (Venoms) were among other British units to participate in the event.

A shortage of serviceable FGA.9s back at Khormaksar was partially resolved by flying an armed T.7 (XL613) as escort to solo FGA.9s on strike sorties. The first such duty was flown on 16 March when the squadron OC, Squadron Leader Knight, attacked a target at Museinah in FGA.9 XE654. Both T.7s were utilised on similar attacks on the 16th (XL613) and 23rd (XL615) of the month.

The first Hunter flagwave was carried out on the 21st, when five aircraft flew low over targets at Suadi Point, Bat Hat Y Al Sa'd, Khaburah Mukhailif and Al Sohar to ensure that potential troublemakers were aware that the RAF possessed a noisy and powerful new weapon. The pilots for this auspicious occasion were Flight Lieutenants Russell (XE600), Leach (XF455) and Lydiate (XF424), Pilot Officer Volkers (XG135) and Flying Officer Baxter (XG169). Further flagwaves were flown over the same locations on the 23rd and 28th in a bid to quell inter-tribal feuding.

Continuing trouble in the Museinah area, however, only subsided following a rocket strike performed by a pair of FGA.9s flown by Flight Lieutenant Brown (XG136) and Flying Officer Bobbington (XE654).

208 Squadron converts

For the first few months of 1960, 208 Squadron continued to fly its Venoms over Kenyan territory, mostly on co-operation exercises with Army formations and units, 24 Brigade in particular. As preparations were put in place for the conversion to the Hunter, time-expired Venoms were despatched to 133 MU at Eastleigh for scrapping, several having only recently been replaced by examples retired from 8 Squadron. One aircraft (WR493) was retained for display by the officers' mess.

Towards the end of March the Squadron was declared non-operational and its pilots and ground crew flown back to the UK for conversion training on the Hunter at RAF Stradishall. Three months later, thirteen gleaming FGA.9s (XE544, XE597, XE607, XE609, XE618, XE623. XE643, XE647, XF376, XF421, XG134, XJ643, XJ687) and a T.7 (XL597) were flown out to Embakasi Airport, Kenya. The high-altitude (5,300 feet) of the RAF airfield at nearby Eastleigh and its relatively short runway had been declared unsuitable for Hunter operations but this was not the case at Embakasi where full advantage could be taken of the 5,000-yard-long runway. Even so, extra vigilance was needed on hot days as a heavily-laden Hunter needed a lot of runway to take off safely at that height.

Venom swansong! Armed 208 Squadron aircraft on the pan at RRAF Thornhill during their final visit to Rhodesia in late 1959 (Pete McLeland).

Hunter Baptism

The situation in the Aden Protectorates began to deteriorate rapidly through the early months of 1960. Anarchist leaders of the 'National Liberation Army' (NLA), the military wing of the South Arabian League, had organised an inflow of Egyptian arms

Getting to grips with the Hunter. One loaded and one empty gunpack trolley indicates that FGA.9 XE620-F will have its pack changed during the turnround, in the Spring of 1960. The aircraft is also configured with eight rocket rails (Ronnie Hush).

8 Squadron pilots and airmen under the command of Sqn Ldr Rex Knight, pose for their first official photograph in front of a Hunter at Khormaksar on 17 September 1960 (Ronnie Hush).

as a prelude to a planned uprising, using routes through the Yemen and by dhows using the Red Sea. The NLA had a long-held desire to create an independent and united states of South Arabia encompassing both the Yemen and Aden, an ambition the British Government would not accept.

Operation CANISTER

The Hunter was about to face its first real baptism as a ground-attack fighter. Flying as part of a joint operation with the Shackletons of 37 Squadron and aircraft from the carrier HMS *Centaur* operating in the Red Sea a border and coastal blockade was put into force. As a prelude to a major offensive scheduled for late April, using a steady stream of RP and cannon strikes, 8 Squadron was tasked with softening up insurgent groups gathered in the Mafhid area in an operation codenamed Operation CANISTER. Nine FGA.9s departed Khormaksar in waves of three through the morning of 12 April and the pattern was repeated during the afternoon, the following day and on the morning of the 14th. A total of thirty-five strike sorties were flown by the Hunters in support of CANISTER. Over the same period, Royal Navy Sea Hawks, Sea Venoms and Gannets were kept busy, pounding a rebel stronghold on Jebel Hanak with rockets and 20mm cannonfire during daylight hours, leaving the Shackletons to maintain continuity, dropping sticks of 1,000lb bombs over the same target area during the hours of darkness.

Operation OUTMOST

With an 8 Squadron pilot acting as Forward Air Controller (FAC), 4th Battalion the Aden Protectorate Levies (APL) was ordered to carry out a damage assessment resulting from CANISTER. Based on their findings, a second phase of the operation, codenamed OUTMOST, commenced at first light on 25 April. The aim of this operation was to locate a dissident group led by Al Bubakr Bin Farid and drive them into the Yemen. Troops of the 3rd Battalion APL were accordingly dropped by Beverley transport aircraft of 84 Squadron into the Mahfid area. From there they headed north into the proscribed area of Museinah, the vacated space in Mahfid being filled by the 4th Battalion. One 8 Squadron pilot was attached to each battalion in the role of FAC to guide the Hunters onto the requisite targets.

Operation OUTMOST accounted for much of 8 Squadron's flying commitment during the first two weeks of May. Groundcrews were fully occupied keeping the aircraft serviceable, refuelled and armed with rockets and guns throughout the daylight hours. APL troops quickly cleared a path into the Aulaqi Khor area, to the south of Museinah and, as the month progressed, were able to drive the dissidents westwards through Marzaqi and Rabizi country. Local inhabitants were warned not to provide any form of support to the dissidents, via a leaflet drop carried out by Flight Lieutenant Morris (XK150) and Flying Officer Webb (XK151), and a 'sky-shouting' Pembroke from the station flight under escort by a second pair of armed Hunters.

Dissident tribesmen were not the only targets; soft targets such as camels, donkeys and goats were struck to deprive the rebels of transport and food. A dawn strike south-west of Museinah on 7 May, for example, was reported to have killed fifteen to twenty camels and a large number of goats. Eleven camels were killed during a strike on another target in the same area, and forty goats and four camels during a third strike later that morning. As the strikes continued, livestock casualty numbers increased steadily until, finally, the Bubakr tribe yielded; enough was enough and they fled across the border into the Yemen. The operation had achieved its goal and was brought to a conclusion on 23 May. An uneasy peace descended on the area.

The heavy flying commitment (325 hours) undertaken during the operation, took its toll on aircraft serviceability. On average, three or four Hunters were declared Aircraft On Ground (AOG) on most days due to a shortage of spares and much valuable time was spent robbing unserviceable aircraft to keep others flying. A high number of engine starter failures was attributed to battery drainage and sticking starter valves due to the high temperatures the aircraft were subjected to while standing on the pan. The situation became so serious that a T.7 (XL613) was pressed into flying on three strike sorties on 16 and 18 May.

Hazell's day!

At 06:00 on 11 May, Flight Lieutenant Dennis Hazell had led the first pair of the day on an Operation OUTMOST sortie, but instead of heading north towards the target area he turned south and flew low and fast over HQ MEC at Steamer Point and the Governor's Palace nearby. His intention was to demonstrate how 'on-the-ball' the squadron was. He took off for a second sortie at 09:00 but, on sustaining damage from a bird-strike, returned to Khormaksar. For his third sortie of the day his wheels remained firmly on the ground as it involved a quick drive home and a change into best No. 6 uniform before reporting to the AOC, the C-in-C and Governor to make his apologies for arousing them so early. On his return to the squadron, he was informed that he had been assigned to the role of B Flight Commander designate. They were clearly not that angry!

As the Hunter was the first aircraft in the Middle East capable of breaking the sound barrier, new regulations were issued to protect the Colony from the effect of sonic bangs. 'Boom Flights' would only be permitted above 30,000 feet and when heading out to sea, the pilots having first notified air traffic control (ATC). However, it was soon realised that a sonic bang had a more practical use. Arab tribesmen were unable to distinguish between the sound of a sonic bang and that of a 1,000lb bomb

XG136, one of the first FGA.9s to join 8 Squadron, sits on the new Hunter pan at the eastern end of Khormaksar airfield. Note that strengthening struts were not fitted to the 230-gallon drop tanks at this time (Des Meek).

detonating in a neighbouring wadi. A few well-directed sonic bangs could give the impression of a heavy bombardment and the tactic was used sporadically as a ploy to deter dissidents from embarking on hostile activities.

Aircraft losses

One of the inherent dangers of low flying is the constant threat of a bird-strike. In this respect, one of the most deadly creatures in the Aden skies and one that pilots had no wish to confront was the 'shitehawk', a huge, ugly, vulture-like bird that was large enough to bring an aircraft down. Back in March, the pilot of FGA.9 XF424 managed to land his aircraft safely back at Khormaksar after one such encounter but the damage was sufficient for the aircraft to be written off.

The loss of a second Hunter soon afterwards had a marked effect on squadron morale. On 1 June Flight Lieutenant A. Devine and Flying Officer M. Walley were killed when their T.7 (XL615) crashed near Little Aden while on a nightflying exercise. A full account of the accident can be found in Appendix 1

Operations for the month of June consisted almost entirely of flagwaves over the Rubat area where Marsatta tribesmen were stirring up trouble with their neighbours in Bauri, Dhubi, Maflahi and Hadram. The show of force was sufficient to reduce tensions both there and subsequently in the Al Kara area, where tribesmen had been levying an illicit tax on camel trains passing through their area from the Upper Yaffa. The tax was swiftly withdrawn!

Goodwill detachment to Rhodesia

On 5 July nine FGA.9s (XE581, XE620, XE651, XF455, XG128, XG136, XG169, XK150 and XK151), departed Khormaksar for a three-week, goodwill visit to the Royal Rhodesian Air Force base at RRAF Thornhill in Southern Rhodesia. Although four aircraft were declared unserviceable on arrival at Embakasi, the only scheduled stopover, they were able to continue to Thornhill on the following day. The long distances, varied climates and unreliable weather forecasting experienced in the Middle East theatre required a good deal of accuracy when calculating fuel loads. On this trip, for example, it was discovered that, without rocket rails, a fuel saving of around 3 to 4 per cent was achievable.

During the detachment training flights were carried out alongside RRAF Vampire FB.5s and T.11s, and interceptions against the force's Canberra B.2s. A good deal of publicity was given to the visit with calls for formation flypasts over Salisbury, Bulawayo, Kariba, Blantyre, Livingstone, N'dola and a number of smaller towns en route. Night stops were also made at Livingstone and N'dola, where the squadron received further plaudits. The detachment concluded on 26 July when six aircraft returned to Khormaksar; leaving three in AOG state at Thornhill, along with three pilots and eight airmen.

A number 1 Squadron Vampire FB.9, RRAF-113, in the hangar at RRAF Thornhill in July 1960 (Barry Shaw).

Still looking in pristine condition, 8 Squadron FGA.9 XK151 receives attention during the three-week detachment to RRAF Thornhill in Southern Rhodesia in July 1960 (Bill Horspole).

Hunter FGA.9s, XK151-X and XE620-F, contrast well with the beautiful scenery as they fly low over the Kariba Dam (above) and the Southern Rhodesian bush during the 8 Squadron detachment to RRAF Thornhill in 1960 (both, via Roy Hollow).

APRF disbands

Back at Khormaksar, apart from a couple of flagwaves, August was most notable for the disbandment of the Aden Photographic Reconnaissance Flight and the redeployment of its four Meteor FR.9s and two T.7s onto the 8 Squadron inventory where it became B Flight.

Despite the return of the three delayed Hunters from Thornhill in early August, the failure for a long-awaited order for spares to be fulfilled resulted in a critically low number of serviceable aircraft, only ninety-six hours being flown during the month.

Support in Oman

It was not uncommon for the Command to come to the aid of neighbouring states experiencing internal strife, and one such request was received from the Government in Oman in September 1960. Dissidents in a number of villages along the Wadi Batha in the south of the country had been warring with each other for some time and, despite attempts by the Sultan of Oman's Air Force (SOAF) Piston Provosts to separate them, the skirmishing continued unabated. Following an appeal from the Sultan, 8 Squadron flew several aircraft up to nearby Sharjah to mount a series of flagwaves over the area. Having never seen jet aircraft before, the noise and potential threat posed by the low-flying Hunters was sufficient for the rebels to agree to a ceasefire.

Armed with four 3" rockets, eight 25lb bombs and two .303 machine guns, Sultan of Oman Air Force Piston Provost WV501 was captured undergoing an engine run at one of the force's airfields (Richard Grevatte-Ball).

An arm dangling from the cockpit, a pair of legs from the radio bay and a bowser pumping fuel are signs of the groundcrew carrying out a turnround on 8 Squadron T.7 XL613 at Khormaksar (Des Meek).

A period of relative calm in the Aden hinterland came as a relief for 8 Squadron, especially as eleven of its sixteen Hunters were AOG awaiting spares. Agreement was reached with 208 Squadron for its T.7 to be flown up from Kenya, but it was declared unserviceable on arrival.

With a detachment to Cyprus in the advanced stages of planning for early October, the groundcrew clocked up 1,700 hours overtime to ensure enough serviceable aircraft were available. On the 4th six Hunters departed Khormaksar for the two-week detachment, together with a complement of eight pilots and forty groundcrew. Flying via Sharjah and Teheran, the aircraft arrived at Nicosia on the following day. A fortnight of intensive air-to-air firing practice was followed by a move across the island to Akrotiri to participate in an exercise designed to test the Island's defences against high- and low-level attacking aircraft, Canberras and Valiants comprising the enemy force. The Mediterranean climate seemed more amenable for the Hunter as high serviceability rates were achieved over the duration.

Operation NIGGARD
Meanwhile, back in Aden, the leader of the Shamsi faction within the Rabizi tribe, Salem Ali Manar, continued with his policy of destabilising the government. When he failed to attend a meeting with the political officer by the deadline of 30 September to

discuss the government's proposals, Operation NIGGARD was mounted by the 1st, 2nd, and 4th Battalions of the APL, together with elements of the National Guard. Their objective was to seek out and destroy the seventy-five to eighty Shamsi rebel tribesmen holed up in the Upper Aulaqi area.

Close air support for the operation was provided by the Meteors of B Flight 8 Squadron together with a flight of four 208 Squadron Hunters, which had flown up from Embakasi to cover the Cyprus detachment, and ten RRAF Vampire FB.9s on a reciprocal, goodwill detachment from Rhodesia. Initial sorties consisted of armed recces over the area but, on 7 October, RP and cannon strikes were launched by Flight Lieutenants Morris (twice, in XK151 and XF455) and Leach (XE655) on pre-briefed targets ahead of APL units advancing towards the Shamsi area where the rebels were determined to hinder the APL advance. Two further strikes were carried out on the same targets on the 8th by Flight Lieutenant Leach using XF455 and XE655.

Having settled back in at Khormaksar, it did not take long for 8 Squadron Hunters to be called into action. Strikes on the Palace of Mohammed Aidrus in the Lower Yaffa by Flight Lieutenants Leach (XF455), Retief (XE655) and Morris (XE581) on the morning of 30 October were intended as retribution for disturbances carried out by his followers to the east of Al Qara. In the afternoon Flight Lieutenants Morris (XE655), Leach (XF455) and Elgey (XE581) attacked and destroyed one of his ammunition

A detachment of ten Vampire FB.9s from number 1 Squadron, Royal Rhodesian Air Force, on the Hunter pan at Khormaksar during a good-will visit in October 1960 (Ronnie Hush).

stores with rockets and cannonfire. As the evening sun began to set, Flight Lieutenants Trowern (XE581) and Retief (XF455) carried out strikes on one of a pair of five-storey houses owned by Mohammed Aidrus in the village of Suruq. The pattern was repeated on the following day with strikes on both houses by Flight Lieutenant Leach (XE655) and Group Captain Merifield (XE581) in the morning, Flight Lieutenants Leach (XE655) and Morris (XF455) at midday and Flight Lieutenants Retief (XE655) and Trowern (XF455) in the early afternoon. Both buildings were reported as being completely destroyed.

Operation NIGGARD continued into early November, but the only request for air support during the month came on the 4th when Flight Lieutenants Leach (XE654) and Hazell attacked Shamsi dissident tribesmen in the Wadi Asher.

Life at Khormaksar was not all work and no play. An open day held at Khormaksar on 18 November saw the squadron performing a series of formation flypasts and Flight Lieutenant Ken Hayr giving one of his trademark solo aerobatic displays.

While performing a low-level flagwave at 400 knots over Am Dhard on 8 December, Flight Lieutenant Kelly's Meteor FR.9 was struck by seven rounds of 7.62mm ammunition, fired from a light machine gun. Initial checks revealed no serious damage, but further inspection discovered a direct hit on the main spar and the aircraft was SOC.

December was another relatively quiet month, giving the groundcrew sufficient time to carry out much needed maintenance on the aircraft in preparation for a forthcoming exercise codenamed WARDEN. This exercise was devised to test the mobility and potential for intensive flying by 8 and 208 Squadrons in support of an emergency in the Persian Gulf should one arise. The alert having been issued, one flight from each squadron was scrambled and flown to Sharjah. Live strikes were performed on the Jebel Dana and Ras Hassain ranges over a three-day period, followed by a return to Khormaksar. This was the first occasion in which the two Hunter squadrons had worked together and, having exposed a number of weaknesses, the exercise was deemed of great value. No one could have anticipated, however, that the lessons learned would be put into practice for real some six months later.

Fears that the imminent expiration of a truce between the Shamsi and Illahi tribes would end in conflict following demands by the Shamsi for its renewal were allayed by flagwaves flown by two pairs of Hunters. The first was performed along a number of wadis to the south of Khaurah on the 28th and the second along the wadis Bahab and Dura two days later. As with many such episodes, the flagwaves were sufficient to dissuade the parties from resorting to arms, at least for the time being.

A replacement for the T.7 lost in the June crash, XL565, arrived from the UK on 18 December and had cleared acceptance checks before the year was out.

The airmen's Christmas bar-building competition saw 8 Squadron take a well-deserved second place. To celebrate, many a can of 'Slops' (Allsops beer) was downed

A rear view of the Hunter pan at Khormaksar depicting the line chiefie's caravan on the left and a line of 8 Squadron FGA.9s headed by a pair of T.7s (Des Meek). The caravan and hut were subsequently moved from the hardstanding onto the sand further to the left, it having proved a hazard to taxiing aircraft, especially at night.

in the 'One over the EIGHT pub' by the pilots and airmen. Fifteen pilots also managed to appear on AFBA radio on Boxing Day to give their polished rendition of 'Land of Hope and Glory' in aid of charity. A target of 600 shillings was set with the ensemble being tasked to sing nonstop until that figure had been reached. Their raucous performance had the desired effect as it only took eight minutes for listeners to put everyone out of their agony.

The Hunter had completed its first year of service as a ground attack fighter, its performance in the role exceeding most expectations. High unserviceability levels during the early months were due partly to the learning curves for both pilots and groundcrew, poor spares replenishment levels and defects that could be attributed to the hostile climate. The experience gained and lessons learned found the squadron in a better position and ready to handle the turbulent times that undoubtedly lay ahead.

Chapter 6

1961 – Kuwait Crisis

Activities at the beginning of the new year continued where they left off in the previous December, or, as the 8 Squadron ORB states, 'An exciting month with considerable air effort in the Upper Yaffa'.

On 4 January 1961, flagwaves were flown by 8 Squadron Hunters in the Hilyan area to break up an inter-tribal feud and to dissuade dissidents from continuing with their attacks on APL troops in an area near Mahfid. Four aircraft were also deployed to provide top cover for a 233 Squadron Valetta engaged in dropping supplies to friendly tribesmen in a nearby area.

Hunter Fatality

After the family house belonging to Amir Haddar, the second son of the Sultan of Upper Yaffa, had been attacked with 3-inch mortars by a dissident group under the command of the First Negib of Mausatta, it was decided to supply Amir Haddar with 2-inch mortars and ammunition via an air drop on 13 January. A planned leaflet drop at Hilyan by two Hunters over the area was called off after Flight Lieutenant Swain was killed when his FGA.9 (XG128) crashed into a hillside in Wadi Yahar. During the search for him and his aircraft, an 8 Squadron Meteor FR.9 and a Hunter FGA.9 were hit by groundfire. In response, two FGA.9s were despatched to strafe the nearby villages of Am Dharb and Gaffa under the guidance of the station commander, Group Captain Merrifield, flying in a third Hunter.

Having turned their attention to robbing camel trains passing through the Mahfid area, dissident tribesmen were dissuaded from continuing with this plundering pursuit by a firepower demonstration on the 19th carried out by four FGA.9s using rockets and ball ammunition. The pilots for this mission were Flight Lieutenants Edmondston and Kelly, and Flying Officers Haig-Thomas and Perreaux.

208 Squadron detachment to Bahrain

The beginning of the year also saw 208 Squadron's FGA.9s keeping busy flying close air support for 24 Infantry Brigade in the Archer's Post area of northern Kenya as part of Operation RHINO. Six aircraft, two in reserve, were then fitted with long-range 230-gallon underwing tanks in readiness for a detachment to Bahrain. With Flight Lieutenants MacDermid, McLeland and Bell and Flying Officer French at the controls, the aircraft departed Embakasi at 06:30 on 11 January and headed for Khormaksar to refuel and the pilots refresh before continuing to Bahrain via Sharjah. This was the first occasion on which 208 Squadron had the opportunity to fly its Hunters from Nairobi to Bahrain in a single day. Thirty-one airmen and three spare pilots followed on in a 30 Squadron Beverley, their 16-hour ferry flight being broken with a night-stop at Khormaksar. Continuing the following day, refuelling stops were made at Salalah and Sharjah, enabling the Beverley to reach Bahrain during the evening of the 12th.

It soon became apparent that the flying commitment at Bahrain was much heavier than anticipated. Several days were planned for live firing on the Jebel Dana range, reconnaissance and flagwave sorties through the mountainous region of Jebel Akhdar and naval co-operation exercises with the frigate HMS *Loch Fada* off the coast near Abu Dhabi. The two Hunters held in reserve in Kenya were flown up from Nairobi by OC 208 Squadron, Squadron Leader Ramirez and Flying Officer Telford on the 31st and their arrival could not have been timed any better as two of the original four aircraft had sustained ricochet damage while firing at targets, one to the port intake and the other to an aileron.

Back at Embakasi, an average of four aircraft per day were available to fly and on one occasion one of the pilots had a lucky escape when his brake-chute deployed as he broke from the formation on arriving over the airport. As he had not touched the streaming control, an inspection of the remaining aircraft revealed several defective brake-chute assemblies. Unfortunately, no diagnosis report or resolution was recorded in the ORB.

Back in Aden, supply drops by 233 Squadron Valettas in the Am Dharb area on 7 February were accompanied by 37 Squadron Shackletons as 8 Squadron Hunters provided top cover. Two days later, despite the threat posed from above, groundfire was detected by a Shackleton crew while performing a leaflet drop. Two Hunters were scrambled with instructions to fire warning bursts close to the area in which the culprits were ensconced. When this was ignored, a second pair of aircraft was despatched to strafe a nearby fort as another pair attacked a village and nearby fort at Red Hill. One aircraft sustained a bullet strike in the process. A further four strikes were carried out on the same targets the following day. A short lull then ensued but, when tribesmen began firing at low-flying aircraft once again, two pairs of Hunters were despatched on the 24th and 25th with instructions to destroy livestock belonging to the Illahi tribe living in Wadi Rihab, as retribution.

8 Squadron detachment to Sharjah

Despite the increase in anti-social behavior up-country, 8 Squadron felt able to release A Flight for a detachment to Sharjah, beginning on 13 February. Under the command of Flight Lieutenant Edmondston, its objectives were; to undertake live range practice in unfamiliar surroundings and to perform flagwaves over rebellious tribesmen in the Jebel Akhdar area. With no local second-line maintenance facilities available, keeping

The official BFAP display team for 1961 (above) was based at Eastleigh and comprised four 208 Squadron pilots; Sqn Ldr 'Pancho' Ramirez and Flt Lts Cohu, Biddiscombe and McLeland (Pete McLeland). The shield and two spears presented by Masai tribal Chief Simeone Ole Pashato to the Squadron (below) in recognition of its display at Ngong in late 1960 (Aviation Bookshop).

The British Forces Arabian Peninsular display team comprising four 208 Squadron Hunter FGA.9s took full advantage of the proximity of Mount Kilimanjaro for its 1961 photoshoot (Pete McLeland).

the aircraft serviceable proved a difficult proposition for the groundcrew, Flight Sergeant Welsh (I/C), Corporal Clark (the sole electrician) and SAC Meek (engines) being singled out in the ORB for their splendid efforts.

During the early part of February, 208 Squadron concentrated on low-level navigation and high-level battle sorties. Formation aerobatics were perfected by the squadron's four-ship display team, in preparation for an official visit to RAF Eastleigh by the Governor of Kenya, Sir Patrick Renison KCMG. Led by Squadron Leader 'Pancho' Ramirez, and with Flight Lieutenants Cohu, Biddiscombe and McLeland flying in positions two to four, the team's display comprised mainly of close formation flying by a section of three aircraft interspersed with solo aerobatics by Pete McLeland.

On 9 March, the 8 Squadron detachment at Sharjah was busy conducting an Army co-operation exercise with the 11th Hussars. The ORB reported that:

This proved to be good value to both sides, gave the Squadron some much needed experience in attacking moving targets, such as tanks and Ferret cars, and spoke volumes for the efforts and keenness of the groundcrew.

As preparations for the return to Khormaksar were getting underway, the pilots were instructed to make a hasty departure to avoid a fierce sandstorm heading for the Sharjah area. The Hunters made it in time but the airmen's departure was delayed until the 24th.

The squadron's B Flight, meanwhile, was heavily involved in Exercise ROULADE, its task to provide air cover for Royal Marine Commandos being landed from HMS *Bulwark* at Ker Unsa and during the subsequent 'battle' along the coast at Ras Imrea. A total of 124 sorties was flown over the five-day period with scramble times from alert to lift-off averaging an impressive 4.25 minutes.

Due to a lack of spare Hunter mainwheel tyres throughout the Command, aircraft availability once again became a serious concern, more especially for 208 Squadron. Only three sorties were able to be flown by its Hunters during March in support of a demonstration of Forward Air Control (FAC) for the Royal Inniskilling Fusiliers, Flight Lieutenant Derek Bell undertaking the role of FAC.

Change of Command

Important personnel changes observed during March included the arrival of two new squadron commanders. Squadron Leader Mike Goodfellow succeeded Squadron Leader Ramirez on 208 Squadron on the 14th while, three days later, Squadron Leader Laurie Jones took over from Squadron Leader Rex Knight as OC 8 Squadron.

No flying was undertaken by 208 Squadron on 16 March to observe the presentation of a shield and two spears from Chief Simeone Ole Pasha of the Masai tribe in recognition of the flying display performed at the Ngong show in the latter part of 1960.

The only operational sorties called for in Aden during April consisted of a flagwave over the Al Qara and Mudiyah areas by a pair of 8 Squadron FGA.9s. Over the weekend

23 and 24 April, Squadron Leader Jones led four aircraft up to Bahrain to participate in an Army exercise at Jazirat Al Yas, a small island off the Trucial Oman. Having achieved the monthly flying target (330 hours) on 27 April and provided ten serviceable aircraft for the Queen's Birthday flypast, 8 Squadron personnel were stood down for three days. Time off was not a common luxury for the operational squadrons but, it being good for moral, the opportunity was taken on the rare occasions it could be authorised.

In order to provide the quickest response to urgent requests from ground force commanders during periods of intensive operations, a quick turnround time was essential. Aware that they could be called on to share the Aden commitment at any time, 208 Squadron decided to spend time perfecting the procedure. It found that by adhering to the Fighter Command 'Operational turnrounds' instruction, the time taken averaged sixty-five minutes from touchdown to take off. After several practice attempts, a new procedure was devised whereby this figure was reduced to just under fifteen minutes.

Meteor replacement

From a Command perspective, and that of 8 Squadron in particular, the undoubted highlight in April was the arrival of three Hunter FR.10s (XE589, XE614 and XF436) on the 29th as replacements for its ageing Meteor FR.9s. A fourth FR.10 (XE579)

Old and new! (above)The 8 Squadron turnround team pause for the camera before getting back to work on Meteor FR.9 WX978 in 1960 (Aviation Bookshop). (opposite) One year on and its replacement, Hunter FR.10 XF436, receives attention on the Squadron pan at Khormaksar (Des Meek).

arrived on 11 May to complete the fighter-recce allocation, while a fifth aircraft
(XE599) was placed in store with 131 MU as Command reserve.

Increasing dissident activity in May saw forty-eight sorties being flown by 8 Squadron
aircraft, many in conjunction with 37 Squadron (Shackletons) and 233 Squadron
(Valettas) in a two-phase operation. The objective for the initial phase was to flush out
a habitual troublemaker, Mohamed Aidrus, from his various hideouts in the Al Qara
and other areas nearby and to destroy his house in the process. Using the element of
surprise, four FGA.9s dived out of the sun from a height of 20,000 feet and at some six
miles distant, before unleashing salvos of rockets and 30mm cannonfire on the solidly-
built residence. Having destroyed the main dwelling, attention focused on removing
Aidrus from Aden altogether but this objective was not so successful as he was able to
escape the attack and run to ground.

FAC and the Dhala convoy

A key role not often relished by some Hunter pilots was that of Forward Air Controller
(FAC), on the Dhala convoys in particular. Composed entirely of military vehicles
loaded with supplies destined for up-country Army garrisons, the prime task of the
FAC was to keep 8 Squadron informed of each convoy's progress and to call for air
support should they come under attack, a regular occurrence. His job then was to
direct the Hunter pilots via a radio link onto the source of dissident fire. On 3 May a
convoy was ambushed five miles south of Thumeir; one vehicle being hit but with no
casualties reported. A pair of Hunters was called up but by the time they arrived on
scene, the culprits had vanished.

Typical composition of an Army convoy on the Dhala Road captured from a nose camera of an 8 Squadron FR.10 by Peter Lewis (Peter Lewis).

A nightmare detachment!

In early May 208 Squadron groundcrews began fitting long-range tanks (two 100 and two 230) and harmonising the guns on six aircraft in readiness to participate in an APC in Cyprus and an exercise in Libya. As Embakasi is situated at a height of 5,300 feet asl, two sorties were flown to ascertain whether the climb figures given in tables contained in the *Pilots' Notes* were applicable for the lengthy flight they were about to endure. The test allayed any lingering doubts as to their accuracy.

At 07:30 on 7 May, as the Hunters completed their start up, two aircraft suffered radio failures and were shut down for the problems to be fixed. A third was shut down to wait for them, leaving the three remaining to head off for Khormaksar. Immediately after take off, one of the pilots reported a red light on his nosewheel undercarriage indicator but, as a visual check by the other pilots confirmed that the wheel was in the fully retracted position, they continued to Aden. The radio problems were quickly resolved, allowing the delayed aircraft to depart fifteen minutes later. They reached Khormaksar at 10:10, just ten minutes behind the first three. The AOC, AVM Sir D. Lee CB CBE and station commander welcomed the pilots who were hosted to an early lunch by pilots from 8 Squadron. At 12:10, the six Hunters took off and headed for Sharjah and an overnight stop. Meanwhile, the support party, comprising thirteen officers and fifty-seven NCOs and airmen, followed in a 30 Squadron Beverley and 70 Squadron Hastings.

An 09:25 departure from Sharjah on the 8th saw the Hunters taking off in pairs at two-minute intervals, the gap being sufficient for the sand to resettle on the runway, and setting course for Teheran. Some 300 miles short of their destination, one aircraft sustained a total hydraulic failure, leaving the pilot to complete the leg in manual control. Having dropped his outboard tanks and stop-cocked the engine on crossing the threshold, the aircraft touched down without incident. BOAC engineers greeted the pilots and refuelled their aircraft.

The five serviceable aircraft then headed off, leaving the disabled aircraft behind with its pilot to await the arrival of the groundcrew. The stage was flown over total cloud cover and, with no radar aids in the area, navigation was accomplished by dead reckoning. To avoid passing over UAR and Iraqi territory, the formation routed via Askaray in Turkey before turning for Nicosia. The abandoned aircraft was repaired at Teheran and flown to Nicosia a few days later.

With the APC completed, the Hunters left Cyprus and headed for RAF El Adem in Libya, the first leg of the flight back to Kenya. The intention had been to fly on to Khartoum in the afternoon but when XE643 failed to start, both it and a second aircraft were left at El Adem, leaving the remaining four to continue to Khartoum. A radio failure shortly after take off forced one aircraft (XG134) to return to El Adem.

The accompanying Beverley and Hastings departed Nicosia soon after the Hunters were safely on their way, en route for a night-stop at Khartoum. On the approach to Khartoum, the Hastings' captain reported an engine problem, one that would subsequently lead to the aircraft being stranded at this remote location. As the first three Hunters remained serviceable, they continued on the final leg to Nairobi. The problems on the trio left at El Adem had, in the meantime, been rectified and the aircraft prepared for departure. When the starter on XE643 failed again, the decision was taken to leave it there to await an engine change and allow the other two to continue on their way.

The personnel on the stranded Hastings were left to make their own way back to Nairobi by hitching a lift on one of the rare RAF transport aircraft that happened to pass through Khartoum en route to Khormaksar. Twelve days were to pass before a final group of eighteen dishevelled airmen arrived back at base, bringing to an end the most unforgettable of detachments.

On 26 Jun, four 8 Squadron aircraft were tasked to carry out a rocket strike on Messalio House in the village of Dhi Surrah as a reprisal for dissident activities. Post-strike photographs taken by an FR.10 proved inconclusive, so the house was struck again by a further pair the following day.

Oil supply threat

Kuwait is a tiny oil-rich country nestling in the top corner of the Persian Gulf. Surrounded on three sides by powerful neighbours Saudi Arabia, Iraq and Iran, its strategic location and massive oil reserves continue to make it one of the world's richest countries per capita. One of the primary reasons Britain retained such a large military garrison on Arabian soil was to protect the main route through which a high percentage of its oil was transhipped.

Kuwait had held longstanding treaty agreements entrusting Britain to safeguard its independence. An exchange of notes between the two governments on 19 June 1961, however, signalled a desire to end these agreements, while retaining the spirit of closeness that had endured for many years. Fortunately, the commitment for Britain to come to Kuwait's assistance in times of crisis remained in force.

Iraq had laid claim to its tiny neighbour for many years on the premise that it was part of Basrah. On being informed of the loosening of its ties with Britain, the Iraqi leader, General Kassim, issued a proclamation on 23 June 1961 reinforcing that claim. Two days later, he ordered his troops and armoured divisions to move towards the border with Kuwait. Kassim's intentions had been known in Britain for some time and contingency plans were in place for the mobilisation of forces within Middle East Command should he try to implement them.

At Khormaksar, the excitement among 8 Squadron ranks for an impending detachment to Rhodesia changed to one of anti-climax when, on the morning of 26 June, news came through that General Kassim was massing his troops along the border with Kuwait.

Operation VANTAGE

In the early hours of 29 June 8 Squadron was brought to immediate standby and the order to move to Bahrain at all haste was received at midday. All serviceable aircraft had been fitted with long-range underwing tanks, and aircraft spares and tools packups prepared for loading onto a Beverley transport. Everything was ready by late afternoon. At 21:30 an advanced party of pilots and airmen left Khormaksar in an 84 Squadron Beverley on an overnight flight to Bahrain.

At 08:45 on the 30th the first section of four Hunters departed Khormaksar for Bahrain, completing the 1,300 miles (2,100km) nonstop flight in a little short of 2.75 hours. A second section comprising four aircraft took off at midday. They were joined in Bahrain by a further four aircraft and second party of airmen on 1 July, leaving six pilots, twelve airmen and pairs of FGA.9s, FR.10s and T.7s, plus the four Meteor

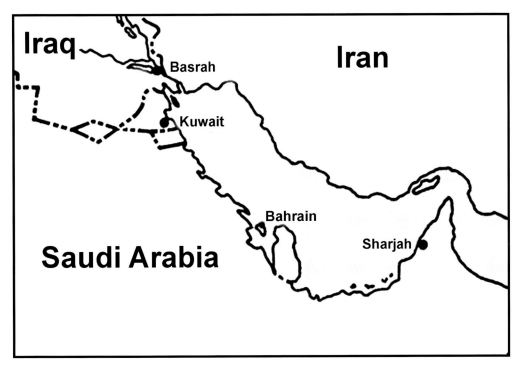

Map of the Persian Gulf illustrating the location of Kuwait relative to the countries surrounding it and the RAF stations at Bahrain and Sharjah.

FR.9s, to maintain order in the Protectorates. Two Shackletons from 37 Squadron were flown up to Bahrain to provide recce and SAR facilities and, if necessary, a bombing capability should the rapidly increasing British force require it.

Hunter movements from Khormaksar to Bahrain

Date	Serial No.	A/C Type	Pilot
30/06	XG169	FGA.9	W/Cdr Neville
30/06	XK150	FGA.9	S/Ldr Jones
30/06	XE581	FGA.9	F/Lt Edmondston
30/06	XE614	FR.10	F/Lt Elgey
30/06	XE654	FGA.9	F/Lt Powell
30/06	XE579	FR.10	F/Lt Volkers
30/06	XE600	FGA.9	F/Lt Ferguson
30/06	XE620	FGA.9	F/Off Stott
01/07	XF455	FGA.9	F/Lt Hayr
01/07	XG136	FGA.9	F/Lt Gathercole
01/07	XE651	FGA.9	F/Off Blackgrove
01/07	XG135	FGA.9	Not recorded

8 Squadron aircraft remaining at Khormaksar

A/C Type	Serial No.	A/C Type	Serial No.
FGA.9	XE655	FR.10	XE599
FGA.9	XK151	T.7	XL565
FR.10	XE589	T.7	XL613

Having arrived with the advanced party, Flight Lieutenant Sandy Burns was flown into Kuwait in a 152 Squadron Pembroke to assess the suitability of its two airports, Kuwait Civil (Old) and Kuwait New, for Hunter operations. Although still under construction and with a solitary 2,500-yard runway and fully surfaced taxiways, Flight Lieutenant Burns advised that Kuwait New would be the more suitable of the two. The recently laid surface on the apron was still a little soft and, with no grids or metal plates for the aircraft to stand on, there was a risk that they could sink into the tarmac. Water, electricity and oxygen supplies were limited or non-existent in some places and construction of buildings and associated facilities was very much a work in progress. A small building was taken over for use by the aircrew, GLOs, Tactical Operations and a Tactical Air Commander. A major concern was the lack of anything resembling Air Traffic Control.

At 09:00 on 1 July a force of Royal Marine Commandos was landed at Kuwait New from HMS *Bulwark* by Whirlwind helicopters of 848 Squadron. Their orders were to secure the airport and its boundary and once this had been accomplished, authorisation was issued for the Hunters to move from Bahrain to Kuwait.

208 Squadron moves north

Following Kassim's declaration of intent, 208 Squadron was ordered to prepare its Hunters for a move to the Gulf. Rocket rails and 230-gallon tanks were fitted and the aircraft cannon harmonised, a task requiring the groundcrew to work from dawn till dusk over a three-day period. VHF radios were re-crystallised to match the Khormaksar specification and pilots not involved in air tests were given lectures on intelligence on the Kuwait local area, long-range navigation techniques, and Iraqi aircraft and tank recognition.

At 14:00 on 29 June 208 Squadron was placed at 24-hour readiness. Three hours later the order, 'Make first destination–Khormaksar–daylight hours, 30 June 1961' was received at the squadron HQ.

At midnight on the 29th a 30 Squadron Beverley departed Embakasi for Khormaksar en route for the Gulf. On board were the advanced party comprising five pilots, twenty airmen and 5,000lb of equipment and spares. At 06:45 on the 30th the first three Hunters were flown to Khormaksar by Squadron Leader Goodfellow and Flight Lieutenants Biddiscombe and McLeland. A second section of three Hunters was flown up to Khormaksar a few hours later by Flight Lieutenants Renshaw and Tate

RAF Bahrain on 1 July 1961 shortly after 208 Squadron's Hunters, seen at the far end of the Hunter line, joined those of 8 Squadron on the first full day of Operation Vantage. A mix of support aircraft types is visible on the right (via Alan Lowe).

and Flying Officer MacNab, leaving Flight Lieutenants Sawyer and Marshall to follow on in the final pair at 13:00.

On arrival at Khormaksar the pilots were briefed that they were to continue to the Gulf the following morning. Squadron Leader Goodfellow, however, believed there was sufficient time to reach Bahrain before nightfall and permission for them to depart was granted. The aircraft took off in two sections of three, staging through Sharjah en route to the Gulf. Following their arrival, the two squadrons were integrated as a wing – Khormaksar Wing.

The two 208 Squadron stragglers arrived at Khormaksar at 15:35 but, too late to press on, the pilots decided to remain there overnight. The Beverley carrying the 208 Squadron advanced party had, meanwhile, sustained an engine defect and was stranded at Salalah, leaving the 8 Squadron groundcrew to maintain the eighteen Hunters sitting on the pan at Bahrain. The delayed Beverley eventually made it to Bahrain at 16:30 on 1 July but, due to the fatigue incurred on the 40-hour-long trip, 208 Squadron personnel were stood down until the following morning.

In the UK, 1 and 54 Squadrons were placed on three-days' readiness to move their Hunter FGA.9s to Bahrain, as 42 Squadron received orders to prepare its Shackleton MR.2s for a move to the Persian Gulf at 24-hours' notice. Other Shackleton units were placed on extended standbys for operations in a troop-carrying role should they be called for.

Into Kuwait

Following a briefing by OC Khormaksar Wing, Wing Commander Neville, at 08:00 on 1 July, a Beverley from 84 Squadron began the airlift of 8 Squadron groundcrew into what they believed to be Kuwait New. It was soon realised, however, that the aircraft had landed fifteen miles to the north at Kuwait Old by mistake, an error attributed to the poor visibility. Without stopping, the Beverley taxied back to the runway and took off on a heading for the correct destination.

Visibility in Kuwait tended to be good in the early hours but decreased rapidly after 09:00 due to haze and dust. Temperatures of 115°F (46°C) in the shade and 139°F (59°C) in the cockpit together with humidity levels reaching 99 per cent made life extremely uncomfortable for both pilots and groundcrew.

Armed with 4 x 135 HE ammunition, 2 x HE and 4 armour-piercing rockets, eight 8 Squadron aircraft departed Bahrain at 09:00 on 1 July, en route for Kuwait. At 15:00, just one-and-a-half days after being given the order to move from Khormaksar, the squadron was declared in a state of readiness and its aircraft placed on 30-minute standby. From 06:45 on the next day, pairs of Hunters were despatched every ninety minutes to carry out reconnaissance and flagwave sorties following a trajectory along the Iraqi border. Nothing untoward was reported.

Kuwait New Airport in July 1961 and 8 Squadron FGA.9 XF376 taxies back to the line at the completion of a recce sortie along the Iraq border. Note the 'zap' on the nose, a gift from the 208 Squadron groundcrew (Ray Deacon collection).

Ready for action at Kuwait New Airport; 8 Squadron FGA.9s XE654-E, XG136-C and XE651-M armed with pairs of HE SAP-headed rockets on the outer rails and four of the armour-piercing variety on the inners (Mike Halpin).

On 3 July two 8 Squadron aircraft were scrambled at 09:30 to identify vehicles moving near the border but no suspicious activities were detected. Four aircraft from 208 Squadron were flown into Kuwait from Bahrain during the morning, raising the total complement to twelve FGA.9s. The reconnaissance flights continued until 15:15 when flying was curtailed due to poor visibility.

Events were moving fast and the pilot briefing on the 4th was brought forward to 04:30. Wing Commander Neville announced that he would move to Kuwait together with a second section of four 208 Squadron Hunters, leaving Squadron Leader Goodfellow as his deputy at Bahrain. Armed with full HE gunpacks and a mix of six HE and SAP 60lb rockets, the aircraft departed Bahrain at 09:00 and were on the ground at Kuwait New by 09:50. As the crews familiarised themselves with the minimal facilities available, visibility steadily dropped below 1,000 yards and no further sorties were flown. Several transport aircraft tried to land but, due to the poor visibility, either turned back, or inadvertently, landed at Kuwait Old.

The pilots remaining at Bahrain were given every opportunity to familiarise themselves with the forward operating area by performing armed reconnaissance flights along the Kuwait/Iraq border.

By midday on the 4th all eighteen FGA.9s and the two FR.10s were serviceable, armed and ready. Two pairs were placed on 15-minute readiness from dawn to dusk as a further two pairs performed dawn recces along the border. A fifth pair was allocated to fly co-operation exercises with the carrier HMS *Bulwark* to assist with the calibration of VDF equipment recently installed at Kuwait New. A rota system was established in which responsibility for the dawn-to-dusk patrols alternated between the squadrons.

Practice scrambles were frequently practised to keep the squadrons on their toes, the best recorded time from alert to wheels-up being seven minutes. Due to the intense heat, pilots on standby were unable to sit in their cockpits to await the call to scramble, resulting in a le Mans-style dash whenever an alert was triggered. Within a short space of time, scramble times from alert to wheels-up, reduced to a mere 2.25 minutes.

Reinforcements

In anticipating the need to augment the strike force in Kuwait, the Hunter FGA.9s of 43 Squadron were redeployed from RAF Leuchars to Cyprus. The establishment of an interdictor/bomber capability was fulfilled by flying four Canberra B(I).8 and eight B(I).6 aircraft of 88 and 213 Squadrons respectively from Germany to Sharjah, and a similar number of UK-based Canberra B.6s to Cyprus. Additional offensive power could be called upon from the Scimitar and Sea Vixen squadrons embarked on HMS *Victorious*, which arrived in the Gulf at just the right time. All in all, a formidable deterrent for Kassim to consider before taking the fateful decision to cross the border! Over that initial four-day period, no fewer than 4,300 men and 1.4 million pounds of freight was airlifted from Aden to Kuwait by MEC transport squadrons.

During the period 5 to 10 July a routine was implemented which required a pair of Hunters to be held at 15-minutes' readiness and two pairs at 30-minutes, each aircraft configured with two 100-gallon drop tanks, fully-loaded HE gunpacks and six HE/SAP rockets. Although intelligence suggested that the Iraqi military build up was ongoing, there were no engagements with its forces throughout this period. With no sign of activity on the other side of the border, the decision was taken to move the 8 Squadron aircraft back to Bahrain and be prepared to rotate with 208 Squadron on a five-day cycle. This would relieve congestion on the apron at Kuwait New and overcrowding in the groundcrew accommodation hangar.

The 8 Squadron aircraft departed Kuwait for Bahrain on the 10th with squadron personnel following in a Beverley. To avoid the disruptive effect of rotating the squadrons, the decision was subsequently revised: 8 Squadron would remain in Bahrain until the end of the month. However, three of its Hunters were flown back to Kuwait on 30/31 July to participate in a joint exercise with 208 Squadron and elements of the Army.

(above) 8 Squadron armourer Mike Halpin gives a friendly pat to an armour-piercing rocket at Kuwait New (Mike Halpin). To help distinguish RAF Hunters from those of the Iraq Air Force, 8 Squadron FR.10 XE589 had white bands painted round the rear fuselage and mainplanes, as can be seen in the photograph (below), taken outside the 131 MU hangar at Khormaksar. As events transpired, they were not needed (Simon Morrison).

Hunter fatality

At 07:15 on 11 July six 208 Squadron aircraft were brought to 15-minute readiness for an Army co-operation exercise. At 08:00 two pairs were given the order to scramble but when both leaders' aircraft failed to start, the number twos took off as a pair. Visibility

Living conditions for the ground crews in Kuwait were basic to say the least as these two photographs clearly illustrate. (above) An orderly queue has formed at the 'Mess' to sample the simple menu, while (below) sleeping under the stars was the coolest way to get a good night's rest (Mike Halpin).

in the exercise area was much worse than forecast and the lead pilot decided not to make his attack. The pilot of the second aircraft, Flying Officer Hennessy (XG134), decided he would make his attack and was killed when his aircraft struck the ground.

To retain the high standard of morale following the accident, shopping trips were run to Kuwait City for 208 Squadron personnel and hockey and water polo matches played against local teams. Personnel were also entertained by local families, a bath, a meal and an air-conditioned room to sleep in being much appreciated.

As Iraqi troops began to pull back from the border area, the readiness state was extended to ninety minutes on 13 July. Frequent exercises continued to be staged to ensure a smooth running operation should Kassim and his commanders have a change of heart. A new routine was implemented whereby a pair of Hunters carried out dawn recces along the Iraqi border as singletons; pairs and fours concentrated their attention on FAC training. Flying ceased at around 11:00 each day to avoid excessive activity during the hottest part of the day, although a recce along the border was flown by a pair of aircraft at dusk.

Recognition

The following extract from the 8 Squadron ORB acknowledges the appreciation expressed by the pilots for the contribution made by the groundcrew during the Kuwait crisis.

Although the cancellation of the detachment to Rhodesia was a big disappointment, the groundcrew pulled their weight throughout their stay in Kuwait, despite the rough going. Aircraft serviceability was excellent. The airmen worked day and night for the first few days, not only maintaining our Hunters but many transport types passing through, such as the Britannia, Hastings, Valletta, Beverley and Twin Pioneer. These were quickly turned-round and refuelled to facilitate a continuous flow of troops into and around the Persian Gulf. Over fifty transport aircraft were turned-round during the first few days and sixty-eight sorties flown by the Squadron's Hunters. This alone was due to the hard work and team spirit of the NCOs and airmen on the Squadron.

Accommodation in Kuwait was basic to say the least, a half-built hangar having been requisitioned by airmen for use as a billet. No fans, no air conditioning and temperatures of 130°F (54°C)! The pilots had the luck to obtain accommodation in the Kuwait Oil Company's guest house. During the rest-up period in Bahrain, everyone was able to relax and the month concluded with a Squadron bash.

Squadron Leader Jones added: 'Although hot in body the means by which to cool it down were amply provided.'

Mention was also made of the sterling work done by the airmen who kept the aircraft flying at Khormaksar.

T.7s pressed into action

While the excitement of the Gulf had continued to dominate the conversation, back at Khormaksar, two 8 Squadron Meteor FR.9s were kept busy flying armed-recces and flagwaves in the Wadi Idim and Wadi Hawayrab areas on 1 and 2 July. On the 3rd three Hunters were despatched to carry out rocket strikes on a fort at Binjebu, completely destroying the structure in the process.

Operations in the WAP steadily increased as the month wore on. Making full use of the Hunters at its disposal, including one of the T.7s, the depleted contingent completed a creditable twenty-seven strike sorties. Several were directed towards the drive to flush Mohamed Aidrus from whichever of his properties he was using as a bolthole. To this end, every house in which he was known to have taken refuge in the Sara region, to the south of Al Qara, was attacked with cannonfire and squash-head rockets and destroyed. No defensive fire was detected, probably due to an element of surprise.

Meteor swansong

During the early part of July, attacks by Awabitma and Khamma tribesmen on military vehicles using the Mukalla-Hadhramaut road had steadily increased. On the 19th the Mukalla Regular Army and Hadrami Bedouin Legion sent their forces into the area with the objective of bringing the offenders to heel, but the operation ended in disaster. Dissidents, who were lying in wait for the military column, carried out a well-planned ambush in which twenty-eight troops were killed and twenty-two injured.

Following a request for air support, an 8 Squadron B Flight Meteor FR.9, WH546, with Flight Lieutenant Seabrook at the controls, was despatched to RAF Riyan on 20 July. Working jointly with a GLO acting as FAC from a 78 Squadron Twin Pioneer, Flight Lieutenant Seabrook flew twenty-three strikes against dissident targets. In all, he fired 10,000 rounds of 20mm ammunition, destroyed around 1,000 goats, a few donkeys, camels and probably a few rebel tribesmen in the process.

Five further strikes were carried out by 8 Squadron Hunters flying directly from Khormaksar while 37 Squadron used its Shackletons to bomb and strafe targets in the Al Qara and Sara areas. The Hunters were forced to jettison their 230-gallon drop tanks in order to deliver a maximum useful load onto the targets which were completely destroyed.

Having taken a severe pounding, the insurgents surrendered on 23 July, releasing the Meteor to return to Khormaksar on 31 July and into retirement. The FR.9 had proved an invaluable asset during its short sojourn in Aden and was the last of this impeccable breed to fire its guns at an enemy target while in front-line service with the RAF. Following its withdrawal, WH546 was placed on static display outside 131 MU.

Bahrain/Kuwait

By early August, with the threat of an Iraqi invasion receding, 208 Squadron carried out an air defence exercise with HMS *Centaur* which had joined *Victorious* in the Gulf. Five pairs of Hunters were placed on five-minute standby and scrambled to intercept naval aircraft approaching low and fast. The average scramble time was recorded as two minutes forty seconds.

The decision was then taken for 208 Squadron to exchange places with 8 Squadron and move to Bahrain, the changeover taking effect on 8 August. Two 208 Squadron Hunters remained in Kuwait together with a number of pilots and groundcrew. A pair of 84 Squadron Beverleys were used to transfer men and equipment between the two locations.

Around half the pilots and airmen on 208 Squadron were then flown down to Eastleigh by RAF Britannia for two weeks' leave on 8 August, leaving the remainder to attend to the defect and maintenance backlog. On their return to Bahrain on the 22nd, the second tranche of personnel was flown to Eastleigh for their period of leave.

On arrival in Kuwait 8 Squadron was placed on 15-minute readiness due to reports of troop movements on the Iraqi side of the border. As the readiness state remained at this level through to the end of the month, a pair of fully armed aircraft was placed on standby from dawn to dusk and a shift system established for all members of the squadron. A short respite enabled the squadron to participate in exercises with the Army. Under the codename FIREBIRD, they were intended primarily for air support and FAC training. The standby pair was scrambled on three occasions during the month, once to intercept unidentified aircraft approaching the Kuwait border, which to everyone's relief were confirmed as a pair of Indonesian Navy Gannets on delivery flights, and twice for unintentional border infringements by Iraqi Hawker Furys. The appearance of an Iraqi Air Force Hunter might have proved interesting!

No respite in Aden

While the focus of attention remained firmly fixed on events in the Gulf, the 8 Squadron contingent at Khormaksar maintained its focus on seeking out Mohamed Aidrus and his cronies as they were still causing problems. Following an attack by members of his group on an Army post at Serar, three FGA.9s, XE655 (Flight Lieutenant Ferguson), XG136 (Flying Officer Stott) and XF455 (Flying Officer Free), were despatched at 09:00 on 2 August to destroy the house of one of the ringleaders. Seventeen rockets struck the target, causing severe damage to the rear of the property. A further dozen rockets fired by XE655 (Flight Lieutenant Powell) and XF455 (Flying Officer Stott) later that morning, inflicted further damage to the main structure and lookout tower. On the next day, three aircraft, XE655 (Flight Lieutenant Powell) and XF455 (Flight Lieutenant Ferguson) and FR.10 XE599 (Flying Officer Stott), carried out rocket and cannon strikes on Fort Bin Jebli, completely destroying it. Two weeks later, despite cover from FR.10 XE589 (Flying Officer Perreaux), a 233 Squadron Valetta sustained a bullet through the tailcone while performing a leaflet drop over the same area.

Another fatality

Flying Officer Volkers, who was on his first tour since leaving Cranwell, was killed on 8 August when his FR.10 (XE579) flew into the ground while on final approach to a target on the range near Zinjibar, north-east of Aden. A replacement FR.10 (XF460) was flown out from the UK later in the month.

Kuwait/Bahrain

Apart from recurring faults with pressure instruments on the Hunters operating from Kuwait New, which were thought to be due to extremes in temperatures ranging from 150°F (65°C) on the pan to -50°F (-45°C) at 40,000 feet, a serviceability rate of 75 per cent produced an average of nine out of the twelve aircraft being serviceable at all times. The 8 Squadron ORB concluded:

> During the month, the groundcrew did a grand job in keeping the aircraft flying in what can only be described as difficult conditions. The majority of personnel were in Kuwait where working conditions through heat and lack of equipment, were far from ideal. A shift system was evolved and spread across the 16-hour working period. Aircraft serviceability was excellent with only the odd snag cropping up.
>
> The groundcrew at Khormaksar did a good job as they had the rough end of the stick, in so much as they had to maintain aircraft being exchanged with those in Kuwait, in addition to those needed to fulfil the WAP commitment.

To keep its pilots skills honed, 208 Squadron began a two-day period of rocket and gun firing on the Ras Sadr range on 1 September, followed by landings at Sharjah. Refuelled and re-armed, a second session was carried out on the range before heading back to Bahrain.

On the morning of the 8th six 208 Squadron aircraft flew to Kuwait to relieve 8 Squadron, its two remaining aircraft (XE607 and XE643) being flown down to Khormaksar for scheduled servicing. All but four 8 Squadron aircraft (FGA.9s XE649, XE651, XE600 and T.7 XL565) then departed Kuwait and returned to Bahrain. On the 14th Squadron Leader Goodfellow took over as OC Tactical Wing as Wing Commander Neville decided the time was right for him to leave Kuwait. On the 22nd 208 Squadron was tasked to 'show the flag' with a formation flypast over Ahmadi, Kuwait City and various Army units located in desert areas to help keep their spirits up. Weather permitting, these were flown at 07:00 and again at 16:00 as nine-ship formations, leaving a pair on standby.

With the alert state relaxed, time was found to form a new 208 Squadron aerobatic team, practice displays taking place in the afternoons to avoid the training schedule. As the month drew on, the four remaining 8 Squadron Hunters were flown to Bahrain, where the squadron took the opportunity to relax while raising aircraft availability to a maximum. Apart from swimming and sailing, the only activity of note was a pilots-versus-airmen cricket match. Played under strict 'a beer-a-wicket' rules, the wickets needless to say fell quickly, causing play to be abandoned due to inebriated and incapable players, and umpires unable to follow the line of the ball. No change there then!

Gulf Ranger

Not wishing to let their planning and preparations for the Kuwait emergency go to waste, 1 and 54 Squadrons were each detailed to despatch a flight of four Hunters to the Persian Gulf. Having flown by way of Luqa, El Adem, Khartoum, Khormaksar and Sharjah, they were greeted by members of 8 Squadron on their arrival in Bahrain on 23 September. Two days later, they flew into Kuwait New where they were hosted by 208 Squadron. During their stay they took the opportunity to perform sector reccees over the Kuwait area before departing for RAF Stradishall on the 27th using the Teheran and Nicosia route.

One of four 54 Squadron FGA.9s to fly out to Kuwait on a Gulf-ranger, XE650 sits on the pan at the New Airport, September 1961 (author's collection).

Number 1 Squadron also flew a quartet of FGA.9s on the Gulf-ranger to Kuwait. One of them, XG207, is seen here alongside a pair from 54 Squadron and a fourth from 208 Squadron. The rocket rails were removed before departure from the UK to comply with international regulations (author's collection).

While carrying out a photo-recce over the Wadi Satman and Upper Yaffa areas on 5 September, Flight Lieutenant Hayr's FR.10 (XE589) was struck by a bullet from a dissident gun, causing Category 3 damage. In another operation carried out on the 20th, two FGA.9s, XE654 (Flight Lieutenant Hayr) and XE655 (Flight Lieutenant Morrell), were despatched to destroy a target near Jamili, but only six rockets hit home, one aircraft having to abort. A second strike carried out later in the day, by the same pair in the same aircraft, completed the task.

Kuwait standdown

No operational flights were flown by 8 Squadron from Bahrain during the first week of October as it continued to maintain the Kuwait standby. Operation VANTAGE was brought to a close on 7 October, a little more than three months after its initiation. As preparations began for 208 Squadron to pull back to Bahrain, a nine-ship flypast was flown over Ahmadi and Kuwait New to signal the end of the RAF's short tenure in the tiny state. On arrival back at New, the aerobatic team broke away from the formation to give an impromptu display. Later that morning, General Mubarak, C-in-C of the Kuwait Forces, was treated to a flight in a T.7 (XL597) with Squadron Leader Goodfellow at the controls. The next two days were occupied with preparing the aircraft and packups for departure, which took place on the morning of 10 October.

Once settled in at Bahrain, 208 Squadron joined 8 Squadron on a 6-hour readiness state in case they were called on to fly armed missions along the Kuwait/Iraq border. A 12-hour readiness state was brought into effect should the call come to redeploy the Hunters to Kuwait. Routine flying was, nevertheless, back on the agenda and the 208 Squadron aerobatic team gave a performance for the OC Middle East Command. Suitably impressed, he nominated it as the official Command Aerobatic Team.

On 14 October the alert state was terminated, releasing 8 Squadron to return to Khormaksar. No sooner had it arrived there then it was brought to 6-hour readiness state.

With the permanent redeployment of 208 Squadron to Khormaksar set for mid-November, Squadron Leader Goodfellow flew down to Aden on 24 October to inspect the newly-completed Khormaksar Wing hangar and office accommodation at the east end of the airfield. The arrival in Bahrain from the UK of two refurbished aircraft (XF388 and XF462) allowed the two loan aircraft to be returned to 8 Squadron. A further two refurbished Hunters (XE552 and XK140) arrived on 2 November, releasing XF421 and XE544 to be flown back to the UK for refurbishment.

Stubborn target

When a local *caliph* in the Dhi Surra area stood accused of causing the death of a government official, 8 Squadron was instructed to carry out a rocket strike on the offender's house as retribution. It was a solid structure, built of stone, 70-feet tall, 60-feet wide and perched on top of a hill. The attack took place on the morning of 3 November with a force comprising three FGA.9s, XF455 (Squadron Leader Jones), XE620 (Flying Officer Griffith) and XK150 (Flying Officer Voller). All eighteen rockets hit the target but only superficial damage was caused. A second wave of four aircraft, XK150 (Squadron Leader Jones), XE654 (Flying Officer Gosnell), XE581 (Flight Lieutenant Hayr) and XE649 (Flying Officer Blackgrove), was despatched in the afternoon in an attempt to complete the task. Badly damaged and with much of the structure remaining inhabitable, a third strike was carried out on the 7th by two aircraft, XE654 (Flight Lieutenant Edmondston) and XF455 (Flying Officer Horsley), followed two days later by yet another attack by XG135 (Flight Lieutenant Elgey) and XF455 (Flying Officer Gaiger). Analysis of the G.90 gun-camera film confirmed that the building had been completely demolished. That such a high number of rocket strikes was needed to destroy the building led to the conclusion that it was constructed of much stronger materials than previously experienced.

Bi-monthly detachments

To ensure that General Kassim fully understood the situation and that invading Kuwait was not in his best interests, the decision was taken to permanently base a Hunter squadron in Bahrain. However, when it became clear that the local ruler was still refusing to allow any form of offensive force to be permanently based on the island,

The immediate crisis over, troops walk out to the 84 Squadron Beverley waiting on the tarmac at Kuwait New in October 1961. Their departure would be followed by that of 208 Squadron's Hunters (Aviation Bookshop).

agreement was reached for the Hunters to operate from Bahrain but only on short-duration detachments. A new routine was devised in which the two MEC squadrons would spend two months at Bahrain on a rota basis.

The routine was introduced on 15 November when 8 Squadron flew eight FGA.9s up to Bahrain to relieve 208 Squadron. The latter's Hunters then departed for Khormaksar, three aircraft night-stopping at Sharjah and five at Salalah. Having failed to start, two of its aircraft remained at Bahrain, where the pilots decided to wait for a third aircraft, undergoing a fuel tank change, in order to accompany it down to Aden. A point to note is that single-engined RAF aircraft were not permitted to fly solo between MEC airfields. The ten 8 Squadron aircraft (four FR.10s and six FGA.9s) remaining at Khormaksar were employed on joint operations with 208 Squadron.

The logistics of rotating squadrons on a regular basis was fairly straightforward for 208 Squadron; all of its aircraft would, in theory, move to Bahrain at the apposite time, although one or two were often left behind with snags or on scheduled servicing. As 8 Squadron only took around half of its aircraft allocation up to the Gulf, more thought was required by its administrators to ensure a balanced number of tradesmen were available at each location.

As much of the territory around Aden was unfamiliar to 208 Squadron pilots, no time was lost in working up. On 17 November two 208 Squadron Hunters were sent to reconnoitre a village called Dhi Surrah but were unable to locate it. A second sortie by another pair proved more successful. Three days later 208 Squadron was briefed to provide a pair of aircraft at thirty-minutes' readiness to cover the Dhala convoy and allocate an officer as FAC. Four pairs of aircraft were flown along the route to familiarise the pilots.

Arabian Protectorate Levies (APL)

On 30 November 208 Squadron flew a six-ship flypast over an Arabian Protectorate Levies (APL) parade to mark the change of name to Federal Regular Army (FRA), following the formation of the South Arabian Federation. The formation was then joined by a further three aircraft for a diamond-nine flypast over Steamer Point and Khormaksar.

Runaway tailplane

A dangerous phenomenon that became known as 'runaway tailplane' was believed to have been the cause of the loss of an 8 Squadron FGA.9 (XE581) on 22 November. While participating in a tail chase, Flying Officer Gaiger was unable to recover his aircraft, even though he had placed his foot firmly behind the control column. At a height of around 15,000 feet, and in a steep dive, he decided to eject but was killed due to the collapse of the seat pan at the beginning of the ejection sequence.

A subsequent runaway tailplane was experienced by Flying Officer Webbon on 12 December, also during a tail chase. He too decided to eject but was unable to due to the high negative 'g' forces preventing him from reaching either pull handle. Instead, he tried to regain control using his feet to hold the control column fully forward and managed to recover his Hunter at 4,000 feet before landing safely back at base.

Independence Day blues!

Taking advantage of a lull in up-country activities, three 208 Squadron aircraft (XF454, XF462 and XK139) departed for Eastleigh to participate in rehearsals to mark the independence of Tanganyika, soon to become Tanzania. While flying in a practice formation over Mombasa, the pilot of FGA.9 XF454 experienced fuel-flow problems. Having jettisoned all four underwing tanks, he was able to return to base and make a safe landing. On 7 December a pair of FGA.9s (XE609 and XK140) departed Khormaksar for Mombasa, carrying spares for the defective aircraft, leaving a final section of four (XE552, XE643, XF388 and XJ687) to join them on the following day. Independence Day, 9 December, dawned and eight aircraft (two as spares) taxied out. Due to a lack of power, the pilot of No. 2 (XE643) in the front section aborted his take off and swung across the runway as the undercarriage retracted. On seeing this, the pilot of No. 3 (XE552) in the second section decided

Mombasa airfield firemen spray a precautionary layer of foam over the stricken 208 Squadron FGA.9 XE643 (author's collection).

to abort his take off and, in trying to avoid his No.1's aircraft, his Hunter left the runway and slithered to a stop on soft ground. Little damage was incurred by this aircraft. The damage to XE643 was initially classified as Category 4, but subsequent inspection revealed it to be Category 5 and it was struck off charge.

December proved to be a relatively quiet month for 8 Squadron with no operational sorties recorded. Much of the time was spent on six-hour readiness following reports of renewed activity by Iraqi forces near the Kuwait border. This was raised to immediate readiness on the morning of the 27th when HQ Persian Gulf (HQPG) warned of a possible invasion, but this was relaxed once the threat had receded.

Due in part to there being no Hunter stores facility in Bahrain and the pack-up kits having been allowed to run down after the Kuwait emergency, eighty-four items were now on AOG back order. Serviceability levels dropped accordingly, allowing just 150 hours to be flown during the month. The situation eased when the Hunter stores kit arrived from Eastleigh.

The year 1961 had been an eventful one for both Hunter squadrons and the high activity levels underlined the need for closer co-operation between the two. The relative peace of the past few months had enabled attention to focus on re-settling personnel returning from Kuwait while digesting the lessons learnt from Operation VANTAGE. The year ended with two 8 Squadron FR.10s flying top-cover sorties for a helicopter carrying a political agent between Mukeiras and Hilyan.

Chapter 7

1962 – All change!

Having endured a turbulent twelve months, hopes were high on Khormaksar Wing for a return to a more settled routine in the year ahead. By the end of 1961 the British government had finally persuaded the leaders of Aden Colony that they should unite with the Protectorates and form a Federation of South Arabia. The move was not popular, however, among the more troublesome tribesmen, the Yahari and Sa'adi in particular, who began to agitate the unrest that simmered beneath the surface. In an attempt to quell rising tensions and bring rebellious tribesmen to heel, Hunter operations were concentrated on another well-known troublemaker and dissident leader, Musi Hammud. Warning leaflets were dropped over his area of influence but when these were ignored, the Hunters and Shackletons were despatched to attack villages and destroy crops.

Shackleton Offensive

As events transpired, a 37 Squadron Shackleton MR.2 was credited with the first offensive strike of the year. Following a leaflet drop on New Year's Day, a total of fifty-two 20lb fragmentation bombs was dropped on various Yahari and Sa'adi targets on 2 January. Similar raids were carried out on targets in the same area over successive days, Flight Lieutenant Castle and Flying Officer Wilkie narrowly escaping injury when a bullet passed through the nose section of their aircraft. On 7 January, Wing Commander Neville, OC Khormaksar Wing, flew as the bomb-aimer on one sortie and achieved very satisfactory results. The tempo increased on the 8th when a pair of MR.2s dropped fifty-two 20lb fragmentation bombs on dissident strongholds and the same pattern of attacks continued over the next two days.

The first of two runs carried out on the 11th took place during the morning when fifteen 1,000lb medium capacity (MC) bombs were dropped in Wadi Beihan, with the objective of destroying Qat and wheat crops. Qat (or Khat) is derived from the leaves of the shrub *catha edulis* which, when chewed like tobacco or used to make tea, has the effect of a euphoric stimulant. An estimated 85 per cent of the adult population used it on a daily basis. The second Shackleton's weapon load comprised fifty-two 20lb bombs and was dropped during the afternoon. Single Shackleton bombing runs were then flown over each of the next four days, each load consisting of fifty-two 20lb fragmentation bombs. At 22.55 on the 19th, Flying Officer Burden and his crew took

The 37 Squadron Shackletons performed a vital role as a heavy bomber during the Aden campaign. Here, MR.2 WR959 was receiving attention to the starboard outer Griffon when photographed at Sharjah in 1962 (Simon Morrison).

With the help of local manpower, 37 Squadron armourers roll a bomb trolley into position beneath the Shackleton's cavernous bomb-bay (Sandy McMillan).

off on a night attack and encountered small-arms fire from the village of Abil Am Had in the Wadi Yahar. In all, 115 1,000lb MC bombs and 1,146 fragmentation bombs were dropped in the period of a week.

As Hunter support was not required for this offensive, 208 Squadron began the year with a programme of air-to-ground firing on the Khormaksar range. This was interrupted when a series of flagwaves was called for over the Nubat Dukaim area following a request from the FRA. A squadron pilot was attached to the FRA as FAC for the duration.

Bahrain/Khormaksar

Their New Year hangovers a distant blur, the two Hunter squadrons prepared for the Bahrain/Khormaksar changeover. On 15 January nine 208 Squadron FGA.9s departed Khormaksar and headed for Bahrain, there to relieve 8 Squadron on the Kuwait standby. Two aircraft became unserviceable en route, one being able to return to Khormaksar as the other diverted to Salalah. Both aircraft, and a second pair which had been delayed at Khormaksar, were able to fly to Bahrain on the following day. No. 8 Squadron's aircraft staged through Masirah on their passage south, leaving the spare pilots and groundcrew to fly direct to Aden in the relative luxury of a Transport Command Britannia.

The Shackletons, meanwhile, continued their offensive, dropping fifteen 1,000lb MC bombs on cultivated pastures on the morning of 16 January. A further raid in the afternoon was flown by the OC 37 Squadron, Squadron Leader Kingshott, with the station commander, Group Captain Davis, as co-pilot.

The versatility of the Shackleton and its ability to perform several roles in a single sortie was often exercised. On the morning of the 17th, for example, having dropped their load of fifty-two 20lb fragmentation bombs, a Shackleton crew was instructed to carry out a photographic overlap of Wadi Sarar. The captured images were used to produce maps and plans for the building of a road along Wadi Sarar towards Yafa.

With no sightings of significant Iraqi troop movements in southern Iraq, the sole 37 Squadron Shackleton still in Bahrain was flown back to Khormaksar on 26 January. Back on home soil, it joined the other three on operations against Yahari dissident tribesmen in the Lower Yafa. The target area had been extended farther south in order to destroy more Qat and spring wheat plantations.

An eerie calm greeted 8 Squadron on its return to Khormaksar, the only operational sorties called for during the remaining days of January being top cover sorties for a helicopter carrying a political agent from Mukeiras to Hilyan on the 30th and 31st. The rest of the time was taken up with recce training and rocket and cannon firing on the local range.

Kenya Detachment

In preparation for a ten-day detachment to Kenya, 8 Squadron formed a four-ship display team under the leadership of Squadron Leader Jones, the remaining pilots comprising Flight Lieutenants Edmondston, Powell and Morrell. Practice displays were performed on most days and by the end of January they were ready to demonstrate their formation-changing routine over Khormaksar airfield.

After what had been six unsettling months, seven 8 Squadron Hunters departed Khormaksar on 18 February and headed for the lush green plains of East Africa, accompanied by six additional pilots, the EO, and forty airmen. To familiarise the pilots with their new environment, long-range, low-level recces were flown over Kenyan and Tanganyikan territory. A number of exercises were flown in conjunction with 24 Brigade to help bring its Forward Air Controllers up to speed. The detachment concluded with a demonstration by the display team for the Duke of Gloucester.

Following their return to Khormaksar the squadron prepared to host visits by a team of Day Fighter Combat School (DFCS) examiners from West Raynham and a detachment of 43 Squadron Hunters from Cyprus. On 27 February, following reports of an FRA fatality near Ataq, sustained when one of its patrols was fired on,

Three 8 Squadron FGA.9s, XE651, XE649 and XK150, an FR.10 XE599, plus a USAF Albatross share the line at Embakasi in January 1962 (Alan Lowe).

8 Squadron FR.10 XE614 awaiting an air test at Khormaksar in 1961. The oblique camera in the forward fuselage is clearly visible ('Mac' McLauchlan).

Flight Lieutenant Hayr led a pair of aircraft (an FR.10 and an FGA.9) to perform a flagwave over the area.

No operational sorties were called for in early March as the uneasy peace continued. To maintain their high concentration levels, 8 Squadron held a reconnaissance contest for its pilots over a three-day period. The objective was for each pilot to produce a series of photographs depicting each of seven turning points located on a circular course and prepare a written debrief on two other targets. The sorties were flown in the FR.10s and points were awarded for planning time, sortie duration, length and quality of the debrief, and quality of the resulting photographs. The winner's name was not recorded in the ORB!

Bahrain ↔ Khormaksar

As the month drew on, preparations were put in place for the bi-monthly Kuwait standby exchange. On 15 March eight 8 Squadron FGA.9s departed Khormaksar and headed for Bahrain, staging through Masirah en route. The pilots remaining at Khormaksar continued with recce training, practice display flying for a forthcoming station open day and mutuals in the T.7s, during which, recently-arrived pilots were given familiarisation flights over the WAP.

Meanwhile, eight 208 Squadron aircraft departed Bahrain and headed in the opposite direction, leaving two aircraft behind, AOG, awaiting parts. As two of the eight aircraft had to return to Bahrain with technical problems, four continued to Masirah and two to Salalah for overnight stops. The next morning the six aircraft continued south to Khormaksar where they were joined later in the day by the pair that had returned to Bahrain.

No sooner had 208 Squadron settled in than its aerobatic team initiated an intensive period of display flying practice for the open day. The pilots in the team comprised the OC, Squadron Leader Goodfellow, Flight Lieutenants Marshall and Westropp, and Flying Officers Doidge and Harper. The rest of the squadron were meanwhile, engaged in flying top cover sorties for supply drops by the Beverleys and Valettas of 84 and 233 Squadrons respectively. Several flagwaves were called for in the Wadi Hatib area and time was found to engage HMS *Ark Royal*'s defences with dummy attacks. The arrival of two refurbished Mark 9s, XJ632 and XJ688, from the UK enabled XE607 to be lent to 8 Squadron for use on the open day.

Khormaksar Open Day

To improve relations with the Colony's population, a public Open Day was held at Khormaksar on 30 March. The flying programme opened in front of some 60,000 spectators with three 8 Squadron FGA.9s diving down from 20,000 feet and breaking the sound barrier on nearing the airfield. Two aircraft approached from the west with the third, the loan 208 Squadron aircraft (XE607), arriving from the east. To everyone's disbelief, XE607 failed to pull out of its dive and crashed onto the military barracks on the north side of the runway, killing the pilot, Flying Officer Blackgrove. Despite there being very little of the aircraft remaining, examination of the tailplane actuator ram led to the conclusion that another runaway tailplane incident had occurred and that this was the cause of the crash.

Ten operational sorties were flown by 8 Squadron FR.10s over the period 2 to 5 April to provide top cover in the WAP for troops engaged in an operation code-named SWAT. During the same period 208 Squadron Hunters were flown in support of FRA units engaged in a show of force in the Wadi Retieb area. When time allowed, the opportunity was taken to acquaint pilots with the diversion airfield at Djibouti across the Red Sea, some ninety miles (150km) to the west. A total of sixty-five sorties was flown over the four days despite the grounding of a number of aircraft due mainly to items on AOG. A further seventy-four sorties were flown by just four aircraft over a six-day period beginning 9 April. The serviceability rate for the squadron's Mark 9s was a lowly 42 per cent while that for its solitary trainer (XL597) was 17 per cent. This aircraft gained a reputation as being a bit of a rogue as much of its time was spent under repair, failing hood seals being a particular problem.

Towards the end of his tour in 1962, 233 Squadron Valetta pilot Keith Webster hitched a dawn ride on SAR Flight Sycamore XG518 in order to take photographs of the airfield and two of the resulting images are depicted here. (above) Looking west along the Hunter line towards the 37 Squadron/SAR Flight pan. Approximately half of the 8 Squadron allocation of FGA.9s, at the far end of the line, would have been in Bahrain at the time. (below) A view of Khormaksar approaching from the west showing Transport Wing pans occupied by Valettas, Argosys, Beverleys, Canberras and a Hastings (both, Keith Webster).

Napalm tests

Although the 30mm cannon and 3-inch rocket were the preferred weapons of choice during the Hunter's period of operation in Aden, napalm offered a third option should it ever be needed. To assess the practicality of using napalm, a pair of 100-gallon drop tanks fitted to the outboard pylons of an FGA.9, were filled with water and sea dye markers and dropped on the Khormaksar range on 18 April. Several more drops were made at heights of 50 and 80 feet and the behaviour of the tanks in flight and the scatter patterns on impact filmed for subsequent review.

In readiness for long-range recces into the far extremities of the Eastern Aden Protectorate, the FR.10s were fitted with pairs of 230- and 100-gallon underwing tanks on the 20th.

Much of the early part of May was occupied with pilot training, both in Aden and in Bahrain. The 10th of the month, however, was an important day in the 208 Squadron diary for two reasons. While flying in support of a ground operation, codenamed CHARADE, in the Hilyan area, Flight Lieutenants Tate (XE552) and Slaney (XE623) were instructed to open fire on a dissident target, the first occasion on which the squadron's Hunters had fired their guns at an enemy target. However, it soon became apparent that a mistake had been made and they had been directed to the wrong target, requiring a revision to pre-strike procedures to ensure such incidents did not recur.

Bahrain ↔ Khormaksar

Eight 208 Squadron aircraft departed Khormaksar early on 18 May to take over the Kuwait standby at Bahrain. By the time they arrived 8 Squadron had flown its aircraft away for the return to Khormaksar. Following repairs, a further two 208 Squadron aircraft were able to join the remainder at Bahrain five days later.

Down at Khormaksar, 8 Squadron was soon back in action, this time helping to separate warring factions within the Illahi tribe. Twenty sorties were flown between 25 May and 1 June in support of Operation DESPERADO, a joint operation involving two battalions of the Federal National Guard (FNG) and the Queen's Royal Irish Hussars. Two FACs, one from 45 Commando and Flying Officer Stott from 8 Squadron, were attached to the force for the duration of the operation. As 2nd Battalion FNG advanced along Wadi Dura and on into Wadi Rehab, 1st Battalion took an alternative route via Mukeiras and Wadi Hatib, then over the mountains to Husan Sufra in Wadi Rehab. Peace was restored by the 30th, allowing the FNG and Irish Hussars to stand down.

In the early part of June, an operation codenamed LANDSWEER was launched after a Hunaidi tribesman murdered another from the Mohamedi over the border in the Yemen. The political officer for the Upper Aulakki area, Mr W. Heber-Percy, paid a visit to the leader of the Rebeezi tribe, a sub-tribe of the Shamsi, in Wadi Hatib. The gruesome killing had been carried out in a manner contrived to incriminate tribesmen from the

Low-flying at its most exhilarating! A photograph taken by Sandy Burns in 1962 from the forward-facing camera of his 8 Squadron FR.10, depicts a second FR.10 giving a village a high-speed early morning call. Several villagers spotted the aircraft making their run-in and can be seen looking towards their direction (Sandy Burns).

Shamsi. At the request of Mr Heber-Percy, 8 Squadron performed two flagwaves to act as a warning while a pair of FR.10s took photographs of the area. The meeting was considered to have been a success, despite no action being taken against the perpetrator.

Up in Bahrain 208 Squadron spent most of the first five days of June on the ground, due to the majority of its aircraft being on primary star servicing or AOG awaiting spares. The unusual situation was attributed to the exceptional amount of flying that had been undertaken during the previous month and a backlog of work that exceeded its first and second line servicing capabilities.

On 19 June the Sheikh of Dubai formally opened a new Jeb-a-Jib air-to-ground range, located some fifty miles along the coast to the west of Sharjah. No. 208 Squadron was offered the first chance to use it but, as there were no charts or surveys from which to produce a reliable map, the pilots found it difficult to find.

Khormaksar was often favoured by UK-based squadrons for Internal Security Training (IST). Having flown from their home base at RAF Ballykelly in Northern Ireland, a pair of 210 Squadron Shackleton MR.2s arrived at Khormaksar in late June on a month's detachment. Internal Security was the contemporary politically correct term for colonial policing. During their detachments to Khormaksar, Shackleton squadrons would often relieve 37 Squadron crews by taking on some of its up-country commitments.

Black day on the range
On 25 June, having flown two height-check passes on the Khormaksar range, Flying Officer Pete Webbon was instructed to return to base by the RSO (Range Safety Officer)

The Range Safety Officer (seated), liaises with pilots as they fire their guns at targets on the Khormaksar range (Roger Wilkins).

as both passes were below the stipulated safe height. Flying Officer Webbon then requested and received permission to fly a further height check across the range. Instead, he made a direct approach towards the RSO at a height estimated by witnesses as five feet and at an estimated speed of 150 knots, with undercarriage and flaps fully extended. As the aircraft (XE600) passed close by the hut, the throttle was opened and the nose raised to the vertical, but when 150 feet or so from the ground, the aircraft stalled, turned over and crashed, killing the pilot. A board of inquiry concluded that; 'the pilot intended to make things uncomfortable for the RSO by blasting his hut with sand and that such flagrant indiscipline usually has some history'.

Bahrain ↔ Khormaksar

With no operational flying called for during early July, 8 Squadron turned its attention to flying low-level recces, range firing and a weapons competition. On the 14th eight FGA.9s and a T.7 were flown up to Bahrain via Sharjah to relieve 208 Squadron, with thirteen officers and fifty groundcrew in support. Leaving three unserviceable aircraft behind, seven 208 Squadron aircraft departed for Khormaksar where they arrived after a night-stop at Masirah. Flying at Bahrain consisted mainly of exercises with the Army and Navy, the majority of them over the island of Yas, some 170 miles distant. This was the only area where Gulf states would allow the military to carry

Every so often, Hunter pilots were assigned to Army units and accompanied them on their patrols. These two views depict 8 Squadron pilot 'Mac' McLauchlan on a recce along the Beihan-Nuqub road. With sidearm at the ready, Mac is pictured (above) with local tribesman alongside his Land Rover as another group (below) look on. Of interest are the FRA soldiers sitting on the wall and a profusion of Jambiyas borne by the tribesmen, an essential item of their attire (Mac McLauchlan).

out exercises. Other training consisted of cine-weave, cine-tailchase and cine-rocket firing exercises.

Down at Khormaksar 8 Squadron retained a sizeable force of six FGA.9s, four FR.10s and a T.7 with which to carry out its normal commitments. Several of these were used as training initiatives on long-range recce sorties, flying into the Wadi Hadhramaut, deep in the EAP. No. 208 Squadron had meanwhile commenced a programme of familiarisation of the more remote areas of the WAP and maintaining a pair of aircraft on Dhala convoy standby.

Flying Officer Owen Truelove joined 8 Squadron on 25 July as Engineering Officer in place of Flight Lieutenant Mike Murden who became tour-expired. Lieutenant Notley RN also joined the squadron on exchange posting from RNAS Lossiemouth as a replacement for Flight Lieutenant Hayr, who had returned to the UK.

Parts of three Auster AOP.9 observation aircraft are evident in this photograph taken by an 8 Squadron FR.10 pilot of a second FR.10 as the pair beat-up an AAC up-country airstrip on 19 October 1962 (Sandy Burns).

SADA – an improved firing technique

On receiving authorisation for pilots to fire their guns while flying at angles of less than 23 degrees, 208 Squadron Pilot Attack Instructors (PAI) were allocated three days in August to devise other techniques that could benefit Hunter pilots. Their report concluded that the best results were achieved with the aircraft flying at 100 feet above ground level, as long as it could clear 500 feet when climbing away from the target. In total, fourteen sorties were flown on the range and the resulting cine film used to define a pattern of attack known as Shallow Angle Dive Attack (SADA).

Both squadrons' PAIs were then tasked to train the rest of the wing's pilots in the execution of the SADA technique. A programme was devised whereby pilots flew a series of three cine attacks followed by a live firing. To assist the RSO in making an accurate setting for his height gauge, a 37 Squadron Shackleton carried out low-level runs over the range. Live firing using the new technique commenced on 7 August but it soon became apparent that in order to adhere to the 500-feet safety limit, pilots were over-stressing their aircraft. Wing Commander Neville deemed the height limitation unrealistic and issued an instruction for it to be lowered to 400 feet. It was drinks all round for Flight Lieutenant Renshaw for, much to his surprise, he achieved a 100 per cent hit rate.

Exercise FIREBIRD 10

Air tests and fuel-flow checks were the priority for 208 Squadron during the first week of September as it prepared for FIREBIRD 10, an exercise scheduled to take place in Kenya. Flight Lieutenant Marshall and Flying Officer Dawson flew two aircraft (XE544 and XF462) to Embakasi on the 2nd of the month to give a demonstration of the Hunter's capabilities to the Kenyan High Command who were considering forming a Kenyan air force. The main section consisting of six Hunters (XE530, XE552, XE647, XF388, XJ688 and XK140) departed Khormaksar for Embakasi four days later. They were subsequently joined there by the AOC Middle East Command.

The exercise was held jointly with 24 Brigade and took place in the Kajiado region, 35 miles south of Nairobi. Recces were flown over the area on the 7th and a programme of FAC training began on the 10th. Both cine and rocket strike sorties were flown on the 11th and, despite poor weather, the exercise was completed in the allocated two-day timescale.

While taking off as number four in the 208 Aerobatic team, Flight Lieutenant Robert's aircraft (XE544) began to vibrate as a fire-warning light came on. He aborted his take off at 150 kts, causing a tyre to burst as the undercarriage was in the process of raising. The aircraft swung off the runway and sustained Category 5 damage. Nevertheless, the

Covered in a thin layer of sand, rocket rails removed, 208 Squadron FGA.9 XE647 awaits departure from Khormaksar for refurbishment in the UK (Keith Webster).

team was able to close the Royal Show on the 29th with a fine aerobatic display over Mitchell Park, Nairobi.

The AOC then departed and headed for Aden in his white Canberra, accompanied by an FGA.9 (XF445).

A runaway tail trim and hydraulic malfunction en route, forced the Hunter pilot to divert his aircraft to Djibouti. The following day, Flight Lieutenant Gleen and Flying Officer French flew down from Khormaksar to collect a repaired XF445, accompanied by an aircraft (XG169) borrowed from 8 Squadron.

Revolution in the Yemen

Apart from the Kuwait emergency of 1961 and one or two other key incidents, the Hunter era in Aden had been one of relative tranquillity. That was about to change! When the Imam of the Yemen, Ahmed bin Yahya, died on 19 September 1962, he was succeeded by his son, Mohammed Al-Badr. He was overthrown within a week of taking power by an Egyptian-backed revolutionary group which declared the country a republic under the rule of General Sallal. Hostile anti-British propaganda intensified and local radio stations began pumping out a continuous stream of broadcasts encouraging the people of South Arabia to rise up and rebel against British and Federal rule. Thus began the steady and often brutal decline of life in southern

Arabia and, with it, the unconventional lifestyle that had been amenable to British servicemen over many years.

43 Squadron takes a turn

Up in Bahrain the 8 Squadron detachment had been keeping itself busy, with simulated attacks on the Royal Navy frigate HMS *Loch Fyne*. The ship's captain signalled: 'The attacks were copybook; that was the best gunnery practice we've had this commission'. The detachment reached its conclusion on 25 September when the Hunters and personnel of 43 Squadron arrived from Cyprus to take over the Kuwait commitment. No. 8 Squadron returned to Khormaksar after an overnight stop at Masirah. With two fully-equipped squadrons and a complement of thirty-three aircraft, the Hunter wing at Khormaksar had formidable firepower at its disposal.

Ugandan Independence

The impending independence of Uganda was celebrated in true African style and verve, with many festivals being held during the preceding week. To mark the occasion, eight 208 Squadron Hunters flew down to Entebbe on 5 October to be greeted with the sight of an airport festooned in the new national colours of black, red and yellow. The squadron aerobatic team and leader of the formation flypast used the next two days to practise their routine and timings at various locations, followed by a dress rehearsal at the Entebbe Regatta in front of their Royal Highnesses the Duke and Duchess of Kent, who were representing HM the Queen.

At the conclusion of the Independence Day celebrations on 9 October, Flight Lieutenant MacDermid led a formation of two Hunter 'box-fours', astern of an RAF Britannia and a Valiant bomber in a flypast over Kampala Stadium, marking the handover of power to Milton Obote.

The Hunters flew on to Nairobi, there to take part in an exercise codenamed FIERY WINGS, scheduled to begin on the following day. Using the format of an Iraqi invasion of Kuwait, the squadron was tasked with giving close air support to 24 Brigade. After a short break, the aircraft returned to Khormaksar on the 16th and detachment personnel stood down for a few days.

Yemeni incursions

In an unprovoked rocket and gun attack on 21 October, Yemeni Republic Ilyushin Il-2s struck a number of villages in the Nuqub area, close to the border near Beihan. One child was killed and a number of inhabitants wounded. The Il-2 was a piston-engined ground-attack fighter that bore a close resemblance to the Fairey Battle. Together with its successor the IL-10, it achieved the highest production run of any aircraft with over 42,000 built. Despite its Second World War heritage, the IL-2 was still an effective weapon when used on missions such as these.

Operation BEIHAN

In responding to these attacks, both Hunter squadrons were brought to an immediate state of readiness and a dawn-till-dusk standby implemented. For 8 and 208 Squadrons the standard 07:00–13:00 working day in Aden was about to become history and life on Khormaksar Wing would never be the same again. Using a pattern of alternating 24-hour shifts, the squadrons were rostered to start their shifts at midday on alternate days. As the standby in itself had no deterrent effect, the ready state was changed from reactive to proactive. A steady stream of Hunters would in future patrol the border with the Yemen, from dawn to dusk, a pair of aircraft taking off every ninety minutes, seven days a week. Codenamed Operation BEIHAN, the first patrols were flown on 22 October by 8 Squadron pilots Flight Lieutenants Morrell and Powell, following a briefing by Wing Commander Neville.

Instructions were issued for any hostile aircraft caught crossing from the Yemen into the WAP to be shot down. No fewer than 108 border BEIHAN patrols were flown by 8 Squadron between the 22nd and 31st, leading to an increase in its total operational flying hours for the month to 434. On the 30th two pilots reported seeing explosions on the north side of the Yemen border and an aircraft was spotted but no action was taken.

Internal Security Training had become a regular feature for a number of UK and Mediterranean-based Shackleton squadrons during the year, two MR.2 aircraft of 42 Squadron, RAF St Mawgan, arriving for a 3-week IST detachment in November. Most of the training comprised medium-level bombing and air-to-ground firing exercises, but the opportunity was also taken to relieve 37 Squadron of part of its border patrol commitment.

In spite of a declaration on 9 November by President Sallal, in which he implored 'his brothers in the occupied south to join the battle against colonialism', the capability of a newly-installed Victor Conway radar system at Nuqub would give sufficient warning of invading aircraft, allowing the number of patrols to be reduced. From 11 November one border patrol was flown by a pair of Hunters per day; a second pair remained at 60-minute readiness with a third pair at 90-minutes. As the commitment was shared between the two squadrons, their pilots had sufficient time to recuperate and the airmen time to maintain their aircraft. The 8 Squadron ORB noted that 'The Beihan commitment placed considerable strain on the groundcrews but it did not impair their efficiency or morale'.

Nevertheless, despite these precautionary measures, a Yemeni aircraft managed to cross the border near Beihan on 23 November, causing a return to the full dawn-to-dusk border commitment by the Hunter squadrons.

Most of the early air-to-ground rocket trials carried out on the Hunter had been with 100-gallon underwing tanks fitted. As most operations in the Middle East were flown with 230-gallon underwing tanks on board, 8 Squadron decided to carry out a

42 Squadron Shackleton MR.2s, WL801-B and WL754-F, on the Khormaksar pan during a 3-week IS training detachment, December 1962 (author).

weapons test on the Khormaksar range to ascertain the optimum range drum setting for rocket-firing with the larger tanks in place.

The arrival of new topographical maps was gratefully received by the pilots. Their greater detail helped to produce excellent results from cross-country recce training in terms of accuracy and in pinpointing targets.

1 Squadron arrives

With the increase in rebel activity up-country requiring the attention of two fulltime Hunter squadrons, number 1 Squadron was detailed to fly its Hunter FGA.9s from the UK to Persian Gulf to take over the Kuwait Standby commitment from 43 Squadron. Ten aircraft departed RAF Waterbeach on 18 October and headed for Khormaksar via the southern route. During its stay in Aden, 1 Squadron pilots were given the opportunity to gain experience in operations over the barren hinterland. On one such sortie on 28 October, Flight Lieutenant Scofield's FGA.9 (XG253) suffered an engine failure, causing the pilot to pull the ejection handle some thirty-seven miles from Khormaksar. He was uninjured and was quickly picked up by a SAR Flight Sycamore. The squadron then flew up to Sharjah for a short-duration APC on the Jeb-a-Jib range, before moving on to Bahrain to relieve 43 Squadron.

(above) Following a long flight from the UK, 1 Squadron FGA.9 XE650 is pictured taxiing in at Khormaksar on 19 October 1962 (author). Eight 1 Squadron FGA.9s share the Bahrain line (below) with a 208 Squadron FGA.9 and a 13 Squadron Canberra PR.9 on 1 December 1962, during the second phase of their Middle East detachment (author's collection).

On 26 October Pakistani exchange officer Flight Lieutenant Akbar led four 1 Squadron aircraft on a three-day detachment to Karachi. At its conclusion, the aircraft were flown to Bahrain, there to await the rest of the squadron when it moved up from Sharjah.

As the end of its period on border standby came to an end, six 208 Squadron aircraft were flown up to Bahrain on 30 November, allowing 1 Squadron to fly its aircraft back to the UK. With only six serviceable aircraft at its disposal and the rest of its pilots and groundcrew still at Khormaksar, 208 Squadron recognised that it would be in an exposed position for a few days. By 2 December the T.7 and a further three FGA.9s were ready to move to Bahrain. The 208 Squadron groundcrew had to wait another five days for the first available transport aircraft, an RAF Britannia, to fly them up to Bahrain. To cover their absence 1 Squadron groundcrew were obliged to stay on and maintain 208's Hunters until 6 December, when they were relieved of their duties and flown back to the UK in the same Britannia.

As December drew on, the Yemen border patrols were reduced to two pairs per day, interspersed with occasional scrambles to keep everyone on their toes. The policy must have had some effect as no further incursions were reported during this period.

A photograph taken from the port camera of an 8 Squadron FR.10 by Sandy Burns captures sister aircraft, XE599, flying high along the length of Ma'alla Straight (Sandy Burns). The apartment blocks housed service men and their families and were built on land reclaimed from the harbour.

Bahrain ↔ Khormaksar

The Beihan border standby continued through the Christmas period making this festive time of year a little less cheery than normal. On the 28th 8 Squadron departed for Bahrain, there to relieve 208 Squadron on the Kuwait Standby. The trip began with high morale and without incident until a bowser failure at Masirah led to a lengthy delay for the main party. Having made the most of a five-day Christmas break, 208 Squadron departed from Bahrain on the same day.

Chapter 8

1963 – A New Wing

'No need to unpack, you're not stopping!' These were the welcoming words that greeted 8 Squadron personnel as they stepped off their aircraft on arrival at Bahrain. A two-phase exercise code-named CANTELOPE was scheduled to take place during the periods from 8 to 12 and 21 to 30 January 1963. During these periods, personnel

DFCS F.6 XG204 and 8 Squadron FGA.9 XE618 roll down the Sharjah runway (above) for a session on the Jeb-a-Jib range on 24 January 1963. F.6 XG204 and T.7 XL591 on the Hunter pan at Sharjah on the same day. Of interest are the gunblast deflectors fitted to the F.6 (both, author).

from 23 Squadron (Javelin FAW.9Rs) and 90 and 214 Squadrons (Valiant tankers) would be arriving from the UK and requiring the only available accommodation. No. 8 Squadron was instructed to relocate to Sharjah for the duration of both phases and return to Bahrain at the end of each.

DFCS appraisal

A simulated Kuwait-style operation carried out immediately on arrival at Sharjah on the 21st ended with a live-firing exercise on the Jeb-a-Jib range. The squadron was accompanied by a team of examiners from the Day Fighter Combat School (DFCS) who had flown a pair of F.6s (XG204 and XG209) and a couple of T.7s (XL591 and XL595) to Bahrain from RAF West Raynham in the UK. The purpose of their visit was to appraise the Command's Hunter pilots on their capabilities when flying low-level intercepts, air-to-ground rocket and cannon firing, and high-level battle formations.

Having 'imbibed heartily of the cheering cup', 208 Squadron entered the new year by ensuring that its recent intake of pilots were able find their way around the Aden Protectorates. To everyone's surprise, the mission was accomplished without losing anyone. Otherwise the squadron concentrated its flying task on dawn-to-dusk border patrols in the Beihan area. With a visit by the DFCS team scheduled for the end of January, 208 Squadron began a programme of weapons and tactical training.

While the RP scores were good, those for gun firing were lower than anticipated. From the 14th to the 18th of the month, G-suit straps were tightened a little more than normal for a period of practice low-level evasion tactics. The pressure eased after a few days, enough to allow the squadron to practise a seven-ship flypast marking the inauguration of a local Sultan at Zinjibar, capital of Fadhli.

The four DFCS Hunters shortly after their arrival in Bahrain on 19 January 1963. The Flight comprised; F.6 XG204-B, T.7 XL591-M, F.6 XG209-C and T.7 XL595-O (author).

When news came through that the DFCS team would be arriving a few days early, a further period on the range brought a marked improvement in results. The team arrived at Khormaksar on 26 January and remained with 208 Squadron well into February. As the squadron ORB stated, 'It was generally felt that great benefit had been derived from the visit and the hope was expressed that they in turn had learnt something of the conditions in which the Khormaksar squadrons operated'.

Aden Colony joins the Federation

In November 1962 Britain declared that it would not recognise the republican regime in the Yemen and would continue to support plans for the incorporation of Aden Colony into the Federation of South Arabia. On 18 January 1963, and with the full support of the British government, Aden Colony became Aden State and the twelfth member of the Federation. This inevitably led to a deterioration in relations with the Yemeni government and to the closure of the British mission in Taiz.

Expedition tragedy

The situation was exacerbated when forty-five members of HQ Middle East Command strayed over the unmarked border in the mountains north of Aden while on an adventure expedition. Yemeni forces opened fire on the group, killing four people and wounding a further two. Twenty-one were captured by Egyptian soldiers and taken to Taiz for interrogation as the remaining eighteen managed to escape and make their way back to Aden. Those taken prisoner were released unharmed ten days later following intense diplomatic activity.

54 Squadron detachment

The Khormaksar squadrons were given a break from duty on the Kuwait standby on 2 February when seven 54 Squadron Hunter FGA.9s flew into Bahrain on detachment from the UK. While in the Middle East the opportunity was taken for squadron pilots and groundcrew to experience front-line operations and familiarisation of the area, should they be called upon during a future emergency. Rocket rails had been fitted by next morning, allowing five 8 Squadron aircraft to return to Khormaksar in the afternoon, three staging through Salalah and two via Masirah. A further pair departed on the 4th leaving two aircraft on loan to the visiting squadron.

As this was one of the rare occasions on which both Khormaksar squadrons were in Aden at the same time, the Yemen border patrol commitment was shared on a rota basis. A shift system was put into operation whereby one squadron undertook standby and border patrol duties from midday on one day until midday on the next, leaving the other to catch up with tactical training, range-work, aircraft maintenance, etc.

During the quieter periods when no air support was called for a routine evolved in which two pairs of aircraft were flown on border patrols by both squadrons. Following a border infringement near Beihan on 23 February 8 Squadron brought pairs of FGA.9s

Soon after the DFCS visit, 54 Squadron took the opportunity to pay a visit to the Middle East. Here we see FGA.9 XF523 on the line at Bahrain shortly after flying in from the UK (author).

Following a period on the Kuwait standby, 54 Squadron moved down to Khormaksar where FGA.9 XG155 heads the Hunter line (author).

and FR.10s to 60-minute readiness and its remaining aircraft to 120-minute standby. These states remained in force throughout the next few days and were concluded on the 26th when two pairs dropped warning leaflets over Wadi Ablah. Nevertheless, a lumbering Yemeni Air Force Yak II light bomber dating from the early 1940s, was able to cross the border, strafe the airstrip at Ayn and return home undetected by a pair of Hunters patrolling at 7,000 feet. To reduce the chances of this recurring, the border patrol profile was changed; one aircraft would fly at 7,000 feet and the second at 2,000 feet. After twenty minutes or so, the pair would exchange positions for the next twenty minutes, and continue interchanging until it was time to return to base.

Bahrain ↔ Khormaksar

On 25 February nine 208 Squadron FGA.9s departed Khormaksar for Bahrain, there to relieve 54 Squadron on the Kuwait standby. A further FGA.9 accompanied by a T.7 (on loan from 8 Squadron) staged through Salalah en route to Bahrain

(above) An early morning view looking across Khormaksar airfield from Hunter line towards the salt pans and beyond to the Radfan mountains some twenty miles distant. Such a clear view was unusual, the horizon being obscured for most of the year due to the haze. (below) Armourers were some of the fittest tradesmen in Aden. Having disconnected the Master Armament Safety Break (MASB) plug from the lead aircraft (XF440), Jock Harman dashes back to repeat the process on number two (XF445). The MASB was connected and disconnected on the peritrack to ensure that guns and rockets could not be accidental discharged in the vicinity of an aircraft pan (both, author).

a day later, leaving two of the squadron's aircraft at Khormaksar on second- line servicing. One of them (XF445) was re-allocated to 8 Squadron. The Bahrain detachment was under the temporary command of Flight Lieutenant Oswell as Squadron Leader Goodfellow, having become tour-expired, remained at Khormaksar to await the arrival of his successor, Squadron Leader Gordon Lewis.

Number 54 Squadron in the meantime had left Bahrain and flown down to Khormaksar for a brief period to enable its pilots to gain experience in operational flying in a hostile environment before returning to the UK.

43 squadron arrives

A few days before Christmas 1962 43 Squadron was informed that it would be moving to Khormaksar on 1 March 1963 on a permanent basis. In the meantime it continued with a training programme and various exercises in the Cyprus area up to the end of February. The groundcrew were then put to work ensuring that the Hunters were brought up to the same modification level, packing and returning equipment and carrying out the multiplicity of tasks inherent with a unit redeployment.

AOC-in-C NEAF, Air Chief Marshal Sir Dennis Barnett, took the salute at a farewell parade on 22 February and several functions were attended by squadron members. A landing ship was provided to transport equipment, heavy personal baggage and members' cars from Cyprus to Aden.

Headed by FGA.9 XJ683, a line of 43 Squadron Hunters on the Khormaksar pan following their redeployment from Cyprus in March 1963 (author).

On the morning of 1 March, under the command of Squadron Leader P. Peacock, the squadron's ten FGA.9s and lone T.7 departed Nicosia and headed for El Adem for a refuelling stop. After an overnight stop at Khartoum, the formation continued to Khormaksar, where it arrived during the evening of the 2nd. Two pilots, Flying Offis Brown and Gill, had in the meantime flown back to the UK to collect a pair of refurbished FGA.9s to bring the squadron allocation up to full strength.

Tactical Wing

Middle East Command now had a formidable strike force at its disposal; thirty-eight Hunter FGA.9s, four FR.10s and four T.7s. The opportunity was taken to restructure the wing under a new name: Tactical Wing (TacWing). The change of name came into effect on 2 March 1963, shortly after Wing Commander John Jennings assumed command from Wing Commander Neville.

1417 Flight reborn

The focal point of the reorganisation was the re-allocation of the four 8 Squadron FR.10s and four T.7s from all three squadrons into a newly reformed 1417 Flight. Flight Lieutenant Peter Lewis was appointed Officer Commanding, with former 8 Squadron colleagues, Flight Lieutenants Morris, Dymond, Rimmer and Burns, completing the

Five pilots from 1417 Flight – Flt Lts Roger Pyrah, Johnny Morris, Peter Lewis (OC), Jim Dymond and Geoff Timms – are pictured in front of one of their FR.10s (Peter Lewis).

Bearing the markings and initials of OC Peter Lewis, 1417 Flight FR.10 XE614 stands alongside T.7 XL613 on the Khormaksar Hunter pan in 1963 (Bryan John).

nominal roll. Although many of the pilots posted to the ground attack squadrons were first-time tourists, the experience and skills demanded for the fighter-recce role were such that only pilots with two or three fast-jet tours under their belts were considered for a position on the flight. No. 8 Squadron airmen retained the responsibility for servicing the flight's aircraft pending the establishment of a dedicated groundcrew. Squadron markings were removed from all eight aircraft and new tailcodes applied in light blue; pilots' initials on the FR.10s and W–Z on the trainers. Based on the shape of an arrowhead, a unit flash was designed and applied to the aircraft as the year wore on. The colours were those of Aden Protectorate (yellow, green and black) with the Khormaksar crest as a centrepiece. The front end was rumpled to represent a camera bellows.

26 Squadron – vertical lift

In recognising the operational overlap, the decision was taken to include 37 Squadron under the TacWing umbrella along with a recent arrival in Aden, 26 Squadron. An interesting addition to the MEC inventory, it was equipped with the Belvedere, a twin-rotor, twin-engined, heavy-lift helicopter. The first two examples arrived in early March having flown all the way from the UK. They were joined by a further two Belvederes a few weeks later and two more as the year drew to a close. As the aircraft's

The first two 26 Squadron Belvedere helicopters to arrive in Aden, XG463-B and XG457-D, were pictured on 1 April 1963 during their work-up in company with an SAR Flight Sycamore (author).

heavy-lift capability would soon be used to good effect in supporting up-country Army units, the decision was taken to assign the squadron to Tactical Wing.

There was no time for relaxation, however, as a constant stream of dawn-till-dusk sorties were being flown to provide top-cover in the Wadi Ayn area in support of an Army operation codenamed JACKKNIFE. The benefits of the third Hunter squadron were soon realised as the pressure eased on both aircraft and crews. The opportunity for a well-earned break came when Sea Vixen FAW.1s from HMS *Centaur* took over the border patrol commitment for a few days.

Mapping

The maps supplied to pilots flying over the Aden hinterland were notoriously inaccurate, the best way of familiarising themselves with the barren terrain being to tag on to experienced colleagues. In an attempt to provide more accurate charts, Canberra PR.7s and PR.9s were detached from the UK, Germany, Malta and Cyprus over several weeks to take high-level photographs of the WAP to provide a source for the production of a more accurate set of maps. On 4 and 5 March 8 Squadron provided a pair of armed FGA.9s as escorts to Canberras performing survey flights.

While acclimatising to their new surroundings, 43 Squadron pilots were briefed on the main difficulties facing RAF pilots flying from Khormaksar, such as; operations,

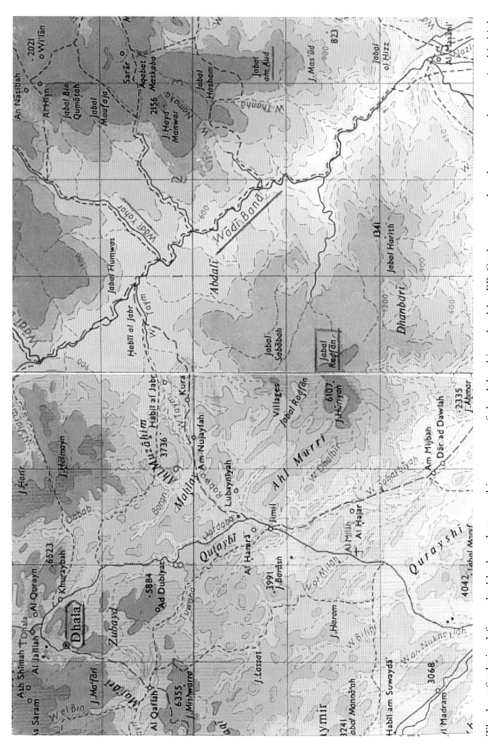

The benefit derived from the blanket photographic coverage of the Aden hinterland by PR Canberras on detachment can be seen in this high definition map of the Radfan mountains produced by MEC cartographers (Alan Pollock).

One of several photograph reconnaissance Canberras detached to Khormaksar in the spring of 1963, 58 Squadron PR.7 WH802 taxies in following a photographic sortie over the Aden hinterland (author).

local politics, weather, air traffic, desert and mountain flying, etc. Their introduction to operational flying in the MEC theatre began on 6 March when 43 Squadron Hunters took over the Canberra photographic escort brief from 8 Squadron.

Operation RANJI

There was little time for 1417 Flight pilots to relax either as they became involved in a new operation that would absorb many flying hours over the coming years. Codenamed RANJI, its prime objective was for its FR.10s to perform sweeps along the WAP coast and identify Arab dhows suspected of making illicit landings while smuggling arms to dissident tribesmen. Six sorties were tasked initially to scour the coast line fifty miles to the east and west of Aden. On this occasion, a Soviet research ship spotted close to the shore line was the only vessel found to be acting suspiciously. A further two sorties were flown by Flight Lieutenants Lewis (XE589) and Morris (XE599) to try to pinpoint the locations of anti-aircraft guns known to exist in the Beihan area.

Five days after its arrival in Aden, 43 Squadron undertook its first patrol in the Beihan border area. In order for the pilots to remain in radio contact with the GCI station at Nequb, one aircraft flew at 15,000 feet while maintaining visual contact with the lead aircraft some 11,000 feet below.

A typical Operation Ranji FR.10 photograph depicting a number of trucks suspected of being involved in arms-smuggling (Peter Lewis).

Having assumed command of 208 Squadron on 17 March, Squadron Leader Gordon Lewis flew up to join his new unit at Bahrain, allowing Squadron Leader Goodfellow to take up his new post with the Air Ministry.

April was a relatively quiet month. The readiness state for the Beihan patrol was reduced to a pair of aircraft at 60-minutes with a further pair at 120-minutes. The standby duty was shared between 8 and 43 Squadrons, the changeover taking place on a weekly basis. Three more Canberra escort sorties were flown by 43 Squadron which was otherwise free to concentrate on cine-weave, high- and low-level gunsight handling, Standard Operating Procedures (SOPs) and combat sorties.

A firm set of rules was imposed for 'dogfight' training. As the maximum four-gun firing time was around seven seconds, only seven seconds of film time was allowed. Any additional film, however good, was disqualified. In addition, the minimum time for a 'killing' burst was two seconds, during which, tracking had to remain steady and the ranging within 10 per cent. These limitations led to a few disagreements but, on the whole, the training value was considered excellent as it taught pilots to use ammunition efficiently and accurately.

On 11 April, 8 Squadron held a parade to mark the arrival of Squadron Leader Tam Syme DFC who, three days later, assumed command of the squadron from Squadron Leader Laurie Jones.

Operation LONGSTOP

The bi-monthly Hunter detachments to Bahrain also received a dedicated codename, Operation LONGSTOP. The name was used for the first time on 29 April when 8 Squadron relieved 208 Squadron in the Gulf. One aircraft was forced to return to Khormaksar with a fuel flow problem, leaving the pilot, the OC RAF Persian Gulf, to find his way up to Bahrain by alternative means.

On its return to Khormaksar, 208 Squadron was stood down for three days with a further three days allocated for aircraft rectification. An intense programme of range work then ensued, with emphasis on the SADA technique for attacking targets. Several senior pilots attained the required level and progressed to the operational one-pass gun-firing phase. Ground-attack skills were further honed with a comprehensive training programme consisting of low-level strikes carried out at 250 feet and 420 knots. Their targets were caves and other landmarks identified from photographs taken by Flight Lieutenant Grimshaw in a 1417 Flight FR.10. A high degree of accuracy was achieved.

Following an APC at Sharjah, Chiefy Appleyard supervises the loading of packup kits for the 8 Squadron move back to Bahrain (author).

ˉOn 13 May 208 Squadron was tasked with providing close air support for the FRA as it penetrated deep into the Wadi Hatib.

New C.-in-C.

On the 30th 208 Squadron performed a farewell flypast in the form of a letter 'E' for the departing C-in-C, Air Chief Marshal Sir Charles Elworthy GCB CBE DSO MVO DFC AFC. Despite poor visibility, the formation arrived over the saluting base in good order and on time. Air Chief Marshal Elworthy was succeeded in post by General Sir Charles Harington GCB CBE DSO MC.

Inactivity along the Yemen border allowed 43 and 208 Squadrons to relieve the pressure on 1417 Flight by sharing the daily coastline patrols on Operation RANJI, along with 37 Squadron. The tempo began to rise in June, however, when twenty-one operational sorties were called for, nineteen on Operation RANJI by 1417 Flight (thirteen) and 43 Squadron (six), and two recces along the Yemen border near Beihan by 1417 Flight due to unrest having been reported in the area.

By now 37 Squadron had completed six years' service at Khormaksar. During that period its aircraft had flown an estimated 3 million miles (5 million km) on operations far removed from those envisaged by the Shackleton's designers. As its primary role, maritime reconnaissance, accounted for only a fraction of its service in Aden, sorties were occasionally flown over the surrounding seas to ensure crews were able to retain their full maritime competence categories.

Throughout this time 37 Squadron had relied on just four aircraft to fulfil the wide range of activities expected of it when the standard Shackleton squadron establishment was six. Detachments by pairs of aircraft from other Shackleton units were often flown to Khormaksar to relieve the workload during busy periods. One such detachment was undertaken by two Shackleton MR.2s from Gibraltar-based 224 Squadron in June, followed by a further pair from 42 Squadron towards the end of July.

Hunters grounded

When a 43 Squadron pilot experienced a broken aileron shackle while flying an up-country mission, he was able to nurse his aircraft safely back to Khormaksar. The problem had been reported previously and although a modification was available to overcome it, all Hunters were grounded for a day for a thorough inspection of every shackle to take place. Although no defects were found, the aircraft were cleared to fly under strict limitations: a maximum speed of 420 knots IAS and guns not to be fired except on operational sorties.

By way of a thank you to Sheik Mactum, the son of the Sheik of Dubai, who generously provided the Jeb-a-Jib range, Squadron Leader Syme flew a T.7 from Bahrain to Sharjah on 15 June to give him a ride in a Hunter. Four days later 8 Squadron performed its last activity of the detachment, a flypast for the first visit to Bahrain of the new C-in-C.

Operation LONGSTOP

The 20th of June marked the end of 8 Squadron's term at Bahrain and its aircraft were flown back to Khormaksar, leaving 43 Squadron to take over the Kuwait standby for the first time since its arrival in Aden. To prepare for a situation where the groundcrew's arrival was delayed, 43 Squadron's pilots were exercised on the main points of turning round their aircraft; removing the outboard drop tanks, repacking the brake-chutes,

Two views from an 8 Squadron Armament Practice Camp at Sharjah with (above), FGA.9 XF376-K touching down on the piano keys as FGA.9 XG237-M (below) looks set to make a three-point landing (both, author).

aircraft refuelling and pre-flight checks. To complete the exercise, they were required to take off and perform a recce sortie over a defined target, all within sixty minutes of having landed at Bahrain.

Taking advantage of the limited flying caused by the aileron problem, the opportunity was taken on 21 June to transfer fifteen airmen from 8 Squadron to 1417 Flight to form the nucleus of a dedicated groundcrew. Accommodation within the wing's compound was found by clearing out the 8 Squadron parts store.

Despite the demarcation, the two units were to maintain a close working relationship over the next four years.

On 8 July a local ruler in the Hilyan area reported that he was under siege in Hilyan fort and exchanging fire with hostile tribesmen. A pair of Hunters were despatched to drop leaflets on the offenders and a flagwave flown early next morning. As these made no impression, pairs of Hunters from 8 and 208 Squadrons carried out cannon strikes on dissident targets during the afternoon. The 8 Squadron pair were flown by Flight Lieutenant McVie (XE620) and Flying Officer Bottom (XE654). A second strike was carried out on the 10th by Flight Lieutenants McVie (XE609) and Constable (XG154) as Lieutenant Notley (RN) maintained top cover in an FR.10 (XE614) borrowed from 1417 Flight. Although this seemed to have the desired effect, top cover sorties were flown to safeguard a 233 Squadron Valetta dropping supplies in the area on the 11th and 15th.

When a USAF SA-16 Albatross amphibian aircraft ditched in the Red Sea, north of Port Sudan, a 42 Squadron Shackleton on detachment to Khormaksar was despatched to locate it. Although it was dark, the crewmen were quickly spotted and two sets of Lindholme gear dropped close by.

When an old feud between the Rabizi and Illahi tribes threatened to erupt in violence, 8 Squadron was detailed to carry out a series of flagwaves in the Upper Aulaqi area on the 27th and 28th of the month, followed by a leaflet drop by the squadron on other tribes in the area, warning them not to get involved. This seemed to have the desired effect as no further trouble was reported.

Ferrying Hunters to the UK

In order to prevent excessive deterioration caused by constant exposure to high temperatures and the ingression of sand, MEC Hunters were returned to one of two maintenance units in the UK – 5 MU at RAF Kemble and 19 MU at RAF St Athan – every two years for a full refurbishment. Basically, this would entail stripping aircraft down to their component parts, replacing a high percentage of the internal equipment, giving them a thorough clean and a fresh coat of paint. The opportunity was also taken to bring them up to the same modification level. As most aircraft differed in some way, it was a complex process and required several months work before a pristine looking aircraft was ready to be flown back to the Middle East.

Approximately every two years, Middle East-based Hunters were ferried back to the UK for refurbishment at one of two dedicated MUs; 5 MU at Kemble and 19 MU at St Athan. FGA.9 XF421 of 208 Squadron (above) was photographed landing at Kemble on 28 March 1962 while prototype FGA.9 XG135, formerly with 8/43 Squadron, had still to pass through the Aircraft Finishing Section when captured at Kemble in October 1966 while taxiing out for an air test (both, author).

Ferrying the aircraft to and from the UK could present interesting challenges for the pilots and many a tale has unfolded of their adventures. No two ferry trips were the same. One that began on 12 July, for example, became a contender for the shortest on record. Flight Lieutenant Adamson and Flying Officer Jarvis were assigned to fly a 1417 Flight FR.10 (XF436) and a 43 Squadron FGA.9 (XJ684) to the UK but were forced to abandon the trip shortly after departing Bahrain. Flight Lieutenant Adamson was unable to raise the undercarriage on his aircraft, forcing both pilots to burn off fuel before landing back at the airfield. On final approach Flying Officer Jarvis's aircraft developed a hydraulic fire in the rear section which became so fierce he was fortunate to touch down in one piece. The rear section, which was assessed as Category 5 damage (scrap), was virtually hanging off as he came to a halt. Air Traffic Control described it as a spectacular sight. As XF436 had incurred a hydraulic pressure problem, both aircraft were left for 43 Squadron to sort out.

Of the nineteen operational sorties flown by 1417 Flight in July, all but two were coastal recces. Two up-country photo recces were flown on the 10th and 11th, the first over the Am Shaq area and the second at Hilyan. FR.10 XF460 was used on both occasions with Flight Lieutenants Lewis and Dymond respectively at the controls.

A serious fire having destroyed the aircraft's rear section in July 1963, 43 Squadron FGA.9 XJ684 was reformed using sections removed from 8 and 208 Squadron aircraft on AOG; hence the dual squadron markings. The photograph depicts 'Jock' McVie taxiing the Hunter out at Muharraq for the flight down to Khormaksar in the following December (author).

On 6 December 1963, three 8 Squadron FGA.9s were flown back to the UK for refurbishment. The pilot of XF455, 'Mac' McLauchlan, took a series of photographs which included, XJ687-E over Khartoum (above) and XE651-M and XJ687-E passing Gozo en-route for Luqa, Malta ('Mac' McLauchlan).

Exercises in Kenya

In order to fulfil the ground–attack element of a couple of exercises scheduled by Army units in Kenya, 8 Squadron despatched five aircraft to Embakasi Airport on 20 July. A further three pilots and thirty-nine groundcrew followed on in a 105 Squadron Argosy later that morning. The exercises took place near Lake Rudolph and to the north of Kilimanjaro, were codenamed CANDYFLOSS and RINGBIRD respectively, and required limited participation by the Hunters. This gave plenty of time for squadron personnel to explore the lush, green environment and leisure activities abundant in the Kenyan countryside. As the squadron record states, 'The unfortunates on the detachment survived unlimited parties and excursions to the game parks, Mombasa and Kilimanjaro'. The OC TacWing, Wing Commander John Jennings, and Flight Lieutenant Talbot flew a further pair of aircraft to Embakasi on 1 August, ostensibly to bolster the number of aircraft available on the line. The detachment concluded on 6 August when the aircraft flew back to Khormaksar.

During the intervening period, a number of flagwaves had been flown in the Upper Aulaqi area by 8 Squadron aircraft still at Khormaksar to deter the Rabizi and Illahi tribes from re-igniting their ancient feud. Leaflet drops were also carried out on tribes living in the surrounding area, warning them not to get involved in the dispute. On a separate front, the remit for Operation RANJI was extended to counter a rise in up-country gunrunning activities in certain parts of the hinterland.

8 Squadron groundcrew set to work on turning round FGA.9 XE620, OC Tam Syme's new aircraft, at Embakasi Airport on 6 August 1963 (author).

No sooner had the Kenya detachment arrived back at Khormaksar, when Squadron Leader Syme (XE620), Wing Commander Jennings (XF435) and Flying Officer Bottom (XE618) were detailed to carry out a strike on targets in Wadi Hatib in support of FRA units hunting a murderer.

The long-awaited arrival and fitting of aileron mod-kits allowed the speed and gun-firing limitations to be lifted during the early part of August. Number 208 Squadron wasted no time in getting back into full swing with a much needed RP programme on the Khormaksar range. The disappointing results were attributed to the low level of experience on the squadron and the long gap since the previous range programme. Concentration then turned to long range, low-level, cross-country sorties ending with run-in and cine rocket attacks on a specified target. A pair of 'enemy' aircraft lingered in the target area to menace the attacking aircraft in order to simulate a hostile air environment while giving the pilots a feel for the challenges they could face while attempting a safe withdrawal. After a few more days perfecting their technique, the focus moved on to air-to-ground gun attacks on the range for newly-arrived pilots in preparation for the next Kuwait standby.

Operation LONGSTOP

On the morning of 22 August Squadron Leader Lewis led six 208 Squadron Hunters north out of Khormaksar to relieve 43 Squadron on the Kuwait standby. Spare pilots and airmen were flown up by RAF Britannia late in the evening, leaving four Hunters to follow on the next day. Due to Bahrain's sole runway being closed for repairs between 12:30 and 18:30, pairs of aircraft were rotated to Sharjah in order to carry out reconnaissance flights over Muscat and Oman. No reason was given in the ORB but many operations over Oman were classified during the sixties.

To cover the initial shortfall of 208 Squadron aircraft at Bahrain, 43 Squadron divided its return to Khormaksar, half of its Hunters departing on the 22nd and the remainder a day later. The groundcrew had to wait a few more days for the first available transport aircraft. As there were no operational duties required of 43 Squadron at this point, priority was given to bringing newly-arrived pilots up to standard. On the 28th pairs of aircraft from both 8 and 43 were placed on two-hour readiness in anticipation of a call for airborne support.

Leaky tanks

Although fuel tank leaks were an accepted norm in the heat of the Middle East, an alarming increase in instances of leaks from the flexible wing-mounted Marston tank over a short space of time gave cause for concern. Number 208 Squadron changed thirteen Marston tanks in September alone! Replacing a wing tank was a laborious task and required several man-hours to complete. Designed for use in milder European climes, the Marston tank was not really suited for conditions in which an egg could

Stan Ovington changing a pair
of defective Marston fuel tanks –
an awkward, time-consuming
activity (author).

be fried on an aircraft's wing. In one incident a tank split during flight causing the
208 Squadron pilot to divert to Sharjah, while a further two of the squadron's aircraft
suffered ruptured tanks while parked on the apron. More aircraft were rendered
unserviceable due to the tank's excessive porosity. The alternative tank was in short
supply, leaving no option but to continue using the Marston product for the time being.

Due to the late arrival of replacement tanks from the UK, 1417 Flight could only
provide one serviceable aircraft (XE614) on a couple of days. Nonetheless, seventeen
coastal recces were undertaken by the flight during August, the most interesting one
being that by Flight Lieutenant Lewis who was tasked to locate the position of a
Russian submarine known to be prowling the area. A further two sorties were flown in
the same aircraft by Flight Lieutenant Rimmer in search of a yacht that was overdue.

The opportunity to fire rockets and guns at splash targets in the Red Sea was rarely
missed and was carried out with the co-operation of the RAF Marine Craft Unit
and, occasionally, Royal Navy vessels on visits to Aden. A more specialised exercise
took place over the period 6 and 13 September when Hunters were tasked to perform
high-speed, sea-hugging runs towards the carrier HMS *Victorious* to assist with the
calibration and testing of its recently installed UHF radio equipment.

Kenya detachment

On 24 September 43 Squadron departed for a short detachment to Nairobi, ostensibly to perform a 15-minute display for visitors to the Royal Show. Shortly after departing Khormaksar, Wing Commander Jennings' aircraft sustained a runaway nose-down trim which he was able to correct and continue on his flight south. The display opened with synchronised aerobatics by Flight Lieutenants Gold and Stoker, followed by a box-four formation led by Squadron Leader Peacock with Flying Officer Law and Flight Lieutenants Doggett and Edwards in the numbers 2 to 4 positions. The display concluded with slow and fast passes by Flight Lieutenants Chapman and Osborne. The proceedings closed with a nine-ship formation flypast to mark the departure of the AOC from Eastleigh, led by Wing Commander Jennings. The squadron flew back to Khormaksar on 6 October and straight into a routine of cine-weaves, air-to-ground firing, Operation RANJI, flagwaves and battle formation tactics.

It was time for OC 43 Squadron, Squadron Leader Peacock, to bid his farewells and relinquish command to his successor, Squadron Leader Phil Champniss. It was an inauspicious start for the new squadron commander who, due to the poor serviceability states of the T.7s, became frustrated at his inability to fly with and assess his pilots, having to base his judgement and supervision on second-hand opinions.

On the morning of 4 October the two 8 Squadron standby pilots were alerted by TacOps to prepare to scramble. As they were being strapped in, the order to scramble came through and, under Champion radar control at Mukeiras, they made a fast dash towards the border to intercept an unidentified intruder aircraft. As was often the case, by the time they reached the area it had flown back into the Yemen. A further pair was scrambled to cover the area between Mudiyah and Laudar but nothing was seen there either.

When it became apparent that some of the high-level photographs taken by the visiting Canberras did not convey the level of detail required, 1417 Flight decided to produce a photographic record of every fort and airstrip within a ten-mile band to the south of the Yemen border.

On 18 October 43 Squadron's 'Battle Flight' was scrambled to identify an aircraft being tracked by Champion radar, the controller having spotted it crossing the border from the Yemen. It passed so close to the radar site that the operators were able to identify it as a twin-engined jet, probably a Russian-built Il-28 Beagle bomber. By the time the Hunters arrived, it had crossed back over the border and permission to pursue it was denied.

Operation LONGSTOP

All too soon, it was time for another Longstop, nine 8 Squadron FGA.9s and a T.7 departing for Bahrain on 24 October. Heading in the opposite direction, 208 Squadron ferried its aircraft down to Khormaksar in three waves, the first two staging through

Nine 8 Squadron FGA.9s on the Hunter line at Bahrain in October 1963. Also of interest are the two 13 Squadron Canberra PR.9s at the far end and the 84 Squadron Beverley in the background (author).

Masirah on the 24th and 25th, as the shorter range T.7 routed via Salalah in the company of an FGA.9. The spare pilots and groundcrew followed in a Beverley.

No. 8 Squadron had time to settle in at Bahrain before playing host to a visit by Prince Sheikh Kalifah Bin Isa Al Khalifah and his entourage. In addition to meeting the pilots, the Sheikh and his guests were treated to a formation flypast by the squadron's Hunters. No operational sorties were flown during November, the opportunity being taken to spend two weeks at Sharjah on low-level flying and live weapons practice on the Jeb-a-Jib range.

Peace and quiet!

As an unlikely peace appeared to have broken out among the warring factions, at least for the time being, 43 Squadron took the opportunity to hone its training programme, the strike phase in particular. In one scenario, four Hunters were flown on both low- and high-level sorties with the objective of locating and effecting dummy attacks on selected targets. The Khormaksar range provided the target for the finale, which consisted of two passes, six rockets being unleashed on the first and thirty rounds of ball ammunition from all four guns on the second.

In addition to operational standbys, 1417 Flight flew fourteen RANJI sorties in November, most of them along the coast to the west of Aden in search of Arab dhows landing illegal immigrants. In an attempt to broaden the understanding of the capabilities of fighter reconnaissance, Flight Lieutenants Cole, Chambers and Neal, accompanied by Squadron Leader Bowie (TacWing Training Officer), gave a series of lectures to local military units, including officers, warrant officers and SNCOs of the King's Own Yorkshire Light Infantry. The sessions were given in the open which gave Flight Lieutenant Grimshaw the opportunity to photograph the assembly from an FR.10 and drop the processed prints some twenty minutes later.

One of the less demanding tasks to be undertaken by TacWing was air experience flights to trainee Forward Air Controllers in a T.7 to help familiarise them with the landscape from a pilot's perspective while flying at high speed and at low level. A demonstration strike was included to illustrate the hazards Hunter pilots faced when attacking targets in treacherous terrain.

The high level of unserviceability continued to afflict 1417 Flight through much of November, only one FR.10 being serviceable through much of the month. Nevertheless, and in spite of completing fifteen operational sorties, the task of plotting and photographing airstrips in the WAP had made good progress, allowing the focus of attention to turn to the numerous forts and police posts scattered across the territory.

Khormaksar Open Day
The Khormaksar Open Day, held on 29 November, gave 43 and 208 Squadron an opportunity to demonstrate their flying skills to the local population. Led by Wing Commander Jennings, the display opened with nine aircraft flying by in various formations, 208 Squadron providing four aircraft and 43 Squadron the remainder. To retain the spectators' attention between each flyby, two 43 Squadron pilots, Flight Lieutenants Golds and Stoker, performed the synchronised aerobatic routine they had perfected in Kenya. This was followed with a solo display by Flight Lieutenant Copplestone of 208 Squadron and a tactical demonstration in which 208 Squadron carried out simulated ground attacks on dummy targets with top cover provided by further Hunters.

The 1417 Flight party piece was to fly an FR.10 along the flight line, take photographs of the display area and deliver the processed prints to the VIP enclosure within thirty minutes of touching down.

The 8 Squadron detachment, meanwhile, concentrated its first few days in Bahrain on a phase of four-versus-two combat, followed by FAC exercises with 2nd Battalion Parachute Regiment. The Marine Craft Unit at Muharraq provided splash targets for the Hunters to shoot at but both were destroyed when the first rocket salvos scored direct hits. The squadron moved to Sharjah on 16 November for a fortnight's weapons practice, starting with a week of precision and operational RP and cannon firing on the Jeb-a-Jib range. For the second week, the accent was on low-level cross-countries ending with RP and cannon strikes on the range.

Two views of 8 Squadron Hunters operating out of Sharjah during an APC in November 1963. (above) Armed with concrete-headed rockets and full gunpacks, FGA.9s XG154-E and XE620-B begin their take-off runs for a practice session on the Jeb-a-Jib range while XG255 (below) prepares to land (author).

Located fifty miles along the desolate coastline to the west of Sharjah, the Jeb-a-Jib range is seen in November 1963 as an FGA.9 discharges a burst of cannon fire at a canvas target. To get there, the range party had to endure a two-hour rough ride in a Land Rover over soft dunes; no road, signposts or map, just a compass and driver's sense of direction (author).

RAF Muharraq

On 1 December 1963 RAF Bahrain was officially renamed RAF Muharraq, the name of the island on which the airfield was located.

Captured!

Following reports that Egyptian reconnaissance aircraft were operating in the Beihan area, dawn-to-dusk border patrols became the main focus of attention for 208 Squadron over the first two days of December. On the 2nd, despite the proximity of patrolling Hunters, a Yemeni Air Force Il-14 Crate transport aircraft was able to cross the border and land at Laudar airstrip, ninety miles north of Aden. The crew, believing they were still in Yemeni territory, had mistaken the strip for one of their own! A quick thinking Army officer prevented it from taking off by driving his Land Rover directly in front of it. The crew were arrested and held for questioning. Minutes later, the pilots of the pair of aircraft that had been scrambled to intercept them, Flying Officers Swain (XF431) and Webb (XJ687), spotted the intruder on the strip.

Later in the day, a second pair, with Flight Lieutenants Grant (XF431) and Dicken (XE647) at the controls, was scrambled to intercept a second Il-14 that had entered

Protectorate territory. They managed to intercept it and direct the pilot to land but, taking a risk, he ignored their instruction, turned and headed for home.

African independence

Number 208 Squadron departed Khormaksar on 5 December for a two-week detachment to Embakasi to participate in celebrations marking the independence of two countries, Zanzibar and Kenya. On the 9th eight Hunters were flown to Dar-es-Salaam in company with a Victor of 10 Squadron in readiness for an Independence Day flypast over the Sultan's Palace in Zanzibar. The flypast took place the next day and, following low-level flybys over nearby islands, the aircraft returned to Embakasi.

The Kenyan Independence Day celebrations were honoured with a nine-ship flypast on the 11th in company with the Victor. The formation was timed to pass over Uhuru Stadium in Nairobi during the first public playing of the Kenyan national anthem. The ceremonial over, the formation proceeded to fly an extended circuit around the country, taking in Thika, Fort Hall, Nyeri, Thomson's Falls, Eldovet, Kakwnega, Kigumu, Kericho, Nakum, Gilgil and Naivagha before landing back at Embakasi.

The solitary 1417 Flight FR.10, XE614-PL, seen sandwiched between 208 Squadron FGA.9s at Embakasi Airport on 5 December 1963, was flown on daily sweeps between Victoria Falls and Mombassa seeking out groups of Mau Mau insurgents. The 30 Squadron Beverly was loaded with rockets and ammunition should they be required (Peter Lewis).

Number 10 Squadron Victor B.1 leads the Kenyan Independence formation flypast over Uhuru Stadium on 11 December 1963. Wg Cdr Jennings led the front box-four and Flt Lt Peter Lewis the rear section (John Jennings).

During the afternoon of the 12th, Flight Lieutenant Copplestone performed a solo aerobatic display for a youth rally that was being held in the Uhuru Stadium.

Assassination attempt

Despite an increase in subversive activities in the Protectorates, the situation in Aden State had remained remarkably stable. This took a dramatic turn for the worst on 10 December 1963, however, when a fatal incident occurred at Aden Civil Airport. The British High Commissioner, Sir Kennedy Trevaskis, was about to fly to London with British Colonial Office officials and leaders of the Federation of South Arabia to attend a constitutional conference. As the delegation walked across the apron towards their Comet airliner, a hand grenade was tossed into the group by a dissident tribesman. Sir Kennedy was pushed aside by his assistant, George Henderson, who took the full blast. He died of his injuries and was posthumously awarded his second George Medal for gallantry, his first having been awarded in 1956 during his service as a political agent in Aden. Two other members of the delegation were killed and fifty-three people wounded. On 30 December Squadron Leader Lewis led a formation flypast over George Henderson's funeral cortege.

In response to this outrage, the border with the Yemen was closed, fifty-seven members of the PSP trade union arrested on suspicion of being involved in the incident, and a state of emergency declared across the whole of South Arabia. It remained in force until the final withdrawal of British forces four years later.

December transpired to be the busiest month for 43 Squadron since its arrival in Aden, with 208 Squadron away in Kenya for much of the period and 8 Squadron on detachment at Muharraq. Following a number of incursions by Yemeni Il-2s in the Beihan area, 43 Squadron was tasked with fulfilling the border patrol commitment on its own. Not the best of timing as several of its pilots were busy elsewhere taking promotion exams. The void was filled by pilots from 1417 Flight and OC TacWing, Wing Commander Jennings.

Problems with the FR.10s

The problem of 1417 Flight FR.10s spending long periods on AOG continued to deprive the command of the aircraft's unique contribution. Flight Lieutenants Lewis and Timms were down in Nairobi with 208 Squadron for the independence celebrations and the FR.10 Flight Lieutenant Lewis had taken with him, had to be left at Embakasi when it went unserviceable. In the interim another of the flight's pilots, Flight Lieutenant Rimmer, had returned to the UK to collect a refurbished FR.10 (XF441) from Kemble, while Flight Lieutenant Dymond was away on FAC duty for the Dhala convoy.

Nevertheless, thirteen coastal recces, one carried out by Squadron Leader Walpole from HQ MEC in FR.10 XF460, and ten border patrols were flown using FGA.9s lent to the flight by 43 Squadron. The Flight performed its hundredth operational sortie on the last day of the year, a feat celebrated in true New Year's Eve style. Just sixteen airstrips remained to be photographed out of a total of seventy-one, intelligence on the rest having been passed to Joint Intelligence in Command HQ.

Operation LONGSTOP

Having recovered from the Christmas grant, 8 Squadron returned to Khormaksar on 30 December. The spare pilots and airmen were flown by 84 Squadron Beverley (XH123) as far as Masirah where the equipment and packups were offloaded by the 8 Squadron groundcrew as the Beverley was needed back at Bahrain and there being no aircraft movements section on the airfield. A 105 Squadron Argosy (XP411) duly arrived and the equipment was loaded for the leg down to Khormaksar.

All flying ceased for 43 Squadron over the Christmas period as it prepared for the move to Muharraq. Having flown via Masirah, where they were refuelled and turned round by 8 Squadron groundcrew waiting for their Argosy to arrive, the first five aircraft arrived in the Gulf on the 30th and were joined there by a further four the next day. Two more were ready to make the trip in the early part of January. Spare 43 Squadron pilots and airmen were treated to the experience and 'comfort' of flying in Beverley and Argosy transports for the first time.

Having landed at Masirah in the 84 Squadron Beverley, 8 Squadron airmen were tasked with turning round 43 Squadron's Hunters en-route to Muharraq on 30 December 1963. FGA.9 XE623 is depicted here (Bryan 'Taff' John).

Chapter 9

1964 – The Radfan insurgency

Day excursions

No sooner had 43 Squadron settled in at Muharraq than the airport authority announced that the runway would close between 12:00 and 18:00 every day for the early part of the new year. To avoid being trapped on the ground, the squadron prepared a programme entitled 'Day Excursions'. In practice, this involved ten armed aircraft departing Muharraq in two sections of five each morning and performing strikes on the Jeb-a-Jib range, followed by a landing at Sharjah.

Having been re-armed and refuelled, they took off and performed a further series of strikes at Jeb-a-Jib before returning to Sharjah. The final sortie of the day was timed to provide an arrival back at Muharraq shortly after 18:00, the opportunity being taken for two-vesus-two combat en route. A total of thirty-three 'day-trips' were flown over a three-day period in February alone.

The Radfan

The Radfan was a merciless region of the Aden hinterland where the accepted rule was 'an eye for an eye' and where disputes and hatred passed from one generation to the next. Following the debacle of Suez in 1956 and the expulsion of British forces from Egypt, General Nasser felt increasingly emboldened to expand his influence in the Yemen. A perpetual stream of noxious, anti-British propaganda from the Sana'a and Aden radio transmitters dominated the airwaves. The Quteibi tribe, who described themselves as 'Wolves of the Radfan', due to their bloodcurdling practices, was one of twelve tribes inhabiting the area. They were lawless, fiercely independent and continually feuding with tribes nearby. As 1963 drew to a close, the authorities were increasingly aware of Egyptian-fostered opposition to the Federation and the serious consequences for Aden State and the Protectorates if the situation was allowed to fester.

The Radfan, which is roughly the size of the Isle of Wight, had become a no-go area for the authorities, a situation that could no longer be tolerated. Up until then, the British government had a policy of reacting to events as they occurred but, following the attempt on the life of the High Commissioner in December, a more proactive policy was employed. A state of emergency was declared across the whole of South Arabia. Border crossings with the Yemen were closed and the decision was taken to teach the dissidents a lesson.

Operation NUTCRACKER

A battlegroup consisting of three British-led Federal Regular Army (FRA) battalions, an armoured car squadron, plus British Army tanks, artillery and engineers, was assembled at Thumier airstrip, sixty miles north of Aden, in readiness to mount an operation aimed at opening up the Radfan. Full air support would be provided by Tactical and Transport Wing aircraft based at Khormaksar.

The AFME establishment consisted of nine squadrons and three flights operating a variety of offensive and support aircraft, as illustrated in the table below:

RAF Khormaksar – 1 January 1964

Tactical Wing		
Unit	Aircraft type	Quantity
8 Squadron	Hunter FGA.9	14
43 Squadron	Hunter FGA.9	12
208 Squadron	Hunter FGA.9	12
1417 Flight	Hunter FR.10	4
1417 Flight	Hunter T.7	4
37 Squadron	Shackleton MR.2	4
26 Squadron	Belvedere HC.1	7
Transport Wing		
78 Squadron	Twin Pioneer CC.1	8
84 Squadron	Beverley C.1	6
105 Squadron	Argosy C.1	10
233 Squadron	Valetta C.1	6
SAR Flight	Sycamore HR.14	4
Other units		
Comms Flight	Canberra B.2	2
	Hastings C.2	1
	Valetta C.2	1
	Dakota C.4	1
Total		96

Codenamed NUTCRACKER, the operation had five objectives when launched on 4 January:

- to give a demonstration of power in the air and on the ground
- to give a show of force in Wadi Misrah, stronghold of the Quteibi tribe
- to enforce the expulsion of twelve named dissident troublemakers from the Radfan

An unusually quiet day on a fully occupied Khormaksar Hunter line. In addition to the three 1417 Flight aircraft at this end, eight 8 Squadron and nine 208 Squadron FGA.9s make up the remainder in this January 1964 view (author).

- to enable a proper road to be built through Wadi Rabwa and on to Wadi Taym, an area dominated by the more hostile rebels
- to convince troublemakers that the Government had the capacity and the will to enter the Radfan whenever it wished

The operation was planned to begin with an airlift of an FRA battalion together with its 105mm howitzers onto mountain ranges aligning the sides of Wadi Rabwa. Six 26 Squadron Belvedere and four 815 Naval Air Squadron Wessex helicopters operating

A RN Wessex helicopter from HMS Hermes, XS880, at one of the up-country airfields, probably Habilayn (Richard Grevatte-Ball).

from Thumier would make the lift in stages using three landing points along the route of the advance. The main FRA force, meanwhile, would advance through the wadi and take the high ground overlooking Wadi Taym before moving along the Bakri Ridge. Top cover and offensive support would be provided by the Hunter and Shackleton squadrons.

Back in action!

No. 8 Squadron had had very little time to re-adjust to life back at Khormaksar when it was thrust straight into action. Almost immediately after the airlift began, a Belvedere sustained a number of hits from small-arms fire as it lowered a howitzer into position, one shot passing through the front fuel tank. Two Hunters, flown by Flight Lieutenants Humphreyson (XF435) and McCarthy (XE618), were called in to provide top cover as the helicopter made a safe and hasty retreat.

When the FRA found itself under attack in the early afternoon, Hunters from 8 Squadron were despatched in pairs at 90-miniute intervals to strike at dissident strongholds. The attacks were flown by Flight Lieutenants Talbot (XE618), Williams (XE609) and Sheppard (XG255), and Flying Officers Baron (XG154), Bottom (XF435) and Johnson (XG169), and continued until fading light brought proceedings to a premature halt. Air support resumed at dawn on the 5th with a two-aircraft cannon strike, the pressure being maintained by pairs of Hunters attacking targets at 90-minute intervals throughout the day. The final pair was led by OC TacWing, Wing Commander Jennings (XF435). Over the five-day period, from the 4th to the 8th, twenty-two top-cover sorties and eighteen strikes were flown by 8 Squadron Hunters against opposition targets.

To deprive the dissidents of much needed sleep and to harass their movements during the hours of darkness, 37 Squadron Shackletons dropped flares to illuminate prospective targets before dropping sticks of bombs onto enemy positions.

As the rebels began to retreat, Royal Engineers moved in to begin the onerous task of constructing the road, using Arab labourers, many of whom would probably have been firing at them only a few days before. When a bout of rifle fire brought progress to a halt on the 13th, three pairs of 208 Squadron FGA.9s were despatched at intervals to strafe the offenders' positions; Flight Lieutenants Grant (XF388) and Lee (XE647) at 10:45, Flying Officers Slade (XE552) and Webb (XJ687) at 13:30 and the same pilots again at 15:55 in XE647 and XF388 respectively.

For 1417 Flight the year had begun with most of its aircraft unserviceable, limiting productive support for the first ten days of the month. An all-out effort by the groundcrew eventually produced three serviceable FR.10s enabling eighty-four hours to be flown over the subsequent fortnight. While Flight Lieutenant Morris was despatched to Nairobi to collect the defective FR.10, OC 1417 Flight, Flight Lieutenant Peter Lewis, was seconded to HMS *Centaur* to brief 892 Squadron Sea Vixen crews on reconnaissance techniques in the WAP.

During the last week of the month, 1417 Flight FR.10s flew four recce sorties in support of NUTCRACKER, providing much needed intelligence and photographs for the FRA and Command HQ.

Due to its instrument panel having been badly damaged by the Egyptian crew, and with no one at Khormaksar sufficiently qualified to fly the captured UAR Il-14 transport from Laudar to Khormaksar, two test pilots were flown out from Boscombe Down to undertake the task. On 14 January, a pair of FR.10s was despatched to escort the lumbering transport on the 20-minute flight while providing a continuous radio link with air traffic at Khormaksar.

No sooner had Wadi Rabwa been secured than the new road was opened, paving the way for NUTCRACKER ground forces to probe deeper into the Danaba Basin and onwards to Wadi Taym. The 3rd Battalion FRA moved swiftly through and advanced up the rugged slopes to Bakri Ridge, taking advantage of the support provided by the Belvederes and Wessex helicopters. Persistent shooting by dissidents hiding behind the boulders and crevices dotted along the rocky escarpment, was brought to an end when eight 208 Squadron Hunters strafed their positions during the afternoon of the 27th. Direction was provided by FACs who had only recently completed their training at Khormaksar. On the following day, eleven more cannon strikes were carried out against dissidents holed up at various points across the mountain range, and on village

Following its capture at Lawdar, EAF Il-14 serial 1148 was flown to Khormaksar and parked behind the SAR Flight hangar (author).

Under the ever present danger from sniper fire, 26 Squadron Belvedere XG467 blows up a cloud of sand as it prepares to lower a load of supplies to troops engaged in Operation Nutcracker (Aviation Bookshop).

hideouts known to be occupied by rebels. When this failed to stop them, 8 Squadron FGA.9s performed a further ten strikes against sniper positions over the final few days of January.

This effectively brought NUTCRACKER to a conclusion. Over 30,000 rounds of HE ammunition had been expended by the FGA.9s during the operation, five FRA troops had been killed and a dozen wounded, while dissident casualty figures were believed to be significantly higher.

During the intervening period, the respective armies in Tanganyika and Uganda decided to stage separate rebellions. Two 37 Squadron Shackletons were despatched to Eastleigh and flew several low-level sorties over the recalcitrant establishments in both countries to act as a deterrent. This was sufficient to bring the situation under control and after a few days, the aircraft returned to Khormaksar.

Operation RUSTUM

Although NUTCRACKER achieved its objectives, FRA forces remained dispersed over a wide area and exposed to attack by dissidents. Plans were quickly formulated for a follow-up operation with the objective of depriving rebel forces of cover, shelter and access to arms. Before the operation, codenamed RUSTUM, could begin, however, 1417 Flight was detailed to capture close-up photographs of rebel-held buildings and high-level oblique shots of suspect structures in areas around Dhala and the Radfan where sufficient detail could not be derived from existing maps.

Based on the intelligence gleaned from the photographs, 8 Squadron was able to get Phase 1 of Operation RUSTUM underway by mounting the first of twenty-four strikes during the early afternoon of 1 February. Early the following morning, two pairs of aircraft on top-cover missions were redirected to attack targets located in their area. A second four-ship strike was carried out on the same targets at noon on the next day.

At 10:25 on 5 February two FGA.9s were scrambled to intercept unidentified aircraft heading towards the border to the west of Mukeiras, but they had turned back by the time the pair reached the area. Later in the day, Wing Commander Jennings flew the AOC, AVM Johnnie Johnson CB CBE DSO** DFC*, on a top cover sortie over the Radfan in a T.7 (XL565). An urgent request on the 7th from the FRA for a specific target to be struck was dealt with by a pair of 208 Squadron Hunters. Three days later, a further pair was despatched by 208 Squadron to perform a strike in a proscribed area of Wadi Taym.

The second phase of Operation RUSTUM was initiated on 15 February and called for a daily routine of cannon strikes on rebel-held buildings in support of FRA forces. When an FRA company encountered intense fire from a village to the east of Dhala on the 24th, Flight Lieutenant Constable (XF435) performed a leaflet drop on rebel hideouts shortly before Wing Commander Jennings (XF376), Flight Lieutenant Williams (XE609), Flying Officer Jarvis (XG237) and Lieutenant Notley (XE620) unleashed volleys of cannon fire at the targets. The message was rammed home with an RP strike performed by Squadron Leader Syme (XG154) and Flight Lieutenant Adamson (XE592) in the late afternoon. As the month drew to a close, a further eight cannon strikes were effected against dissidents who were still causing trouble in the area.

Evacuation of a number of dead and wounded FRA troops was carried out by a 26 Squadron Belvedere. Once this gruesome task had been completed, the reporting line for the helicopter squadron was transferred from Tactical to Transport Wing.

Operation LONGSTOP

No. 43 Squadron's return to Khormaksar at the end of February was spread over several days. Spare pilots and the majority of the groundcrew were flown down in a pair of Argosies on the 24th, followed by six Hunters on the 25th and the remainder on the following day. The remaining groundcrew were flown back at Khormaksar on the 28th. The final days of the month were utilised in converting the radio configuration on 43 Squadron's aircraft from VHF to UHF.

In the meantime an advanced party of 208 Squadron personnel had departed for Muharraq, followed by the main party on the 24th. Once settled in, the squadron

Armed with full gunpacks and concrete-headed rockets, a line of 208 Squadron FGA.9s stand ready for practice firing on the Jeb-a-Jib range; Sharjah 1963 (Les Dunnett).

became engrossed with an APC at Sharjah, FAC exercises with the Trucial Oman Scouts and three co-operation exercises with ships of the Royal Navy.

Renewed turmoil in the Radfan

By the end of February, it had become clear that the FRA forces were spread too thinly on the ground to maintain effective order in the Radfan while at the same time attempting to prevent incursions by dissidents from the Yemen. Accordingly, the decision was taken for the FRA to move its troops out of the Radfan and regroup at their base camp at Thumier. In doing so, a vacuum was created that enabled the dissidents to return and for Egyptian propaganda to claim victory over 'the puppet imperialists'.

Inter-tribal feuding flared-up among the various groups as they re-occupied Wadis Jirdan, Habban and Taym. This was responded to with flagwaves and leaflet drops by 8 Squadron aircraft, but when this failed to bring the miscreants to heel, targets in all three wadis were subjected to a period of sustained cannon and rocket fire, a total of fifty-eight rockets and 4,371 rounds of ammunition being expended in the process.

The high intensity and variety of operations undertaken by the Hunter squadrons required close collaboration with force commanders on the ground, especially when operating in the same area. In early March, for example, while 8 Squadron was busily occupied with feuding tribesmen, 43 Squadron had focused its attention on close air support for FRA units making their withdrawal from Wadi Rabwa. On 3 March 43

In March 1964, 8 Squadron was tasked with assessing colour film for use in Hunter gun cameras. The test was carried out at sea by four 8 Squadron FGA.9s firing cannon and rockets at a splash target towed by Vosper-built Rescue & Target Towing Launch 2767, seen (above) ready to depart the Marine Craft Unit jetty. (below) The crew prepare to launch a splash target under the watchful eye of Range Safety Officer Roy Humphreyson, one of a handful of 8 Squadron pilots and airmen to observe the test. Powered by a pair of Sea Griffon engines, the launch then accelerated to the 30+ knots required to generate a sufficient plume of water. The shadow of Mount Shamsan can be seen in the distance (both, author).

(main picture) Having fired its rockets at the splash target, the FGA.9 pulls out from the dive, leaving plumes of water rising from the surf. The smaller plume, just to the right, is that generated by the target. (inset) Cannon-fire from the lead Hunter produces more of a splash pattern and tends to shield the target from view. Using its gun camera, the second Hunter records the sequence on the Kodak colour film (both, author).

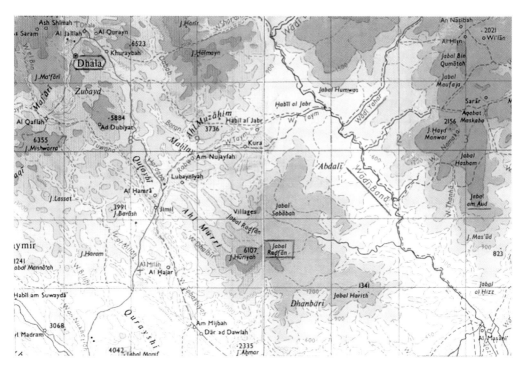

Map dating from 1964 depicting the Radfan mountains and nearby wadis (Alan Pollock).

Squadron aircraft were called in to carry out rocket and cannon strikes in the Radfan and Danaba areas, eleven such sorties being flown in total by Wing Commander Jennings (XE623 and XG296), Squadron Leader Champniss (XG292, XG296 and XJ692), and Flight Lieutenants Stoker (XJ680 and XG292), Osborne (XF456), Forse (XJ692), Chapman (XE550) and Wilkins (XE655).

In a joint offensive carried out in Wadi Rabwa on 19 and 20 March, dissident targets were struck with 2,540 rounds of ammunition, fired by six 8 Squadron and six 43 Squadron FGA.9s. A week later, the 8 Squadron standby pair scrambled to support FRA units mopping up after Operation RUSTUM. Under the direction of a FAC, they flew in low and fast to strafe groups of dissidents causing trouble at Milestone 27 on the Dhala Road, firing 680 rounds in the process.

No. 1417 Flight operations, meanwhile, ranged from performing flagwaves and pre- and post-strike photo recces in the Rajaf and Dana areas to locating and photographing a pair of Russian destroyers in the Indian Ocean.

The attack on Fort Harib
Following the re-occupation of the Radfan by large groups of Egyptian-backed dissidents and a proclamation over Sana'a and Aden radio that they were winning the battle to liberate 'occupied South Yemen', morale among the dissidents began to rise

in line with actions that became more aggressive. Rising incidents of incursions by Yemeni aircraft culminated in an audacious attack by two Yemeni MiG-15 jet fighters and an armed helicopter near Beihan. The defenceless village of Bulaq and a nearby customs post were heavily bombed and strafed. Such actions would be tolerated no longer and, by way of retribution, a Yemeni Fort called Harib was selected for destruction by TacWing Hunters.

At 01:00 on the morning of 28 March Wing Commander Jennings was woken to the news that he was to attack the fort at 06:30. Given that the flight time to the target was thirty minutes, the Hunters would have to be ready for take off at 06:00. Air and ground crews were woken at 03:30 and ordered to report to Squadron HQ immediately; no ablutions or breakfast. As the pilots were briefed, the ground crew set to work preparing the aircraft, two FR.10s (one spare) and ten FGA.9s (one spare). The outer drop-tank pylons were removed on the latter and replaced with additional rocket rails to give each aircraft a configuration of eight HE rockets and a full gunpack containing HE ammunition. Airmen of all trades assisted in carrying out tasks that were alien to them and, in spite of having to work on a dimly lit pan, the aircraft were ready to go as the sun began to rise.

At 08:30 a 1417 Flight FR.10 (XE614), flown by Flight Lieutenant Lewis together with an 8 Squadron FGA.9 (XG237) with Flying Officer Bottom at the controls, departed Khormaksar, their airbrakes stuffed with leaflets warning the occupants of Harib that the fort would be attacked in fifteen minutes. Flight Lieutenant Lewis took photographs of the Mark 9 as it released its confetti-like load over the structure before releasing leaflets of his own. The two aircraft then circled high overhead to maintain top cover for the main strike force.

Led by Wing Commander Jennings (XF440), the force consisted of eight heavily-armed FGA.9s three 8 Squadron pilots – Flight Lieutenants Humphreyson (XG256), Williams ((XE609) and Johnson (XE620) – and four from 43 Squadron – Squadron Leader Champniss (XF456), Flying Officer Hill (XJ692), and Flight Lieutenants Doggett (XE623) and Stoker (XE611).

The leader's rockets made a direct hit on an ammunition store, causing a massive explosion and a mushroom cloud that obscured the target for a few moments. A total of 2,895 rounds of ammunition and sixty-four rockets were fired at the solid stone-walled structure. Photographs taken by the FR.10 before and after the strike revealed hidden anti-aircraft weapons; an anti-aircraft gun was destroyed and lifted off its mountings and a number of vehicles wrecked. The fort itself was completely destroyed. So good were the photographs that warning leaflets could be clearly seen on the ground.

A second, much larger, army fort and barracks at Qataba, further into the Yemen, was earmarked for similar treatment the following week but, following complaints of 'external aggression' by the Yemen government, a resolution calling on both sides to keep the peace was signed by the United Nations. The Qataba attack was cancelled and

These pre-strike (above) and post-strike (left) photographs of Fort Harib were taken by Peter Lewis in his FR.10 on 28 March 1964 and provide a perfect illustration of the devastating fire-power of the ground attack Hunter. The anti-aircraft guns can be seen at the extreme left of the fort (both, Peter Lewis).

incursions by Yemeni aircraft abated for a while but attacks on merchants and caravans using the Dhala Road intensified in an act of defiance. A more worrying development was a growing allegiance between Egyptian-trained dissidents and normally peaceful tribesmen.

At midday on 30 March a pair of 8 Squadron aircraft scrambled to intercept an unidentified aircraft heading for Mukeiras from across the Yemen border but it turned short and landed at a nearby Yemeni airstrip.

During the early months of 1964 four Whirlwind HAR.10s arrived at Khormaksar as replacements for the Sycamores on the SAR Flight. In addition to a role in SAR, the ability of the Whirlwind to carry several armed troops provided an invaluable addition to the MEC vertical-lift inventory. The Sycamores were flown out to HMS *Albion* on 28 March for shipment back to the UK.

The attack on Fort Harib appeared to have had the desired effect as operational activity abated during the first few weeks of April. Border patrols continued to be flown by pairs of 8 and 43 Squadron aircraft, employing a compromise between endurance and tactical air speed so as to stay in the area for as long as possible. The relative quiet was broken on the 10th when the 8 Squadron standby pair was scrambled to intercept a radar contact fifty miles north of Aden. Although the contact had disappeared by the time they arrived, they remained on station under direction of Champion Radar without further incident. When Champion Radar intercepted another target approaching the border on the 21st, a pair of 8 Squadron aircraft on Beihan patrol was directed towards it. When intercepted, the 'target' was identified as an Ethiopian Airways DC-3 en route to Khormaksar!

The lull in operational activity allowed 1417 Flight's pilots to embark on an air-to-ground firing programme on the Khormaksar range. Each pilot flew at least three 'shoots' and one night-flying sortie. The timing could not have been better as they were soon back on front-line duty, taking photographs of targets in the Radfan area for an operation in the advanced stages of planning. High serviceability levels, an additional pilot and a doubling of other ranks to thirty-six NCOs and airmen placed the flight in a much better position to fulfil its commitments.

Operation LONGSTOP

As the 208 Squadron detachment drew to a close its aircraft were flown down to Khormaksar over the two days, 24 and 25 April. Heading in the other direction, six 8 Squadron aircraft departed for Muharraq on the 24th, followed by a further four on the 25th. From the 26th to the 29th, long-range recce flights were carried out over the WAP to re-acquaint 208 Squadron pilots with the area, in preparation for a week as duty squadron from 1 May.

Operation RADFAN

Following a sharp increase in attacks on convoys and vehicles using the Dhala Road by a large pack of some 500 well-armed dissidents, backed by a further 200 Egyptian-trained guerrillas, and fearing that the situation was getting out of control, the decision was taken to restore order through a show of strength the likes of which had never been seen in South Arabia.

A recently appointed garrison commander, Brigadier R. Hargroves, was appointed as GOC for the operation and he quickly set about establishing a small headquarters at Thumier manned by staff officers from all three services. The following objectives were agreed:

- to end dissident insurgency within the Danaba Basin and Wadi Taym regions
- to prevent the tribal revolt from spreading
- to reassert the government's authority
- to stop attacks on vehicles using Dhala Road

Ground force

The scale of the operation can be judged by the composition of the ground force, which became known as Radfan Force (abbreviated to Radforce):

- J Battery Royal Horse Artillery battery – 105mm guns
- one armoured car squadron
- one troop of The Royal Engineers
- 1st Battalion East Anglians
- 45 Commando Royal Marines
- one company 3rd Battalion Parachute Regiment
- two FRA battalions

Air support

Offensive air support and heavy-lift transport and communications requirements would be undertaken by Khormaksar-based aircraft, and elements of the Army Air Corps operating from up-country airstrips:

- 8 Squadron   Hunter FGA.9
- 43 Squadron   Hunter FGA.9
- 208 Squadron   Hunter FGA.9
- 1417 Flight   Hunter FR.10
- 37 Squadron   Shackleton MR.2
- 84 Squadron   Beverley C.1
- 78 Squadron   Twin Pioneer CC.1
- 26 Squadron   Belvedere C.1
- SAR Flight   Whirlwind HAR.10
- 653 Squadron (AAC)   Scout, Beaver, Auster

(above) The first two AAC Scout helicopters XR601 and XR600 to operate in the Middle East pay a visit to TacWing at Khormaksar in March 1964 (author). The versatility of the Beaver is illustrated in this photograph of XP819 at Falaise Camp (below) carrying a load of 25lb bombs on two wing-mounted racks (Richard Grevatte-Ball).

Operation RADFAN – phase one

The aim of the initial phase was to locate and mark a suitable drop zone (DZ) on a mountain peak, codenamed 'Cap Badge', onto which 120 members of 3 Para could be dropped from two Beverley transports. As dusk fell on 29 April, a small party of 22 SAS Regiment was airlifted 5,000 yards inside dissident territory by a pair of AAC Scout helicopters, the only two of the type in Aden at the time. The helicopters' limited capacity, however, forced them to return to Thumier twice in order to move the full complement. The patrol was twenty minutes late in setting off and its progress slower than anticipated. As daylight broke on the 30th, they were forced to 'hole up' in a sangar, some two miles short of their objective, to avoid being detected.

By a stroke of bad luck, a young boy tending his sheep stumbled across the party and ran away to raise the alarm. Very soon the troopers found themselves under sustained sniper fire from forty to fifty rebels. A radio request for urgent assistance was received at Thumier by Major Grey who relayed it on to the Brigade Air Support Officer (BASO), Squadron Leader Bowie, at Khormaksar. A distress call was transmitted in the hope of contacting any Hunter pilots in the area. Fortuitously, Wing Commander Jennings was on a solo mission close by, searching for camel trains carrying arms. Despite the vague description of the location, he managed to locate it and lay down sufficient covering fire to keep the rebels at bay. Within a short space of time, pairs of 43 and 208 Squadron Hunters arrived and unleashed a barrage of cannon and rocket fire onto rebel positions until it became too dark to fly. In total, 127 rockets and 7,131 rounds of HE ammunition were fired that day.

Under cover of darkness, the patrol attempted to break out but tragically, the officer commanding, Captain Edwards, and radio operator, Signaller Warburton, were killed during exchanges of fire as they made their escape.

Letters of thanks subsequently received at TacWing HQ from SAS commanders, Major Grey and Major de la Billière, praised the accuracy of the Hunter strikes. It was one of several occasions on which the pilots had to open fire within twenty-five yards of British troops and their skill undoubtedly saved the lives of those twenty troopers.

When it became evident that there were far more militants in the area than had been predicted, a change of plan was quickly formulated. No. 45 Commando would take on the task of capturing Cap Badge, leaving 3 Para to move on foot through Wadi Taym under the protective fire of the commandos.

To ensure that sufficient Hunters were ready to respond to calls for support, six pilots and three pairs of aircraft from the two squadrons (43 and 208) were placed on permanent RADFAN standby between 05:30 and 18:30, one pair at 10-minutes' and a second at 30-minutes' readiness. They were called out two or three times a day to cover troop movements in the Wadis Rabwa and Taym. The third pair of Hunters was held at 30-minutes' readiness to provide air defence cover should Egyptian MiG pilots be tempted to cross from the Yemen.

Recently returned from refurbishment in the UK, 208 Squadron FGA.9 XE645 is seen on an untidy Hunter line at Khormaksar (author).

Groundcrews were rostered on an alternating two-shift rota, one shift beginning at midday on day one and continuing through to 13:00 on the next day. The next shift began at midday on day two to ensure a smooth handover, allowing the first shift to be stood down for twenty-three hours. Beihan patrols continued to be flown on alternate days by the air defence standby-pair and regular sorties were also flown on Operation RANJI.

Hunter fatality

On 17 April four 43 Squadron pilots were briefed to perform a low-level navex and practice RP strike on a target near Ruseis, approximately 120 miles north-east of Khormaksar. Having completed his strike and begun his pull out, Flying Officer Martin Herring's FGA.9 (XG136) rolled rapidly to the right and crashed into the ground. Top cover was flown over the area to protect the operation to retrieve his body and salvage his aircraft.

Over the first week of May the standby aircraft were scrambled two to three times every day in response to calls from ground forces operating in the Radfan. On occasions pilots found themselves firing at dissidents only twenty-five yards distant from Radforce troops, while flying close to the ground. On at least one occasion a soldier was injured by a shell case ejected by a Hunter as it zoomed in low overhead.

A panoramic view looking across the exposed tops of the Radfan mountains depicting FRA troop reinforcements alighting from 26 Squadron Belvedere, XG468. Dissident tribesmen could be hiding anywhere in the hostile terrain (Aviation Bookshop).

After thirty hours of intense fighting, 45 Commando was able to capture Cap Badge and with it command of Wadi Taym.

The first phase of Operation RADFAN was completed on 5 May, all objectives having been achieved for the loss of two soldiers killed and ten wounded. Airpower continued to be employed in the proscribed areas of the Danaba Basin and Wadi Taym to systematically destroy targets such as fortified buildings being used by snipers.

By the end on the month 43 Squadron alone had flown 158 strike sorties in the Radfan area, expending 1,009 rockets and 50,029 HE cannon rounds in the process.

Intelligence gathering

The high quality photographs captured by 1417 Flight's Vinten cameras were a crucial decision-making element for commanders conducting the air and ground assault. Oblique line overlaps were produced of the main areas of operation for pinpointing targets and for pre-strike briefings. Pre- and post-strike photographs were taken of most targets and the FR.10s were often required to combine recces with HE cannon strikes. The visual intelligence-gathering capacity of the flight's pilots provided an invaluable addition to the operation. The four aircraft exceeded 100 flying hours during May, fifty-eight of them on Operation RADFAN. Full credit was accorded to the groundcrew who worked tirelessly over long hours to keep the aircraft serviceable.

The Mobile Photographic Section (MFPS) also played an important role in the intelligence-gathering process. Attached to TacWing, its work was of a high standard and, by using mass production techniques, F.95 camera prints were processed in very quick time.

From 14 to 21 May 208 Squadron took the lead role in carrying out multiple four-ship strikes on selected targets in support of Radforce. Minor damage was sustained by several aircraft from ricochets and flying debris generated by the exploding force

A marked-up photograph from Roger Pyrah's FR.10 captures another 1417 Flight FR.10, XF441, as it flies low over the infamous Bakri Ridge, scene of some of the fiercest battles during the initial phase of the Radfan campaign (Roger Pyrah).

of HE cannon shells on rocky crags. Two aircraft, XK139 and XJ687, were classified as Category 2, one requiring a new mainplane and the other, a new tailplane. In total, the squadron flew a creditable 105 strike sorties over the eight-day period. This was the last action the squadron would see as, from 26 to 30 May, its attention turned to preparing for a permanent move to Muharraq.

Although the Belvedere had proved very capable aircraft and had performed admirably in the hot desert environment, the Napier Gazelle engines suffered considerably from ingestion of sand which inevitably led to a shortage of engines. With the timely arrival of HMS *Centaur* in Aden waters, six 815 Squadron Wessex helicopters were detached to Khormaksar on 24 May, to assist 26 Squadron with the heavylift commitment.

Operation RADFAN – phase Two

Having encountered intense opposition during the initial phase, the decision was taken to fly 39 Brigade out from the UK and for it to take a lead role at Thumier before moving on to Phase Two. The runway at Thumier had in the meantime been extended to 1,000 yards to enable its use by the higher capacity Beverley, leaving the Twin Pioneers to make full use of two recently constructed airstrips at Paddy's Field and Monk's Field in Wadi Taym.

Under the command of Brigadier Blacker, and with the addition of 1st Royal Scots and remainder of 3 Para to the main force, the second phase of Operation RADFAN commenced on 25 May. Their first challenge involved the elimination of fifty or so dissidents dug in on Bakri Ridge near Qudeishi and along the peaks above Wadi Misrah. Dissident strongholds were designated as proscribed areas and allocated codenames such as 'Carthorse', 'Ramrod' and 'Buffalo'. Using photographs taken by 1417 Flight, every fortified building, watch tower and sangar located within these bounds was attacked and demolished in wave after wave of rocket and cannon strikes by 43 Squadron Hunters. A pair of 224 Squadron Shackleton MR.2s, on detachment from Gibraltar, enabled 37 Squadron to concentrate on strafing targets by day and dropping 1,000lb bombs during the hours of darkness. Having sustained a high number of casualties, the dissidents decided the time had come to vacate their positions, leaving the way clear for 3 Para to occupy Bakri Ridge.

Before the advance could commence on the final objective, Jebel Huriyah, Wadis Misrah and Dhubsan needed to be cleared of dissidents. Wadi Dhubsan was a narrow ravine and still in rebel hands. A company of 3 Para reached the entrance to the wadi but encountered stiff opposition when moving forward. A band of around fifty rebels, some equipped with light machine guns, maintained a continuous stream of fire onto the troops below.

In a combined effort the TacWing Hunter squadrons flew low and fast along the wadi bed, opening fire on dissident positions as they appeared in front of them. Several troops were hit by shell casings ejected from the aircraft as they passed low over their

As the pilot of the 8/43 Squadron FGA.9 banks over to check the accuracy of his work, a Forward Air Controller watches the rockets strike their target somewhere in the Radfan mountains, (Alan Pollock).

heads, a proposition more agreeable no doubt than a round from a dissident gun. The rebels made a hasty retreat, leaving the way clear for 3 Para to reach for their objective.

Jebel Huriyah stands at 1867m (6125 ft) and dominates the whole of the Radfan. It had never been climbed by a European. The assault on the mountain began on 1 June as Hunters and Shackletons maintained top cover. The force comprised the 4th Royal Tank Regiment, 1st East Anglians and 2nd Battalion FRA and, on reaching the village of Shaab Sharah some seven days later, was brought to an abrupt halt by a hail of gunfire from another large band of dissidents hidden along a ridge. The imminent departure of 208 Squadron for Bahrain left 43 Squadron and 1417 Flight to deliver a steady stream of rocket and cannon fire in a determined attempt to dislodge them. When troops moved in on the following day (8 June), they found the village deserted, the rebels having retreated during the night. The battle for Shaab Sharah was the most decisive of the campaign and the capture of Jebel Huriyah gave Radforce uninhibited control over the whole of the Radfan.

During its final month in Aden 208 Squadron flew 150 operational sorties in support of ground forces operating in the Radfan, firing 1,009 rockets and expending more than 50,000 rounds of HE cannon shells in the process.

Mention should also be made of the excellent contribution by 1417 Flight. Having flown 120 sorties and exposed many thousands of frames, its FR.10s also fired over 8,000 rounds of HE ammunition at dissident targets. The unit's strength had by this time increased to six pilots, a warrant officer, two sergeants, eleven Corporals and twenty-two airmen.

Although the tempo of operations could now be eased, air and ground control of the Radfan would remain a priority for the foreseeable future, the policy of unremitting harassment of rebellious tribesmen by the Hunters during the day and the Shackletons at night was maintained until, one by one, the offending tribes decided that they had had enough and began to sue for peace.

Farewell 208 Squadron

Although it could not have come at a more inopportune time, 208 Squadron had begun making preparations for its redeployment to Muharraq during the last week of May. Despite the intensity of operations in the Radfan, authorisation was given for the final Operation LONGSTOP to proceed on schedule.

On 2 June four 208 Squadron Hunters lifted off from the Khormaksar runway for the last time and headed for their new home at Muharraq. Eleven of its aircraft

(left) A watch tower in Wadi Ruqub captured by an FR.10 for pre-strike analysis and (opposite), the remains of a house in a proscribed area of the Radfan following a visit by the ground attack Hunters (both, Peter Lewis).

had arrived in the Gulf by the 6th leaving one under repair at Khormaksar. After two-and-a-half years, the squadron's tenure in Aden had come to an end and it could look forward to operating in the more serene environment experienced in the Persian Gulf.

As the outboard tanks were still fitted, the squadron settled in by flying formations of four and six aircraft on long-range reconnaissance and familiarisation sorties over the Jebel Akhdar region during the period 9 to 12 June, refuelling stops being undertaken at Sharjah.

No. 8 Squadron moved back to Khormaksar via Masirah over the first three days of June and was immediately thrust into a campaign which had acquired the soubriquet 'Radfan War'.

Date	a/c serial	Pilot	Up	Down	Details
01-06-64	43 Sqn a/c	Flt Lt Constable	15:15	16:05	Cannon & RP strike, Wadi Dibaan
,,	,,	Flt Lt Hounsell	,,	,,	,,
02-06-64	,,	Flt Lt Williams	07:45	08:45	,,
,,	XG256	Flt Lt Sheppard	10:45	11:35	,,
,,	XE620	Flt Lt McCarthy	13:45	14:40	,,
03-06-64	43 Sqn a/c	Flt Lt Constable	10:20	11:35	,,
,,	43 Sqn a/c	Fg Off Jarvis	,,	,,	,,
,,	43 Sqn a/c	Flt Lt Humphreyson	,,	,,	,,
04-06-64	43 Sqn a/c	Flt Lt Hounsell	07:05	07:55	,,
,,	43 Sqn a/c	Flt Lt Humphreyson	08:50	09:45	,,
,,	43 Sqn a/c	Lt Notley	11:45	12:35	,,
,,	XF421	Flt Lt Constable	13:45	14:45	,,
,,	XF440	Flt Lt Hounsell	14:50	15:40	Cannon & RP strike, sangars, Wadi Misrah
,,	XF440	Flt Lt Humphreyson	16:00	16:50	,,
05-06-64	XE609	Flt Lt Williams	09:45	10:30	,,
,,	XE618	Flt Lt Sheppard	,,	,,	,,
,,	XE620	Flt Lt Adamson	10:50	11:40	Cannon & RP strike, Wadi Durra'a
,,	43 Sqn a/c	Flt Lt McCarthy	11:55	12:50	RP strike, Wadi Durra'a
,,	XE620	Flt Lt Sheppard	12:50	13:35	Cannon & RP strike, Wadi Misrah
,,	43 Sqn a/c	Flt Lt Adamson	14:15	14:45	Lulu – Cannon strike
,,	43 Sqn a/c	Fg Off Jarvis	,,	15:05	Lulu – Cannon & RP strike, Wadi Misrah
,,	XF440	Flt Lt Williams	16:45	17:35	Cannon & RP strike, sangars, Wadi Durra'a
06-06-64	43 Sqn a/c	Flt Lt Constable	07:20	08:20	Armed recce, Carthorse, Ramrod
,,	XF440	Fg Off Sturt	,,	,,	,,
,,	43 Sqn a/c	Flt Lt Hounsell	08:50	09:40	Cannon & RP strike, Wadi Durra'a
,,	43 Sqn a/c	Lt Notley	10:20	11:10	Armed recce, Carthorse, Ramrod
,,	XF440	Flt Lt Humphreyson	13:45	14:20	Lulu – Cannon & RP strike
07-06-64	XE609	Flt Lt Adamson	09:40	10:35	RP strike, Bakri
,,	43 Sqn a/c	Fg Off Jarvis	,,	,,	,,
,,	XE618	Flt Lt McCarthy	10:55	11:35	RP strike, Wadi Durra'a – Dhubsan
,,	XE609	Flt Lt Williams	12:25	13:25	Lulu – Cannon & RP strike, sangars, Wadi Misrah
,,	XF435	Flt Lt Sheppard	,,	,,	,,
,,	43 Sqn a/c	Fg Off Jarvis	13:45	14:35	Lulu – RP strike, ridges & caves, Wadi Misrah
,,	XE620	Flt Lt Williams	16:15	17:00	Cannon & RP strike, houses & water tower, Wadi Dhubsan

Date	a/c serial	Pilot	Up	Down	Details
"	XF435	Flt Lt Adamson	17:40	18:20	Lulu – Cannon & RP strike, Wadi Misrah
"	43 Sqn a/c	Flt Lt McCarthy	"	"	"
09-06-64	XE609	Flt Lt Johnson	08:50	09:40	Armed recce, Carthorse, Ramrod
11-06-64	XF435	Flt Lt Williams	05:35	06:45	No fire – RP into sea – top cover Jebel Hureyah
"	XF421	Fg Off Sturt	"	"	"
"	XG292	Flt Lt Constable	13:20	14:20	Armed recce, Wadi Durra'a
"	XF376	Fg Off Baron	"	"	"
12-06-64	XG256	Flt Lt Sheppard	09:10	10:10	Armed recce
"	XF440	Flt Lt Johnson	11:05	12:00	Armed recce, Wadi Sigma, Wadi Durra'a
"	XG292	Fg Off Baron	"	"	"
"	XJ692	Lt Notley	13:45	14:35	Armed recce
"	XG256	Fg Off Sturt	"	"	"
"	XG292	Flt Lt Adamson	14:55	15:55	Armed recce – Sha'ab Widina, Wadi Bana
"	XF445	Fg Off Baron	"	"	"
13-06-64	XF435	Flt Lt Humphreyson	12:00	13:00	Armed recce
"	XJ692	Fg Off Sturt	"	"	"

This extract from the 8 Squadron ORB illustrates the intensity of offensive activity during the first two weeks of June.

With sixteen HE SAP rockets mounted under its wings and HE cannon in the gunpack, 8 Squadron FGA.9 XG256 is pictured while en-route for another mission in the Radfan in June 1964 (©IWM).

Centralised servicing

In an attempt to rationalise the engineering functions at Khormaksar, a centralised servicing system was implemented on 15 June. Although pilots retained their individual unit associations, airmen were combined into a single Rectification Flight. The aircraft were allocated to a central pool with tailcodes sequenced from A to Z and the markings of both 8 and 43 Squadrons applied either side of the fuselage roundels. The 1417 Flight FR.10s retained the initials of their pilots while the markings of all three units were applied to the T.7s.

The re-organisation was too much for OC 43 Squadron who wrote in the ORB, 'A sad blow for sentimental reasons but we are assured that the re-organisation will lead to a more efficient utilisation of manpower. The results so far are most discouraging but it is early days yet.'

Of the sixty-three operational sorties flown by 1417 Flight's FR.10s through the rest of June, forty were armed recces while fifteen HE cannon strikes were flown against buildings, sangars and livestock. The recces provided pre- and post-strike photos of targets, area photographic coverage for briefings and visual reports of suspicious activities. From 16 June the flight was tasked with flying the first and last sorties of the day over the Upper Yaffa district to search for and photograph camel trains suspected of supplying arms to rebel forces.

In an attempt to identify arms smuggling camel trains, 1417 Flight flew early morning and late evening recces over their suspected routes (Roger Pyrah).

In spite of only seeing action during the latter three weeks of the month, 128 operational sorties were flown by 8 Squadron. Eight of these were Beihan patrols while two aircraft were scrambled in response to an unidentified aircraft reported in the Dhala area. Relief all round when an Aden Airways DC-3 was spotted on a scheduled flight to Khormaksar! A further nine aircraft were scrambled to support troops being fired on by dissidents still hiding in the Jebel Huriyah area. In the continued pursuance of the drive to remove rebels from the Radfan area, rocket and cannon strikes were directed on houses and buildings believed to conceal troublemakers.

A high level of precision flying was demanded from AFME Hunter pilots. Attacking targets hidden deep inside steep-sided wadis and firing at enemy positions less than thirty yards from friendly forces required a high degree of skill and concentration. On occasions when it was deemed necessary to ground hug an approach along a wadi floor, there was the ever present danger of being fired on from the peaks above. Indeed, as has already been mentioned, the Hunters were flown so low on occasions that troops on the ground were sometimes struck by discarded shell cases as the aircraft passed overhead.

Fleet Air Arm

To relieve pressure on the Hunter squadrons, Sea Vixen FAW.1s of 892 Squadron operating from HMS *Centaur* assumed responsibility for armed recces and top-cover support for ground troops still battling Quteibi dissidents in the Radfan. Strikes

OC 892 Squadron taxies his Sea Vixen FAW.1 XJ605 onto the Hunter pan at Khormaksar, to attend a planning meeting at TacWing HQ. Of interest are the SNEB rocket pods mounted on the inner pylons (author).

against forts and other rebel strongholds by the naval fighters using batteries of 2-inch and 3-inch SNEB rockets proved extremely effective at knocking down stone walls, some up to three-feet thick!

By the end of June, Hunter strikes in the Radfan area reduced in tempo but the readiness states remained in force. In less than two months, Operation RADFAN had achieved its main objectives, but the Egyptian-backed hardliners were not about to capitulate. The table below provides an illustration of the support provided by the RAF units based at Khormaksar:

Aircraft	Sorties	Rockets	Cannon 20/30 mm	Bombs 1,000lbs.	Bombs 20lbs.
Hunter FGA.9	527	2,508	176,092		
Hunter FR.10	115		7,808		
Shackleton MR.2	85		18,195	14	3,504
Aircraft	Sorties	Passengers	Casevac	Freight (lbs.)	
Beverley	9	407		112,084	
Twin Pioneer	324	3,697	161	399,887	
Belvedere	1,027	1,798	48	1,110,515	
Whirlwind	57	95	26	41,140	
Wessex (RN)	409	2,096		192,659	

The demand for air support in the Radfan continued through July. Although the first 8 Squadron strike was carried out at Wadina by a pair of aircraft on the 3rd, the majority of its ninety operational sorties comprised armed recces and flagwaves. Over a number of days, the squadron was detailed to mark targets for the Shackleton crews as they continued to harass troublemakers. Similarly, the majority of 43 Squadron's sixty-five operational sorties were armed recces over the Radfan, usually by pairs of cannon-armed aircraft. If nothing untoward was spotted, their guns were fired off at improvised targets as they headed back to Khormaksar.

Under the direction of an airborne AAC FAC, two strikes were carried out by 8 Squadron aircraft against a dissident target near Mudia on 21 July. The same target was selected for a further attack by a pair of aircraft on the 30th.

Destroying arms dumps

The discovery of an arms cache was dealt with swiftly and forcefully. Locating them was difficult enough but to find two on the same day, as occurred on 28 July, was rare. OC 8 Squadron, Squadron Leader Syme (XF445) led a four-ship cannon strike on a mission to destroy one of the dumps in Wadi Yaheer, along with Flight Lieutenants McCarthy (XJ680), Humphreyson (XE609) and Sheppard (XE592).

Later the same day, his 43 Squadron counterpart, Squadron Leader Champniss (XE609), led a section of four aircraft to perform a rocket strike on the second, a cave containing arms and ammunition. The other three pilots on this mission were Flight Lieutenants Chapman (XF456), Wilkins (XE680) and Stoker (XE592). Sixty rockets and 540 rounds of HE ammunition were fired at the cave, which was recorded as being blown 'wide open'. On the final day of the month, the standby pair was scrambled to strike a position in Wadi Taym from which rebels had been reported firing at ground forces.

Flying activities were curtailed through much of July due to sandstorms and winds of 30kts gusting to 40kts and visibility down to 1,000 yards. The situation was exacerbated by a centralised servicing system that failed to provide enough serviceable aircraft.

Several missions that should have been flown by sections of four aircraft had to be flown as pairs. In quoting from the ORB, OC 43 Squadron commented.

That it was becoming increasingly difficult to maintain a high standard of briefings due to the lack of confidence in the availability in the planned number of aircraft. Furthermore, experienced pilots were increasingly being forced to give up some of their allocated flying hours to allow non-operational pilots reasonable continuity prior to becoming operational.

The pilot of 43 Squadron FGA.9 XE611 unleashes a volley of six HE SAP rockets on a target in the Radfan in June 1964 (©IWM).

Of the thirty-three operational sorties flown by the FR.10s, ten were armed recces over the Radfan area, two of which were converted to HE cannon strikes on selected targets while the aircraft were en route. A further seventeen recce sorties were flown in a search of rebel groups moving around the Wadi Ayn, the Upper Yaffa and Dhala areas. The reduction in the overall operational commitment, enabled 1417 Flight time and space to seek out new targets for use in upcountry ground attack training.

Shortly before departing for the UK at the end of his tour, OC 1417 Flight, Peter Lewis, was promoted to squadron leader and, in recognition of the 119 operational sorties completed during his two-year tour, awarded the AFC. He was succeeded in post by Flight Lieutenant Roger Pyrah.

Although the centralised servicing system was a problem for the ground–attack squadrons, it worked well for 1417 Flight, due to the higher priority attributed to the flight's intelligence-gathering assignments. August continued very much in the same vein as for July. In addition to six flagwaves being flown over the Mahfid, Mudia and Mukeiras areas, 1417 Flight flew a further seventeen recce sorties to capture photographic evidence of dissident activity for intelligence briefings.

The first action of note for August took place on the 5th with 8 Squadron performing a strike on a target on Jebel Farman. Five days later 8 Squadron aircraft carried out two firepower demonstrations, one at Am Surrah and the second at As Sawad. Due to a shortage of serviceable FGA.9s, a T.7 was used to help make up the number. The purpose of a firepower demonstration was to instil a graphic image of the destructive effect of a burst of 30mm cannon shells in the minds of dissident tribesmen. On this occasion, both targets were destroyed, leaving spectators on the hillsides in no doubt as to what would happen if they failed to stop feuding.

Attention now returned to the Radfan where terrorist groups had begun to move back into the region. Fifty-eight armed-recces were flown over a proscribed section known as 'Ramrod'. Since attacks on houses were no longer permissible for this type of mission, pairs of Hunters were authorised to fire their guns into crops and fruit trees over a wide area to deprive the dissident incumbents of their sources of food. A further thirty-two flagwaves were flown in the Hilyan, Al Khabr, Wadi Habib, Mukeiras, Shuqra and Am Surrah areas. Three were combined with leaflet drops to warn of repercussions should the rebels refuse to desist from their insurgent activities. Under the somewhat erratic direction of an FRA Forward Air Controller, a further eight strike sorties were flown by 8 Squadron in the vicinity of Mudia. These consisted of pairs of aircraft firing rockets and cannon onto positions where dissidents had been reported behaving suspiciously. As no movements were detected it was not possible to assess the outcome.

A strike planned for 16 August on a fort and nearby wooded area in Wadi Bana by eight 43 Squadron FGA.9s was abandoned when poor visibility obscured the target. The attack was instead carried out by eight aircraft from 8 Squadron two days later.

Following the pooling of TacWing aircraft and groundcrew, 8 and 43 Squadron Hunters received dual squadron markings as can be seen on this view of rocket-armed 8/43 Squadron FGA.9 XE530 awaiting its next strike mission (Roger Wilkins).

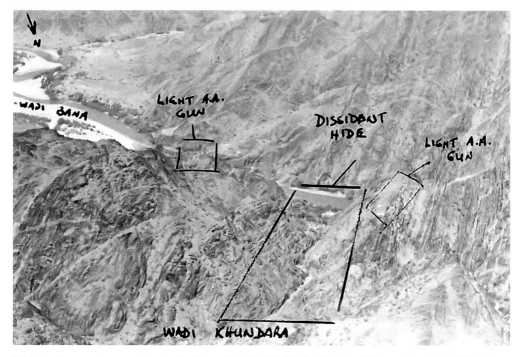

High level recce photograph taken by Roger Pyrah's FR.10 of a dissident hideout deep in the Wadi Bana (Roger Pyrah).

Led by Flight Lieutenant Williams (XF456), the force comprised Flight Lieutenants Porteous (XJ680), Johnson (XE618), Constable (XG296), Cureton (XJ684), Hounsell (XG256) and Flying Officers Baron (XJ692) and Sturt (XE655). Serious damage was inflicted on the building, five camels being used by gunrunners were killed and a large number of rifles destroyed when a stack of twenty boxes of ammunition exploded.

Reports of dissident activity near Dathina was responded to by 43 Squadron with two flagwaves, four firepower demonstrations and a strike on selected targets on Jebel Fahman. On the last day of August Wing Commander Jennings led a formation of eight 8 Squadron aircraft to carry out an attack on rebel-held houses on Jebel Khuder, inflicting severe damage on all targets.

Hunter loss

While flying as No. 2 of a pair of Hunters ten miles north of Khormaksar on 11 August, the engine of Flying Officer Burrows' FGA.9 (XE623) flamed out. Turning back towards the airfield, he tried to relight the engine but was forced to eject when this failed, injuring his back in the process. The aircraft landed itself semi-intact on the salt pans to the north of Khormaksar.

Having achieved its objective of photographing every airstrip and fort within the Western Aden Protectorate, 1417 Flight focused its concentration on a more ambitious proposal, the creation of an extensive photographic library of every town and wadi in the WAP. A minimum of three photographs of each locality was to be captured and filed with the Ground Liaison Officer (GLO) for use as an intelligence aid. With the formation of an Air Reconnaissance Intelligence Centre (ARIC) at the Command HQ, administration of the library was handed over to the new unit.

Following an appreciable increase in reports of dissident movements near Dhala and Mudia, HQ MEC instructed 1417 Flight to take detailed photographs of twenty-six potential targets in these areas. The processed prints confirmed fears that mines were being laid close to Wa'alan and on a road leading to the airstrip at Dhala. No. 8 Squadron was instructed to perform flagwaves over the areas in the hope of dissuading the perpetrators from pursuing such an unwise practice. They heeded the message, but for how long?

Based on evidence gleaned from the photographs, rocket and gun attacks were carried out against targets at Mudia by a pair of 8 Squadron aircraft on 2 September and by a further pair at Jebel Khuder. Two days later two FGA.9s returned to Mudia to perform a rocket and cannon strike on other rebel targets. At 06:20 on the 16th two aircraft were despatched to disperse a large concentration of dissidents with a flagwave over Jebel Misawarra. This was backed up by a second pair two days later to ensure the message was understood.

When dissidents were found to have returned to their minelaying activities at Wa'alan, OC 8 Squadron was briefed to lead a four-ship flagwave over the target area.

All my own work! The devastating effect of a 30mm HE cannon strike from a solo 1417 Flight FR.10 can be judged from these photographs taken of a target before and immediately after. The note at the lower right reads; 'the effect of an attack by myself of 30mm HE' (both, Roger Pyrah).

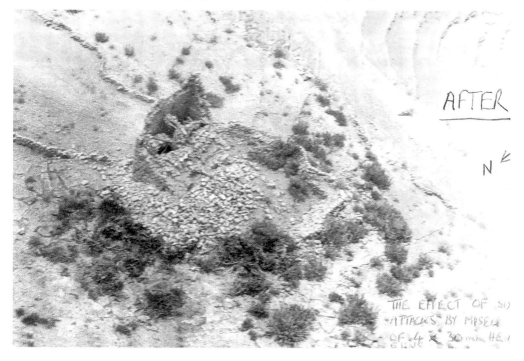

Due to an update from an observant FAC, however, the mission was changed en route to one of a cannon strike. With dissidents in the proscribed 'Ramrod' area continuing to cause trouble, OC TacWing decided that he would lead a four-ship dawn strike against the culprits. Jebel Widina became the focus of further TacWing attention when two pairs of FGA.9s responded to a request for a strike on nearby targets.

For 43 Squadron the month had begun with a strike at Mudia by Flight Lieutenant Chapman (XF456) and Flying Officer Middleton (XG296). The bulk of its operations, however, consisted of sixty-six armed recces in the Radfan area and an air defence scramble to investigate reports of unidentified aircraft crossing the Yemen border near Haushabi. None were seen.

As September drew to a close, both squadrons were detailed to carry rockets while flying armed-recces in the Radfan area and to use them on selected targets in proscribed areas as a means of keeping the militants in check. Houses within these areas were declared legitimate targets once again but for front gun attacks only.

Eastleigh rundown

Having assured the Kenyan Government that the RAF would maintain a presence in the country for one year following independence, the British government issued instructions for the rundown and closure of RAF Eastleigh to proceed. As a first phase 30 Squadron redeployed its Beverleys, not to Khormaksar as originally planned, but to Muharraq.

Armed recces over the Radfan continued to occupy the ground-attack squadrons well into October. Rockets and HE ammunition were carried on all sorties and this proved invaluable on the 6th when trouble flared up near the village of Asaqa, to the east of Dhala. Four flagwaves were flown over the village and when this failed to have the desired effect, eleven 43 Squadron aircraft carried out rocket and cannon strikes on targets in the area. As this was ignored by the warring factions, three pairs of 8 Squadron Hunters were despatched to strike at the dissidents in the early morning of the 9th. Undeterred, the feud raged on! The FRA was ordered in to sort the situation out but this only made matters worse. In a more concentrated effort to stop the fighting, twenty-three strikes were flown on targets in territory occupied by both parties by 8 Squadron FGA.9s over the four days beginning 10 October. This appeared to have the desired effect but when the feuding erupted again almost immediately, twelve strikes were targeted against a specific offender's stronghold. The destruction of further targets in Mudia was the objective for four further strikes on the 29th and the month ended with two flagwaves and four close air support missions under FAC control, near the army base at Blair's Field.

Hunter loss

Despite ten pilots, five from each squadron, and six Hunters being away on detachment at Masirah between the 8th and 16th, 26,000 cannon rounds and 378 rockets were expended by TacWing aircraft in October. The detachment was marred by the tragic

Another before and after sequence in which a house in the Wadi Yahar (left) has been marked with an 'X' to identify it as a target for 8/43 Squadron FGA.9s. The post-strike photograph (right) taken on 6 October 1964 illustrates the precision exercised by the pilots when attacking targets; none of the surrounding buildings were damaged (both, Roger Wilkins).

loss of Flying Officer Ian Stephens whose FGA.9 (XE592) crashed into the sea shortly after a formation take off for the return to Khormaksar.

For reasons not recorded in the ORBs, restrictions imposed on the use of 230-gallon drop tanks in October reduced the Hunter's radius of operation. The FR.10s were configured with four 100-gallon drop tanks, which enabled them comfortably to complete fifteen armed recces in the Radfan and Dhala areas, two combined recces and leaflet drops, and a further two recces to locate and photograph Russian merchant shipping in the Gulf of Aden.

New Hangar

Having settled into a routine of exercises, battle combat, FAC training and APCs at Sharjah, 208 Squadron took possession of a brand new maintenance hangar at Muharraq in October. Sufficient space was provided for up to seven Hunters on primary and minor servicing and others requiring rectification work, removing the need to fly aircraft down to Khormaksar for periodic servicing.

When a 1417 Flight FR.10 suffered a flame-out at Masirah, an engine-change unit and servicing party from 208 Squadron were flown down from Muharraq on the 28th to carry out an engine change.

Peace at last?

On 18 November the Ibdali became the last of the dissident tribes to broker for peace, enabling offensive action over proscribed areas in the Radfan to be scaled back, at least for the time being. The decision was somewhat premature as a strike was carried out on a target north-east of Mudia by a pair of 8 Squadron FGA.9s in response to a call from an FAC. Only thirty operational sorties were flown by 8 Squadron and four by 43 Squadron during November.

Although the tempo of operations by ground forces in the Radfan had been gradually abating, the Hunter squadrons continued to maintain internal security in the area. A reduction in the need for close air support enabled them to concentrate more on much needed training, especially for newly-arrived pilots. A broad-based training programme was implemented which comprised air-to-ground gun and rocket firing, high- and low-level cine-weave, ranging and tracking, one-*vs*-one interceptions and formation flying. Low-level navigation exercises included practice diversions across the Red Sea to Djibouti.

The programme was extended to include co-operation exercises with the Royal Navy following the arrival of the aircraft carrier HMS *Eagle* and the frigate HMS

8/43 Squadron FGA.9 XE649 accompanies a 1417 Flight FR.10, XE599, on a photo-recce mission over the Aden hinterland in late 1964 (Roger Wilkins).

Zulu in the Gulf of Aden. TacWing Hunters engaged in low-level, simulated attacks on the warships while at the same time trying to avoid detection. Cannon and rocket strikes on splash targets towed by the ships brought the exercise to a close. The Buccaneer, Sea Vixen and Gannet squadrons had, meanwhile, landed ashore at Khormaksar to undertake an improvised training programme over WAP terrain.

The outbreak of peace was destined not to last. Renewed trouble in the Radfan on 4 December was dealt with by cannon and rocket strikes by two waves of four 8 Squadron aircraft. Wing Commander Jennings led the first section, followed by the second some thirty minutes later, led by Squadron Leader Syme. On the next day, four 43 Squadron aircraft were despatched to destroy a gun emplacement near Beihan. A request initiated by an FAC for dissident targets to be destroyed in the same area was responded to by a 1417 Flight FR.10 in the company of an 8 Squadron FGA.9. Mopping-up strikes were performed by a pair of 8 Squadron aircraft in the late afternoon.

On the evening of 7 December another band of dissidents decided to direct their gunfire on the tiny airstrip at Blair's Field. Under FAC control, two 8 Squadron aircraft were directed onto the rebel positions. Undeterred, the rebels carried out a second attack on the strip late in the evening of the following day, too late for TacWing to intervene. Notwithstanding, at first light on the morning of the 9th, the dissidents firing positions were struck hard and a number of rebels were spotted making a hasty retreat towards the hills.

Revised Wing Structure

Based on the experience of an extremely busy year and the lessons learned from the numerous operations carried out in the WAP, the Khormaksar flying wings were re-organised into three wings from 14 December 1964. The changes outlined below were designed to improve the efficiency of the station and the operational effectiveness of the squadrons operating from it.

- **Strike Wing**
  Born out of Tactical Wing, it remained under the command of the then OC Tactical Wing. In its revised form the rebranded Strike Wing consisted of 8 and 43 Squadrons (Hunter FGA.9), 1417 Flight (Hunter FR.10), 37 Squadron (Shackleton MR.2c) and the Strike Wing Servicing Squadron.

- **Medium Range Transport (MRT) Wing**
  Placed under the command of the then OC 105 Squadron, MRT Wing comprised 105 Squadron (Argosy C.1), 84 Squadron (Beverley C.1) and the MRT Servicing Squadron.

- **Short Range Transport (SRT) Wing**
  SRT Wing remained under the command of the OC Transport Wing and
  consisted of 26 Squadron (Belvedere HC.1), 78 Squadron (Twin Pioneer CC.1),
  Middle East Communications Squadron (Valetta C.2, Hastings C.4, and Dakota
  C.4), Search and Rescue Flight (Whirlwind HAR.10) and the SRT Servicing
  Squadron.

Although the Hunter ground-attack squadrons had acquitted themselves well and
been the focus of attention through much of the year, many of their successes could be
credited to the high standard of photographic and visual intelligence provided by 1417
Flight. At the end of its first full calendar year, the flight had flown 314 operational
sorties, exposed 693 films, processed 13,355 prints, an invaluable contribution.

Chapter 10

1965 – Maintaining security

Terrorist uprising

In 1964 the British government announced that the South Arabian Federation would become independent by 1968. With no wish to add coal to a smouldering fire, there was no mention of the British forces' valiant endeavours in defeating the 'Wolves of the Radfan'. But that is precisely what that announcement achieved. Believing the time was now right, nationalist factions began to stoke the embers in a determined attempt to drive the British out of South Arabia in a much shorter timeframe. Yemeni, Egyptian and Aden-based dissidents accelerated the flow of weapons, mines and explosives into Aden from the Yemen as a prelude for an all-out guerrilla-style war. The attempted assassination of the Governor at the airport was the first sign of the depths to which terrorists groups were prepared to go. In the final weeks of 1964 the daughter of an RAF medical officer was killed by a grenade thrown through a married quarter window and more than thirty further incidents had been reported before the year was out.

The main political organisations in Aden, the National Liberation Front (NLF) and the Front for the Liberation of Occupied South Yemen (FLOSY) in particular, were not content in directing their wrath towards the 'foreign invader', but on pursuing their individual, centuries-old, inter-tribal feuds. It was against this deteriorating security backdrop, therefore, that British forces would endure difficult times while trying to maintain order across the Federation over the next three years.

Tactical training and assessment

From 4 and 10 January 1965 twelve 8 and 43 Squadron pilots undertook a training detachment to Masirah. Over the period, fifty-six high- and low-level practice strikes were carried out, together with area recces over unfamiliar terrain in Oman and practice diversions to Sharjah.

Shortly after their return to Aden, a team of four DFCS instructors arrived to assess the 'war' potential of Strike Wing pilots. Various mission envelopes were flown, based on four-ship strikes with instructors occupying the numbers two and four positions. To make the task more challenging, the strikes were hampered by pairs of Hunters posing as missile-armed enemy aircraft. The focus then turned to four-*vs*-two combat skirmishes at both high and low level.

The urgent need for more forward air controllers eased after Strike Wing conducted a series of training exercises for British Army officers attached to

As the groundcrew get to work on their aircraft, the pilots of 8/43 Squadron enjoy a cool beer on the Masirah pan following their flight from Khormaksar on 4 January 1965. Visible in the picture are, l to r; John Thomson, John Sweet (OC Masirah), Roger Wilkins, Major Adamson (GLO), Alan Pollock, Phil Champniss, Ron Loader (EO) and Ron Burrows (Roger Wilkins).

225 GL section. In one segment, the students experienced the excitement of flying a dummy strike in the Abyan area from the comfort of the righthand seat of a Hunter T.7. Their ability to direct Hunters onto ground targets had noticeably improved by the end of the course.

Back to the day job!
After the relative quiet of the previous few months the adrenaline began to rise in January as the number of operational sorties flown by the wing increased to sixty-four. Most targets were located in the Dhala, Mudia and Radfan areas. Twelve flagwaves were flown while seventeen pairs were despatched to counter threats to Beverley and Twin Pioneer aircraft whose pilots had reported being fired on while landing and taking off from Mukeiras.

The long route home
When Sudan suddenly decided to deny overflying rights to foreign military aircraft, the RAF was left with no option but to take the longer northern route when ferrying aircraft to and from the UK. This inevitably led to an increase in defects and delays

en route. On one occasion an FGA.9 and an FR.10 being ferried back to the UK by Flight Lieutenants Wilkins (XF421) and Liddle (XE614) experienced so many defects that the trip became something of an epic. Having staged through Masirah, Muharraq, Teheran, Akrotiri, El Adem, Luqa and Nice, they arrived at St Athan five days and thirty-eight flying hours after leaving Khormaksar.

The OC 208 Squadron, Squadron Leader Lewis, was not so lucky either when he and another of his pilots were forced to abandon their ferry of a T.7 and an FGA.9 at Tehran due to bad weather over Turkey and return to Muharraq.

Still in the Persian Gulf, once an area of Yasirat al Yas island had been cleared for use as a range, 208 Squadron carried out a programme of air-to-ground firing practice under the guidance of trainee forward air controllers. This was the first time the squadron had experienced a live-firing exercise using FACs since moving to the Gulf and proved of great value to the pilots and controllers.

Combined strike

On 16 January 1417 Flight pilot Flight Lieutenant Timms (XF460) was briefed to photograph a suspected dissident transit camp in Wadi Yahar. Based on evidence extrapolated from the resulting prints and a briefing by the pilot, eight 43 Squadron Hunters were detailed to strike the encampment and a nearby supply dump with HE rockets and cannon. The mission concluded with a Shackleton dropping eleven 1,000lb bombs over the target area. Several dissidents and animals were killed and their supplies destroyed in the most intensive action by Strike Wing for some time. The 37 Squadron ORB speculated that 'The resultant damage emphasised the effectiveness of one Shackleton versus eight Hunters in this particular role'. Nothing like a little friendly inter-squadron banter to hone the concentration! A further eleven strikes were carried out by 43 Squadron aircraft on the 25th, 26th and 29th of the month, but the targets were not specified in the ORB.

With its serviceability problems seemingly resolved, 1417 Flight comfortably exceeded its monthly 100-hours flying target for January. Included in the total was the time dedicated to a balanced training programme for recently-arrived pilots. Of the operational sorties, one comprised a flagwave, six were photo and visual recces and one, flown by Flight Lieutenant Timms (XF460), was to provide top cover for a Beverley operating out of Mukeiras.

As January drew to a close, Squadron Leader Champniss entered an explicit comment in the 43 Squadron ORB in which he highlighted legitimate concerns about the experience levels of some of his pilots. With three new pilots about to be added to the unit's quota of ten first-tour pilots, he pleaded that 'This is too many! I must be given more flying hours to train them up to an acceptable standard if the overall standard is not to drop below an acceptable minimum'. The question was highlighted in the report produced by the DFCS team following their earlier visit to the squadron.

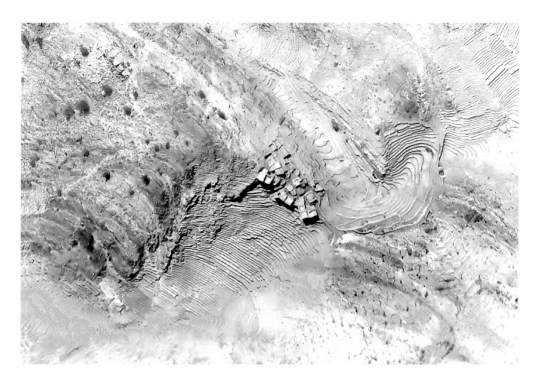

Farar Al Ulya, a dissident training camp in the Wadi Yafar, was destroyed when a 37 Squadron Shackleton dropped 11,000lb of high explosive on it on 16 January 1965 (Sandy McMillan).

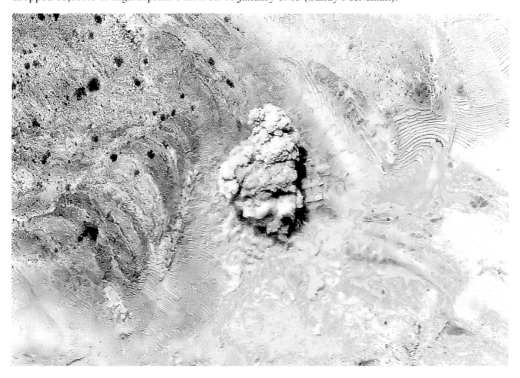

Fresh from refurbishment at Kemble, gleaming 1417 Flight FR.10 XE589 was adopted by Canadian pilot, Flt Lt Ralph Chambers, as his own aircraft. Here, it awaits its master's attention for a post-refurbishment air test at Khormaksar on 20 January 1965 (Ralph Chambers).

Operation CUT

February was a quieter month for air operations. Of the twenty-four operational sorties flown by 8 Squadron, six were Beihan patrols, twelve were flagwaves and a further six were flown on armed recces and leaflet drops near Dhala. When troops came under fire on the Dhala road on the 15th, ten aircraft were scrambled to carry out a strike against the offenders under FAC direction. Ground-controlled strikes by aircraft protecting convoys on major transit routes such as this were henceforth classified under the codename Operation CUT.

In the meantime 43 Squadron kept its pilots occupied on border patrol duties in the area around Beihan and performing flagwaves to the north of Wadi Ruqub, near Musaymir, and over an area east of Dhala. Naval co-operation exercises also featured, eight strike sorties being flown against splash targets towed by HMS *Zulu* as the ship's crew took the opportunity to exercise its radar and fire-control systems. At one stage, *Zulu* steamed in convoy with a tanker under the flag of a Soviet satellite state which encouraged the following comment to be written in the ORB, 'We trust they were duly impressed by the Squadron's accurate firing at the splash targets'.

No. 78 Squadron Standard

The two Hunter squadrons also made time to practise formation flying in readiness for a flypast to mark the presentation of the Standard to 78 Squadron on 11 February. Serviceability levels remained sufficiently high for fifteen aircraft to be flown on five practice runs and, on the day itself, the flypast being flown in a perfectly formed

One of several photographs captured by Frank Grimshaw's FR.10 depicting twelve 43 Squadron aircraft flying in formation on 13 February 1965 (Roger Wilkins).

figure '78'. Two days later, buoyed on by their success, 43 Squadron pilots posed a twelve-ship formation for a photograph captured on one of Frank Grimshaw's FR.10 Vinten cameras. Much of its remaining time was utilised on continuation training for current pilots and operational training for new arrivals.

Air defence

In Aden, the air defence commitment was undertaken by Strike Wing Hunters and generally involved the interception of intruding aircraft from the Yemen. The air defence remit for Bahrain island, where 'enemy' aircraft could approach from any direction, was the responsibility of 208 Squadron, whose pilots were kept on their toes with practice intercepts of 13 Squadron Canberra PR.9s returning from sorties along the Iraq border. As the PR.9s could fly higher than any other aircraft in the region and had a good turn of speed, they tended to make life as difficult as possible for the Hunter pilots. Regular practice intercepts were carried out and on one such exercise two pairs of Hunters were scrambled to intercept two 'intruders' reported to have overflown Kuwait and heading in the direction of Bahrain. Under the direction of HMS *Zulu*'s radar, the Canberras were intercepted but not until one was directly overhead Bahrain. The OC RAFPG flew as number two on one exercise to gain a better understanding of the measures that would need to be taken to provide a better air defence of the island.

Two views of the Muharraq dispersal depicting (above), 208 Squadron XJ632 at the head of a line of armed FGA.9s (Ron Turrell) while a pair of 13 Squadron Canberra PR.9s, XH177 and XH164 (below), bake in the midday sun. The Canberra Squadron operated a regular rotation of aircraft from its base at Akrotiri, Cyprus (author).

A rare formation comprising a Shackleton MR.2 of 42 Squadron on detachment from St Mawgan and four 8/43 Squadron FGA.9s – XF435-J, XJ691-T, XE552-D and XE530-O – high above the Aden hinterland on 10 March 1965 (Peter Sturt).

On 2 February two refurbished FGA.9s (XG255 and XJ691) and a T.7 (XL597) arrived at Muharraq on ferry from 19 MU. The ORB states that both Mark 9s were equipped with VHF radio. As both aircraft were fitted with UHF before returning to the UK for refurbishment the previous year, the entry in the ORB must surely have been in error.

February was generally an uneventful month from a 1417 Flight perspective. Although its target of 100 hours was comfortably achieved, only nine operational sorties were flown, six on visual and photo recce, one on a search for a dissident roadblock in the Urqub pass and a further two to locate and photograph the *Esso Lincoln* as it passed through the Red Sea.

By contrast, 'The busiest period for some considerable time', was how the 43 Squadron ORB portrayed the month of March. Offensive action began on the 4th when Wing Commander Jennings (XG205), led a four-ship strike on targets on Jebel Khuder, accompanied by Flight Lieutenants Porteous (XG237) and Williams (XF454), and Flying Officer Hulse (XJ632). Over the border in the Yemen, the fall of Harib village to the Royalists on 10 March led to a rise in the number of Egyptian MiG incursions in the Beihan area. These were countered with ninety-four air defence sorties along the border by Strike Wing Hunters. Seven were combined with flagwaves over neighbouring areas to remind habitual troublemakers that the 'Queen of the skies' was still in control of the skies of South Arabia. Although MiGs were spotted by the

Hunter pilots and occasionally chased back across the border, no guns were fired, the Hunters' presence being deemed a sufficient enough deterrent at this time.

For the period from 8 to 19 March a flight of seven 8 Squadron FGA.9s and one FR.10 from 1417 Flight flew up to Masirah to embark on a training programme.

In the Dhala area, fourteen sorties were flown by 43 Squadron in support of FRA operations, two leaflet drops, two scrambles, which had to be aborted due to radio failure, and ten armed recces. With half of 8 Squadron away on detachment at a time when Beihan operations were reaching a peak, the 'valiant efforts of the groundcrew in making sufficient aircraft available' was acknowledged in the squadron ORB.

Target detection trial

Under Flight Lieutenant Pyrah's supervision, an exercise was formulated whereby 1417 Flight pilots' target-detection capabilities could be accurately assessed. A civil servant (Mr Spears) and an RAF officer (Squadron Leader Harrison) from the MoD were flown out from the UK to witness the event. As a Whirlwind helicopter, hidden by camouflage was moved around various locations in the Lower Radfan, the pilots were briefed to locate it while flying at 200 feet and at 420kts. Alas, the results from this interesting experiment were not recorded.

Of the seventeen operational sorties flown by the FR.10s in March, three were by 43 Squadron pilots due to a shortage of serviceable FGA.9s, the situation having been exacerbated by the 8 Squadron detachment. Two further FR sorties were flown to seek out gunrunning dhows on the narrow stretch of sea between Perim Island and Mukha.

Operation PARK

Despite the undoubted success of Operation RADFAN the previous year, insurrections were once again on the increase across the breadth of the Federation, the miscreants bolstered by an increase in the supply of Egyptian arms and money. On 11 January, the C.-in-C. reported that dissident tribesmen had been detected making preparations for a major offensive against British interests to the north of Dahla. To counter this threat, Operation PARK was launched in late March, its objectives mirroring those of the Radfan campaign, relying to some extent on the use of proscription.

The number of requests for air support increased sharply during the early part of April. A creditable seventy-four operational sorties were flown by 8 Squadron during the month, including thirty on Beihan border patrols, twenty-two on strikes and a further ten on armed recces in support of Operation PARK. Four more sorties were flown to provide top cover for an Army Scout helicopter on a flight from Habilayn to Dhala, while further pairs were assigned to escort a Comms Flight Dakota (KN452) on a return flight from Beihan.

On 7 April OC 8 Squadron, Squadron Leader Syme (XG296), led a force of six Hunters, piloted by Lieutenant Kerr, RN (XG256), Flight Lieutenants Williams

The pilot of 1417 Flight FR.10 XE599 keeps a close watch on activities in the impenetrable hilltop village of Al Qara as the enclave was regularly used by dissidents as a hideout and store for their weapons (John Severne).

(XE552) and Hounsell (XJ689), Flying Officers Hulse (XF376) and Wharmby (XG237), to perform a strike on dissident targets at Al Qara.

In a rare lighthearted moment, an incident recorded in the 37 Squadron ORB for 26 April, describes a leaflet-drop by a Shackleton sortie in the Yashbum/Ataq area, informing local tribesmen that a truce had been declared in the area.

> At one small village, a wedding was taking place when the aircraft roared overhead at fifty feet, showering the party with leaflets, much to the delight of the locals who treated it like confetti.

Two days later a dawn strike was carried out by four 8 Squadron aircraft on troublemaking tribesmen in Wadi Bana, to the west of Kundhara. When this failed to separate them, a further twelve strikes were performed by a mix of Strike Wing squadron pilots on the morning of the 30th.

With Harib town in Royalist hands, Republican forces regrouped to prepare for its recapture. The options were either to approach via the Al Haqla Pass from the north or via Wadi Ablah in the south but both routes were heavily defended by Royalist troops. As Harib was close to the border with Aden, Strike Wing Hunters were detailed to fly air defence sorties over Yemeni territory to the north of the pass to deter MiG fighters from entering the area.

As the battle for Harib simmered, 43 Squadron aircraft maintained patrols over the area as a precaution. When the Harib–Sana'a road (inside the Yemen) was blocked by Royalists, Republican reinforcements withdrew towards Sana'a. If they were to retake Harib, the only alternative was to approach via disputed Federal Territory, an option which would have been vigorously opposed by Federal forces with the support of Strike Wing Hunters.

Wing Commander Jennings' tour as OC Strike Wing came to an end on 12 April. Much had been achieved by the wing under his guidance for which he was awarded the DFC. He was succeeded in post by Wing Commander Martin Chandler.

On 5 May two 43 Squadron aircraft were despatched to patrol the border near Beihan while providing top cover for a Comms Flight Andover operating in the vicinity. A second pair of Hunters was dispatched later to maintain continuous cover. Three days later, OC 43 Squadron, Squadron Leader Champniss (XG154) led Flight Lieutenant Taylor (XE649) on a scramble alert to Al Khuraibah to perform a strike on a target in which twenty or so dissidents were known to be concealed. Contact was made with a FAC who marked the target using smoke, enabling the strike to be carried out using

The Jungle Bar is the location for this relaxed group of 8 Squadron pilots with, standing l to r, Mike Flynn, Mal Grosse, Mac McKenzie-Crooks, Andy Bell, Chris Cureton, Roy Humphreyson, Alan Dix, Chris Hulse, and seated, Nick Kerr (RN), Graham Hounsell, Tam Syme, Graham Williams, Iain Porteous, Mac McCarthy and Martin Johnson (Mal Grosse).

cannon only. A back-up pair, flown by Flight Lieutenant Liddle (XG256) and Flying Officer McKeon (XF456) struck a nearby fort with rockets and cannon, destroying both it and an arms dump in the process.

A scramble on 11 May saw the 43 Squadron standby pair heading towards Perim Island to intercept an intruding aircraft detected flying over the border; the only aircraft spotted was a friendly AAC Beaver. Everything then fell silent until 29 May when two 43 Squadron aircraft were scrambled to come to the aid of an Army patrol that had come under attack by twenty or so dissidents. Contact was made with the patrol when it fired a red flare to indicate its position. Although the Hunters performed a search of the area and despite firing at suspected targets, no dissidents were seen. Later that morning, a second pair was scrambled to the same area with the same outcome. As the patrol's FAC was in a disadvantaged position, he called for a helicopter to lift him onto a high ridge in the hope of gaining a better perspective. A third pair of Hunters was then despatched but by the time they arrived the patrol had lost contact with the assailants. Under guidance from the FAC, the pair searched several routes along which the rebels might have escaped but no trace of them was found.

Of the fourteen operational sorties flown by 8 Squadron, two were firepower demonstrations by Flight Lieutenant Hounsell (XJ692) and Flying Officer Grosse (XE649) on the 21st to pre-empt possible trouble at Al Mithaf, while two more strikes were carried out against dissident targets five miles to the west of Thumier on the 30th.

Sabotage
Of greater concern was the deterioration in internal security. This was illustrated with dramatic effect when, on 29 May, one of the two RAF Dakota C.4s based at Khormaksar,

The wreckage of Dakota KJ995 lies abandoned on the Khormaksar civil airport apron following the sabotage attack on 29 May 1965 (Roger Wilkins).

KJ995, was destroyed by a bomb while parked on the civil airport apron, close to the Hunter pan. The discovery of a time-pencil detonator confirmed suspicions that the aircraft had been destroyed by an act of sabotage, the explosive device having been placed in the aircraft during a visit to an up-country airfield. As a precaution, RAF flying units were instructed to take precautionary measures regarding the local civilian labour and pay close attention to nooks and crannies when performing pre- and post-flight inspections on aircraft.

Engine defect fear

Meanwhile, in the early afternoon of 6 May, a turbine locking plate from an Avon engine was found on the Hunter pan at Muharraq. All 208 Squadron aircraft were grounded and the one still airborne recalled. The aircraft were subjected to a thorough inspection but no sign of any damage was detected. Following consultation with AFME in Aden, the squadron was instructed to replace the engines on all of its Hunters, four of which were still at Sharjah on detachment. Replacement engines were flown up from Khormaksar by Argosy in batches of three along with two engine fitters from Strike Wing. Eleven days were to pass before the final flight test was completed.

A rare colour photograph of the damage regularly inflicted by Strike Wing Hunters on solid stone-built buildings. It was taken by Roger Wilkins with a hand-held camera while holding the control column between his knees (Roger Wilkins).

The first day of June was another milestone in 8 Squadron's history when Squadron Leader Des Melaniphy assumed command, relieving Squadron Leader Tam Syme to take up a position in the UK. The handover occurred at a time of relatively little rebel activity in the Federation, which was just as well as several aircraft were at Masirah on a three-week detachment with 43 Squadron.

On the same day, 43 Squadron pilots Flight Lieutenants Liddle and Taylor were detailed to carry out a strike on three mortar positions that had been spotted on a ridge overlooking an Army encampment. The attack was timed to take place at dusk in the hope of catching the dissidents in action but, as none were seen, they sprayed their cannon-fire at the targets before returning to base.

The new OC 8 Squadron did not have to wait long before seeing some of his pilots off on a mission. A strike by squadron aircraft was called for on the 3rd against a dissident hideout, followed by an air defence scramble on the 13th after an unidentified aircraft had been detected in the Mukeiras area. No contact was made. The remaining sorties consisted of flagwaves over routes known to be used for the movement of arms and for top cover for VIP helicopters and military convoys.

War games
For 43 Squadron the entire month's training was devoted to a sixteen-day detachment to Masirah starting on 10 June. The full complement of squadron pilots, together

43 Squadron pilots enjoy a refreshing can of beer on arrival at Masirah on 10 June for a two-week training detachment. l to r, Roger Wilkins, Tony McKeon, name unknown, John Sweet, Andy White, Ron Loader and Ron Burrows (Roger Wilkins).

with two pilots from 1417 Flight and a GLO, Major Adamson, were deployed to the island, along with six FGA.9s, a T.7 and an FR.10. The programme began with high-level reconnaissance sorties over the Sharjah/Muscat area, refreshing old memories for some while introducing new pilots to the variations in terrain and areas of operation. A later phase was devised to create a war situation in which the squadron was tasked with breaking up an imaginary advance of ground forces. With bold imagination, Major Adamson produced a realistic scenario which was both fluid and interesting, using photographs of nine airfields and thirty other strike targets provided by 1417 Flight. The experience enabled pilots to quickly become familiar with the new location and accustomed to operating over extreme ranges with minimum navigation aids and basic maps. An additional segment required a pair to fly to Muharraq each afternoon and return the following morning; the objective being for new pilots to gain valuable experience in route flying and operations in the Persian Gulf.

The Wessex arrives

Based on the flexibility displayed by naval Wessex in the early Radfan operations, the decision was taken to re-equip 78 Squadron with the latest version of this versatile helicopter. When the squadron was declared operational on type on 2 June, its Twin-Pioneers were dispersed between 21 Squadron, which had moved up to Khormaksar from Eastleigh, and 152 Squadron at Muharraq.

A lull in operations allowed a number of 8 Squadron pilots to undertake a three-day attachment to Habilayn to learn more of the challenges facing the Army in its up-country habitat. The timing was ideal as 43 Squadron had begun to fly top cover sorties for Army re-supply convoys and flagwaves over feuding Fadhli and Audhali tribesmen.

MiG attacks

On 29 June, Egyptian MiGs crossed the border and attacked a wellhead at Nejd Marqad, killing a woman and wounding a further two. A pair of 43 Squadron FGA.9s, supported by two 1417 Flight FR.10s, scrambled but, despite FAC contact and the Hunters remaining on station for as long as possible, no intruders were encountered. Later the same day, MiG fighters carried out an attack at Bulaiq, killing a Federal guard. The deteriorating situation was upgraded to 'Critical' and border patrols reinstated over the area for the rest of the day. The deterrent effect probably had the desired effect as no more sightings of intruding aircraft were reported.

In the hope of catching MiG pilots off-guard, and at the request of the Sharif of Beihan, the FRA installed anti-aircraft guns at three positions and Strike Wing flew a constant stream of border patrols on 1, 2, 3 and 5 July. Despite the relative calm, Strike Wing HQ continued to receive calls for air support from Army units operating up-country. Four strikes were flown by 8 Squadron pilots Flight Lieutenant Sturt (XJ632) and Flying Officers Mackenzie-Crooks (XG256), Flynn (XF454) and Wharmby (XJ689) on 7 July to relieve an FRA patrol that had come under fire from dissident tribesmen.

To mark the farewell visit of the retiring Chief of the Defence Staff, Admiral of the Fleet Earl Mountbatten of Burma, on 19 July, a formation of 8/43 Squadron and 1417 Flight aircraft performed a ceremonial flypast. And when Air Marshal Sir Augustus Walker paid a visit to Strike Wing, a 1417 Flight FR.10 flew low overhead to capture his arrival on camera. The photograph was presented to him some eleven minutes later, a new record.

Apart from the occasional flagwave, much of the operational commitment throughout July involved seeking out arms-smuggling camel trains in support of an FRA policy of disrupting dissident groups while trying to curb their inter-tribal feuding. The Emir of Hilyan, a loyal British ally, had become increasingly concerned at the sympathy being shown by his people to dissidents using his territory as a supply route. On 2 August, at his request, two aircraft were diepatched to perform flagwaves over Marfad and Al Kharba.

Having long been a haven for dissident activists, the area to the north of Blair's Field was placed under permanent surveillance by 1st Royal Anglian Regiment and, as a result of their observations, a full-time FAC position was established at the airstrip. When a group of thirty or so dissidents was seen acting suspiciously, the controller directed a dusk strike on the rebels' position by a pair of 43 Squadron aircraft flown by Flight Lieutenant Pollock (XF388) and Flying Officer White (XF456). This appeared to have the desired effect, at least for the time being.

Operations over Oman

With the arrival back at Khormaksar of XE614 following refurbishment in the UK, 1417 Flight's FR establishment comprised five Mark 10s (XE589, XE599, XE614, XF436 and XF460). Of the eighteen operational sorties flown by these aircraft in August, eleven were in the Western Protectorate and seven in support of a new operation being conducted to the extreme east and north of the country. An interesting development, surrounded in secrecy, had been sanctioned by HQ RAFPG and was about to commence in the Gulf. Four 208 Squadron FGA.9s were flown to Salalah to prepare for an operation over the Dhofar region of Oman. They were joined there on the 27th by a pair of 1417 Flight FR.10s which had flown up from Khormaksar. The Flight ORB described the main objective of the operation as being 'to seek out and photograph rebel columns and gun-running camel trains known to be crossing the uncharted desert wastes of Oman'. There was no mention of the operation by name

43 Squadron pilots at Khormaksar in June 1965. Standing l to r, Peter Biddiscombe, Alan Pollock, Neil Hayward, Alasdair Liddle, Barney Lydiate, (OC) Philip Champniss AFC, John Thomson, John Osborne, Roger Wilkins; kneeling, Geoffrey Taylor, Don Brown, Anthony McKeon, Nigel Ashley, Michael Fernee, Rod Dean, John Batty, Peter Skinner (Alan Pollock).

in the 37 Squadron ORB, but its Shackletons were reported as searching for Iranian-registered ships suspected of transporting smuggled arms to the country.

On 28 August OC 1417 Flight, Flight Lieutenant Roger Pyrah, handed over command to Flight Lieutenant Ralph Chambers, one of many Canadians to join the RAF in the 1950s, and returned to a posting with the Central Flying School at Little Rissington.

Having read Wilfred Thesiger's book on the Empty Quarter, Flight Lieutenant Chambers bestowed the name THESIGER on the operation and, using his knowledge of the area, decided to fly up to Masirah to join his two colleagues. He wrote of the operation:

Because the maps of the area were out of date and virtually blank pieces of paper, we devised a plan to make our own maps. We flew a triangular route each day looking for rebels. Every time we passed a feature such as a track, house or oil well, we marked it on the map. The next mission we moved the starting track of our triangle by 5°. After several trips we built up a very good working map of the target zone. It was kept secret at the time because, although we were looking for dissidents, we were a long way into the neighbouring country – fortunately we could not be seen.

Two views of Ralph Chambers as he flies his personalised 1417 Flight FR.10, XE589, creating a shadow over a sea of sand (above) and high above the Aden hinterland (below) (both, Ralph Chambers).

Ambush at Jebel Khuder

A notable increase in bands of dissidents moving around the up-country areas of Aden was a sign of impending trouble. The month of September began to the sound of the 43 Squadron standby pair being scrambled in response to urgent calls from 4th and 5th Battalions FRA, whose troops had been ambushed and were under fire from dissident groups ranged along Jebel Khuder. With 5th Battalion FRA pinned-down, the two Hunters expended short bursts of fire at the rebel positions to keep their heads down until more 43 Squadron aircraft arrived on scene. Undaunted by cannon shells exploding all around them, the dissidents continued to rain down fire on the besieged troops. With the situation reaching deadlock, five 8 Squadron Hunters, led by OC Strike Wing, Wing Commander Chandler, arrived to launch a series of strikes against the rebels. The airborne onslaught was hammered home by eight 8 Squadron aircraft later in the evening.

The action resumed at first light on the following morning to the reverberation of 30mm cannon fire from pairs of 8 Squadron aircraft echoing along the wadi. This was a sufficient distraction to enable 5th Battalion FRA to withdraw its troops and evacuate a number of casualties by helicopter. At least five dissidents, including a prominent tribal leader, were reported as being killed and three more wounded.

The wrath of the Shackleton!

Under the leadership of Ahmed Bubakr Bin Saridm, a notorious troublemaker and recent arrival in Aden from the Yemen, the Bubakir Bin Farid dissident group drew attention to itself with attacks on twenty-two houses as they made their way along Wadi Hatib. To dissuade local inhabitants from supporting these terrorist thugs, the opportunity was taken to make further use of the offensive capability of the Shackleton. Two 37 Squadron MR.2s were despatched to the area and dropped thirty 1,000lb bombs on the dissidents. The attack was followed up with a firepower demonstration by six 43 Squadron aircraft. The dissidents melted into the hinterland and peace returned to the area. There was no let up in the pace of 'routine' operational flying, however. In an attempt to destroy a pair of houses belonging to a well-known collaborator in the Wadi Maraban, near Wi'lan, fifteen RP and cannon strikes were performed by 8 Squadron aircraft over a three-hour spell on the afternoon of 3 September.

When a party of British MPs on an information gathering exercise paid a visit to Strike Wing, their arrival was captured on camera by a low-flying FR.10 of 1417 Flight. Nine minutes and thirty-five seconds later, the print was handed to the distinguished group – a new record time that would have been bettered had the nosecone not proved difficult to remove.

On the morning of the 11th a reported sighting of Bin Saridm's rebel group in the Ruseis area was responded to by a pair of 43 Squadron Hunters. A thorough search

The offset gunsight on the FR.10 is clearly visible in this view taken by Ken Simpson as his aircraft rolled down the runway at Masirah (Ken Simpson).

over the area proved fruitless but, later in the day, a second pair of aircraft spotted three of his armed rebel groups making their way across the rocky escarpment. By the time they completed an orbit for a second run, however, the rebels had concealed themselves.

Increasing demand for its intelligence-gathering capabilities required forty-three sorties to be flown by 1417 Flight during September, twenty-seven of them in support of the operation over Oman. Once this had concluded, the FR.10s were flown back to Khormaksar on 11 September by Flight Lieutenants Chambers (XE589) and Johns (XF436), together with Flight Lieutenant Simpson (XF460) who had joined them at Salalah, leaving the 208 Squadron FGA.9s to return to Muharraq in their own time. In the WAP, meanwhile, despite the absence of three aircraft, the flight had been tasked to locate buildings being used to hide dissident sympathisers and their arms caches. The endeavour was hampered somewhat by an inability or, more plausibly, the unwillingness of Arab 'informants' to identify suspect buildings from aerial photographs. By the time the targets had been verified, the rebels had moved on and taken their arms with them.

As the month progressed, the FR.10 pilots were briefed to undertake further Operation RANJI sorties, with a specific objective of investigating and recording suspicious shipping activities within the three-mile limit of the coast line. This

37 Squadron Shackleton MR.2 WR962-A on standby at Khormaksar alongside 38 Squadron MR.2 WR967-Z undergoing an engine change during an IST detachment from Luqa (author).

contributed to the number of operational sorties flown by the flight reaching its highest monthly figure since the Radfan campaign of the previous year.

Visit to Iran

On 13 September three 208 Squadron FGA.9s and the T.7 departed Muharraq and headed north on a liaison visit to the Imperial Iranian Air Force Base at Vahdati. While flying on a low-level sortie with an Iranian pilot in the right-hand seat, the T.7 suffered a bird strike, rendering it unserviceable for the rest of the visit. The FGA.9s meanwhile were engaged in low-level cross-country details accompanied by Iranian F.86 Sabres. The detachment concluded on the 18th when two Mark 9s and a patched up T.7 returned to Muharraq, leaving one aircraft unserviceable at Vahdati. It was not retrieved until 4 November.

Aden constitution suspended

The rapidly deteriorating security situation in Aden State, encouraged by the open connivance of terrorist-supporting members of the Aden government and the NLF, would no longer be tolerated. Following the murders of a British police inspector in August and the British speaker of the Legislative Council a month later, the British

1417 Flight pilots proudly sit for the camera in front of one of their aircraft at Khormaksar - FR.10 XE599-DW. l to r; Frank Grimshaw, Roger Neal, Ralph Chambers, Derek Whitman, Richard Johns and Ken Simpson (Ken Simpson).

government decided to suspend the Aden constitution on 25 September 1965 and impose direct rule. A night-time curfew came into force between the hours of 18:00 and 05:00, all British service schools were closed, bars, restaurants and cinemas placed out-of-bounds, and servicemen and their families ordered to stay in their homes at weekends. The governance of Aden was placed in the reliable hands of Sir Richard Turnbull, the High Commissioner, as the security forces patrolled the streets in case of a reaction. Once again, Aden found itself on the front pages of the world's press.

Squadron Leader H. Davidson arrived at Khormaksar on 1 October and assumed command of 43 Squadron, leaving Squadron Leader Champniss to depart two days later to take up a post as Flight Safety Officer, Maintenance Command.

Disturbances in up-country areas slowly began to ebb in both severity and frequency, requiring just four operational sorties to be flown by 8 Squadron in October. Two were to provide top cover following a disturbance at Am Shudayf, close to the Yemen border, and a further two as top cover for a military convoy travelling from Dhala to Habilayn. Most of the remaining flying time was directed at raising the standard of the squadron's rocket-firing capability. Several days were spent attacking targets on the Khormaksar range and splash targets under tow by Royal Navy ships in the Gulf of Aden.

'Muscat invasion'

The reduction in up-country operations enabled the three Hunter units to participate in an exercise that had been deferred for some time. Its objective was to simulate a situation in which relations with a foreign power had deteriorated to a level that had led to the invasion of Muscat. The two Hunter squadrons took it in turn to fly up to Masirah for the two-week exercise, accompanied by a 1417 Flight FR.10 and one of its pilots. No. 8 Squadron led the way and when 'war' was declared, simulated strikes were carried out on airstrips, forts, wells and lines of communication.

Down at Khormaksar, meanwhile, 43 Squadron was busily engaged in an exercise with aircraft from HMS *Eagle* as it steamed through the Gulf of Aden. Codenamed LITTLE EASTERN, four Hunters were stood at five-minute readiness and scrambled by Champion radar to intercept a mass raid by Sea Vixens and Buccaneers as soon as they appeared on its displays. In a role reversal, the squadron was then briefed to evade naval aircraft waiting to intercept them and perform simulated strikes against the carrier by firing at splash targets.

As soon as the Muscat exercise finished, 8 Squadron returned to Khormaksar, relieving 43 Squadron for its turn to move up to Masirah and participate in the war games.

While the Hunters were otherwise engaged, 37 Squadron was detailed to destroy a dissident hideout which had been discovered at the junction formed by the Wadis Bana and Taym. Two Shackletons were despatched to drop full loads of 1,000lb bombs

Converted from an F.4 single-seater fighter, 1417 Flight T.7 XF321-TZ was photographed in the markings of all three Strike Wing Hunter units while on detachment to Masirah (Aviation Bookshop).

(above) To make an assessment as to whether it would be possible to operate Hunters out of Beihan, several 43 Squadron pilots were flown up to the airstrip in 84 Squadron Beverley XB266 (Roger Wilkins). No reason was given for the 8 Squadron pilots (below) who were let loose on this isolated desert strip having been flown up in the Comms Flight Dakota KN452 (Robin Morrell).

onto the target. Although the building and much of the surrounding area was razed to the ground, there were no reports of casualties.

With several of its pilots assigned to various detachments, 1417 Flight found itself with just two pilots at Khormaksar to fulfil the broad range of intelligence-gathering duties and any unforeseen challenges that would come their way. This unsatisfactory situation continued until 22 November when all six aircrew were back in Aden. Interestingly, the highest number of operational sorties recorded by the wing for the month was achieved by 1417 Flight. Fourteen were standard Operation RANJI sorties and another three in search for a 105mm gun which had been stolen to the west of Beihan. It was never found! Post-strike photographs were also taken of the damage inflicted by the Shackletons on the hideout in Wadi Bana. The final FR sortie consisted of taking a series of photographs of Sheikh Othman for an impending internal security cordon and search operation by ground forces.

As a result of continual harassment of dissident tribesmen by the FRA, hostile activities by the rebels slowly began to diminish, allowing an uneasy peace to linger through much of November. Nevertheless, seven pairs of 8 Squadron aircraft were needed to perform flagwaves in the Ruseis, Al Mithaf (twice), Jebels Khuder and Harrier, and in the Wadi Dulay'ah and Wilan areas, to deter dissidents from re-igniting inter-tribal warfare as they intensified their recruitment efforts.

Otherwise the rest of November's flying was devoted to simulated strikes, range work and practice interceptions. Several of these were combined to take advantage of the modified 230-gallon tank then coming into service. This was fitted with an internal baffle designed to prevent fuel from a partially empty tank from flowing from the back to the front during a dive, thereby reducing the chance of a tank breaking away from the pylon during the pullout. Practice interception sorties were also flown to assist technicians engaged in the re-calibration of Champion Radar.

26 Squadron disbands

The Belvedere's ability to lift heavy guns and equipment to high mountain peaks, move troops into inaccessible areas and transport casualties back to the hospital at Steamer Point had proved invaluable during the Radfan campaign and many subsequent operations. Nonetheless, the Napier Gazelle engine's susceptibility to damage through the ingestion of sand led to the decision to disband 26 Squadron, a disbandment parade being held on 30 November. The heavylift commitment was taken over by the Wessex helicopters of 78 Squadron on the following day. The Belvederes were re-allocated to 66 Squadron and shipped out to the more amenable Far Eastern climate on the deck of HMS *Albion*.

'Normal service resumed in December!' In response to an urgent call for air support from 45 Commando, a pair of Hunters was scrambled to an area to the east of Habilayn. As they were stood down shortly after arriving, the pilots agreed to exercise the skills of the FAC with a practice session on directing attacking aircraft onto a target. The tempo livened up a few days later when the first of forty-two operational sorties, evenly divided between the two squadrons, was flown in support of joint operations by troops from 5th Battalion FRA and 45 Commando in the Dhala, Habilayn and Wadi Taym areas.

Knocking out arms dump

When reports were received that a house in the Yaffa was being used to stash arms, 1417 Flight flew nine sorties to photograph other suspect buildings in the area. When a thorough study of the images, taken by Flight Lieutenants Chambers (XE589) and Johns (XE599), confirmed the identity of this specific house, the pair were despatched to mark the target for a five-ship rocket-strike led by OC 8 Squadron, Squadron Leader Melaniphy (XE649), accompanied by Flight Lieutenants Taylor (XF456), Etheridge (XE617) and Kemball (XE530) and Flying Officer Wharmby (XE546) of 43 Squadron.

In responding to reports that dissident elements had been seen in the Ataq area, the FRA despatched a convoy of troops to round them up. Top cover and reconnaissance reports on the convoy's progress between Mukeiras and Ataq were fed back to Khormaksar by Strike Wing FGA.9s on 20 December. The troops were able to make use of their Land Rovers on the first leg from Mukeiras, but forced to abandon them at Am Surrah due to the perilous terrain and continue on foot as far as Aqabat Talh. Sufficiently rested, they were airlifted to the top of Jebel Fahman by Wessex helicopters on the morning of the 23rd under the protection of a pair of Hunters flying top cover.

As the season of goodwill approached, Strike Wing Hunters flew an eight-ship formation in the form of a letter 'J' to mark the impending departure of the AOC, Air Vice-Marshal Johnnie Johnson DSO DFC. Another eight Hunters were despatched to drop Christmas cards on Army garrisons at Beihan, Mukeiras, Dhala, Ataq, Beihan, Habilayn and Al Milah and perform low-level flypasts over other units encamped in the Wadi Taym area.

The increase in operational flying in December may have gone some way to raising adrenaline levels, but the usual round of intensive partying was strictly limited, due to curfew regulations and sensible advice to remain clearheaded, alert and on guard at all times. The security warnings were heeded; none of the fourteen serious incidents reported over the standdown period involved service personnel.

No sooner had the routine returned to normal than a five-ship strike was called for on a target near Wi'lan. On the final day of the year a further four Hunters were briefed to come to the aid of a 45 Commando patrol that had come under fire in mountainous terrain. Although no rebel movements were detected, the pilots decided to expend their ammunition along a ridge from which the firing had been reported. The loss of one of its number and a further three reported as being wounded was enough to dissuade the rest of the rebel band from continuing with their attacks.

SNEB and Napalm

In his closing comments in the December 1965 ORB, OC 208 Squadron, Wing Commander Rhodes, demonstrated his frustration with the SNEB situation with the following entry:

> Progress is still painfully slow regarding the two weapons for which we are scheduled to have a capability – SNEB and Napalm. Indeed we already have a Napalm capability (from the inboard pylons only) but no sign of our being allowed to practise it. As for SNEB, although there are fifty-five operational launchers at Muharraq, the aircraft are only now starting to be modified to carry them and nothing has been received in the way of flying clearance and training policy.

It would be another year before the squadron was in a position to perform its first proper firing of the weapon.

The year had seen a complex set of challenges facing British forces in Aden, not only in the Radfan but in other up-country areas too. The dangerously deteriorating security situation in Aden State remained a serious cause for concern, although recently erected security fencing around the airfield boundary offered a degree of protection for aircraft and personnel. Similar protection could not be afforded to service families living in hirings in the external community, however, leaving them at increasing risk from terrorist activity. It was against this frightening scenario that British rule would be severely tested in the year ahead.

Chapter 11

1966 – Secret Missions

Fuel Strike

The season of goodwill faded quickly for no sooner had the New Year begun than petroleum workers walked out on a strike that would last a month. Although deliveries to the airfield were severely curtailed, a ration of 20,000 gallons per day was delivered for Strike Wing directly from the refinery at Little Aden.

No. 8 Squadron Hunters were soon back in action. Sixteen operational sorties were flown in January, eight on a strike against a suspected arms cache in Wadi Yahar, six flagwaves and an armed recce in the Duhlman area in conjunction with an FRA exercise. The flagwaves were flown in the Al Khabr and Hada areas in an attempt to separate the Ahl Majawwar and Ahl Fatima tribes, who were engaged in open warfare. A follow-up flagwave by a pair of 43 Squadron aircraft was sufficient to persuade both sides to call a halt to the fighting and to release the hostages they had taken into the capable hands of the political officer.

On 15 January 1417 Flight was detailed to despatch an FR.10 on a search for a dissident arms dump, hidden somewhere in Wadi Yahar. Having successfully located it, Flight Lieutenant Grimshaw (XF436) was briefed to mark the target for a strike by eight FGA.9s from 8 Squadron later that day.

Marking targets

Target marking was normally carried out by 1417 Flight pilots as they would have taken pre-strike photographs and knew exactly which building, patch of mountainside or cave was to be attacked. HE ammunition was used for the purpose as bright flashes from the exploding shells could be seen by the FGA.9 pilots from a distance. Ideally, the FR.10 led the first FGA.9 in the dive with the FR.10 some 800 yards ahead. Having fired a short burst of cannonfire onto the target, the FR.10 would pull away, leaving the FGA.9s to fire their guns and rockets. Once the attack was over, the FR.10 would make a final run over the target to capture post-strike photographs.

On one specific occasion the pre-strike briefing emphasised that the targeted house alone should be struck and there should be no collateral damage – especially to a nearby mosque. Target marking went as planned but at some point during the rocket attack both the mosque and its minaret were hit and destroyed. The FR.10 pilot decided that he would take the post-strike photographs at an angle that excluded the ruined mosque from the frame. OC Strike Wing was not fooled or best pleased when he discovered what had occurred.

The knack of taking good photographs

The technique required to capture good quality photographs of prospective targets for use by the ground-attack squadrons required a high degree of precision flying by the FR.10 pilots, as outlined in this résumé by Ken Simpson:

> The aiming of the sideways facing Vinten cameras in the FR.10 was basically all down to experience. When to press the shutter button was not a big problem because the film was fed at a rate of 100 frames per second. In practice, the rule was to use a minimum amount of film to save processing time and the time Photographic Interpreters spent looking for the target. Lining the aircraft up was down to practice and experience. There were other considerations. Into the shade or down from the sun, for example! Rebels liked sitting in the shade so that was the pilot's preference. When photographing ships, they tried to take oblique corner to corner shots. When marking targets, at least one or two close-ups of the target would be taken plus one or two at the range a rocket would be fired (800 yards), and one more at the turn in point.

Taking advantage of the presence in Aden waters of HMS *Eagle*, an interesting series of naval co-operation exercises was conducted during January. Hunters from both squadrons were pitted against Sea Vixen FAW.2s in two-*vs*-two combat on the 19th and splash targets under tow by the carrier were fired at on the 28th. The combat sorties were of particular value as they gave the Hunter pilots the rare opportunity to test their skills against missile-equipped aircraft. Cine 'kills' were registered followed by a liquid debrief on board the carrier.

The C.-in-C., Admiral Sir Michael Le Fanu, paid a visit to Strike Wing on 27 January and was given a ride in a 1417 Flight Hunter T.7, flown by OC Strike Wing, Wing Commander Chandler. Flight Lieutenant Chambers accompanied the T.7 in 'his' FR.10 to take photographs of the aircraft as the pair flew over the Aden hinterland. A set of prints was presented to the Admiral at the conclusion of his visit.

Fuel supplies returned to normal at the beginning of February, enabling Strike Wing to resume its operational and training commitments. An unusually high movement of 1417 Flight pilots on detachments to Masirah and Bahrain was compounded by the loan of Flight Lieutenant Simpson to RAF Eastleigh for three weeks, as Operations Officer for an airlift of fuel into Embakasi, following the fuel embargo imposed by Ian Smith's regime in Rhodesia.

In spite of the destruction inflicted in Wadi Yahar in January, six 8 Squadron aircraft were despatched to destroy a second arms dump discovered in the area.

Captured on film by the nose camera of Ken Simpson's FR.10 as it steamed at speed through the Gulf of Aden, the deck of HMS Hermes is partially screened by the Sea Vixen FAW.2s and Buccaneer S.2s of 893 and 809 Squadrons respectively (Ken Simpson).

No. 43 Squadron was the busier of the two Hunter units in February, however. On the 1st two aircraft performed a flagwave over Am Wuthia to instil a sense of calm during elections in the State of Dathina. On the following day two aircraft responded to an urgent call from the SAS who had cornered twelve heavily-armed dissidents in the Bilah area during an operation codenamed FLASHBULB FOXTROT. Three dissidents were killed and four wounded in the ensuing skirmish. In spite of further flagwaves being flown over the area, the Dathina elections had to be cancelled because of the continual unrest.

When alerts were triggered by Champion Radar on the 7th and 8th two air defence scrambles were flown by pairs of 43 Squadron Hunters in the direction of Beihan and Mukeiras respectively. Both were called off when the aircraft were identified as RAF Canberras photographing the local topography! No. 43 Squadron was also detailed to carry out flagwaves over Wadis Rihab and Behab following reports that armed dissidents were using them to access the Upper Aulaqi Sheikdom. The sight of the low-flying Hunters was sufficient to persuade the Illahi tribesmen that it was in their best interests to prohibit the use of these routes to dissidents.

Towards the end of 1965 a known dissident troublemaker named Salin Thabit Harbi Al Yahari, blew up a house belonging to the Sheikh of Yahari in a blatant act of terrorism. As he continued to cause trouble, Flight Lieutenant Grimshaw (XF460) was briefed to fly up to Wadi Yahar on 12 January to photograph a pair of houses in the village of Lakamit Al Harbi that were owned by Al Yahari. Two days later, and by way of retribution, Wing Commander Chandler (XJ646), accompanied by Squadron Leader Davidson (XE617), Flight Lieutenant Taylor (XE649) and Flying Officer White (XE530), led a four-ship strike on a mission to demolish both buildings. The final operational sorties of the month comprised four 43 Squadron aircraft flying top cover for an SAS patrol as it tightened a cordon around a village to the west of Al Milah in readiness for a search operation.

Of the thirty-seven operational sorties flown by 1417 Flight during the month, fourteen were by the two pilots on detachment at Masirah. A security blackout prevented details of these operations being reported in the ORB but they were probably Operation THESIGER related.

This spectacular air-to-air shot of 1417 Flight FR.10 XF436-PN skimming a wall of rock puts into perspective the skills required to fly the Hunter at high speed through the hazardous mountains of the Aden hinterland (Ken Simpson).

Independence for South Arabia!

On 22 February 1966 the British government published a Defence white paper which confirmed plans for the South Arabian Federation, of which Aden State was a signatory, to become an independent nation in 1968, and that British forces would be withdrawn from Aden by the same date. This came as a profound shock to Federal leaders who had been led to believe that Britain would retain a military garrison in Aden for the foreseeable future. As the foundations of the Federation had been built on an understanding that it would continue to be supported by Britain beyond independence, they had good reason to be fearful. In the Yemen, Egyptian puppetmasters declared the time had come to liberate 'South Yemen' using all the means at their disposal. Shorthand for terrorism!

Final preparations for the return of the ruler of the Upper Aulaqi Sultanate in March were accompanied by the sound of Strike Wing Hunters performing flagwaves in the skies above and a show of force by the FRA on the ground. To discourage any thoughts of a return to dissident activity following the demolition of the rebel leader's house at Lakamit the previous month, two Hunters, flown by Flight Lieutenant Pollock (XE689) and Flying Officer Lawton (XE649), were despatched on the 5th to perform flagwaves over the village. Nothing untoward was sighted by the pilots, although both aircraft sustained damage from small-arms fire; one bullet striking the leading edge of the tailplane on one and the second entering the leading edge of a wing on the other. A further pair of aircraft was despatched to the same location two days later, under orders only to open fire if fired upon.

On the ground the final phase of a 2nd Battalion FRA operation, codenamed GHIA, involved setting up a base camp prior to carrying out a sweep of Wadis Tiban and Hatib to flush out dissidents who may have been lurking in the area. Two FGA.9s were despatched to carry out a flagwave over the wadis as the operation commenced on 14 March. As a further deterrent, Squadron Leader Davidson led a flight of four 43 Squadron aircraft on a high-speed, low-level run through Wadi Hatib later in the day.

Two more sorties were flown by 43 squadron on the 16th to find a Hadramaut Bedouin Legion (HBL) Ferret scout car which had disappeared during a road test in the region of Husn Al Abr, thirty miles from the Yemen border. Reports that the car had been ambushed but had managed to escape in a westerly direction could not be corroborated.

Up in the Gulf, 208 Squadron flew eleven sorties on a tactical recce over the Dhofar province in search of a convoy of six trucks believed to be carrying dissident fighters towards Salalah. Pilots were briefed to commence their search forty miles north of RAF Salalah at midday and check the four routes leading to Dauka through Wadis Atina, Ghudun, Haluf and Duka. Unfortunately, there is no mention of the outcome in the ORB.

Six Operation Thesiger pilots taking a break at Masirah are, Terry Thornton (208 Sqn), Andy Maitland (208 Sqn), Dick Johns (1417 Flt), Stuart Eastwood (208 Sqn), Peter Day (208 Sqn) and Ken Simpson (1417 Flt) (Ken Simpson).

208 Squadron FGA.9 XK151 was captured by the port camera of Ken Simpson's 1417 Flight FR.10 during an Operation Thesiger search for a convoy of dissident trucks smuggling arms through the Dhofar region of Oman (Ken Simpson).

Back to Oman

Due to the high number of sorties being flown by 1417 Flight's FR.10s, its target for March was increased to 120 hours. Of the forty-three operational sorties flown, twenty-seven were over Dhofar State in support of another round of Operation THESIGER. The security clampdown at the time barred any relevance to THESIGER being entered in the ORB but one of the 208 Squadron pilots involved in the operation, Flight Lieutenant Doug Marr, has written a review.

At the end of February 1966 208 Squadron was once again at RAF Sharjah for its routine APC when, out of the blue, we received tasking by HQ RAFPG to mount an immediate operational deployment to Masirah for 'reconnaissance duties'. Our boss, Sqn Ldr Chaplin, briefed the Squadron, sending half back to our base at Muharraq to get ready for deployment before leading the first detachment of six aircraft, each fitted with 2 x 230 gallon and 2 x 100 gallon drop tanks to ensure maximum endurance, straight from Sharjah to Masirah. Here, he was joined by two Hunter FR.10s from 1417 Flight. According to intelligence sources a group of six trucks carrying rebels and armament were believed to have left the Gulf area en route for the Dhofar province, south-west of Oman and north of Salalah. It was suspected that they would follow the 'route of wells' across the inhospitable Empty Quarter.

Rebel fighters had been a threat to the Sultan of Oman and to the airfield at Salalah which was a staging post and storage facility for the RAF and whose security was of concern. The task was to fly a programme of high–low–high reconnaissance sorties over the desert in the hope of intercepting the convoy before it reached its destination.

For those of us who flew our aircraft back to Muharraq it came as a shock to learn that the Central Flying School (CFS) Standardisation Team had arrived to check out our pilots to make sure our handling and knowledge of drills and procedures was up to scratch. What timing! So I and others dutifully flew our standardisation sorties before setting off in our jets for Masirah. I arrived on 5 March and went straight into a briefing for my first operational sortie. The format was for a formation of three aircraft to climb to height, let down to low level north-west of Thumrait (Midway) airfield, and then search for dissidents along routes to Dhuqu, Mugshin and Haima before climbing back up to height to return to Masirah. The low-level part of the sortie was led by one of the recce experts on 1417 Flight, these being Flt Lts Dick Johns and Ken Simpson, whose expertise at identifying vehicle tracks and their freshness was part of their specialisation. When at low level they would fly at fifty feet where the 208 Squadron Hunters would fly as an escort pair at 250 feet scanning a wider area. This inevitably led to questioning about what we did if we came across the rebels. On asking if they were armed it was suggested that they might have Vickers guns mounted on the back of their vehicles. We were to be armed with full Aden gun-packs but 'without the fuses in'! Opening fire could only be approved by higher authority which was no use if the fuses were out!

During this two-week operational deployment a total of fifty-six operational sorties were flown to the enormous credit of our hardworking groundcrew. Each sortie lasted two hours on average, with almost all operational pilots gaining experience in the area – seen as some of the most inhospitable in the world. Though we did not find the convoy we learned that ground forces did, so perhaps we helped. In fact it was hard to imagine anyone in their right mind wanting to drive across the Empty Quarter, which invited the question 'if you were determined to carry out such a mission wouldn't you want to do it at night when it was cooler?' And from our point of view it might have made identifying a convoy easier especially if they had their lights on. Night flying at low-level over an empty desert was, however, not seen as a sensible option.

At Khormaksar, 1417 Flight's regular quota of Operation RANJI sorties were interspersed with searches for missing vehicles. One aircraft despatched to find a convoy of Royal Engineers' trucks was recalled when they were discovered safe and sound back in Normandy Lines, Aden. Flight Lieutenants Chambers and Simpson located a missing bulldozer in the Shabyah area but the reason for it being in such a desolate location was cause for much speculation.

SNEB trial

No sooner had 208 Squadron returned to Muharraq than it was tasked to carry out the much anticipated SNEB rocket trial that would lead to the introduction of the weapon into RAF Hunter service. Although there were fifty-five operational launchers on the station, there was no flying clearance or training policy. The operational pod carried nineteen rockets which could be released as a salvo. It had a frangible nose cone which shattered as the first rocket of the salvo left the pod. Much time had been lost due to the slow pace in which the squadron's aircraft were modified but, on 4 April, Flight Lieutenant Marr flew as the chase aircraft for a Hunter carrying a SNEB pod to observe what happened to the nose cone in normal flight:

As speed built up it shattered. So the operational nose cone had to be strengthened. In the meantime we needed to train using this weapon one-at-a-time and this required a training launcher which carried fewer rockets, did not need a nose cone and was reusable. Suffice to say that it wasn't until December 1966 that we finally started firing SNEB rockets at targets on Rashid range near Sharjah. And what a fabulous weapon it turned out to be. We could fire it using either

208 Squadron FGA.9 XJ687 parked alongside a defective 43 Squadron aircraft on the pan at Sharjah. Of interest is the SNEB pod mounted on the outer pylon and the revised squadron markings on the fuselage (author's collection).

the gyro gunsight or a fixed sight with far greater accuracy than before, and this weapon was to give the ground attack squadrons the teeth they deserved in the anti–armour land battle.

Caught in the act!

One of 1417 Flight's more titillating operations required a number of sorties to be flown in the search for a missing HBL scout car and its crew. A pair of FR.10s despatched to the sandy wastes of the Sabatayn area, their last reported location, proved fruitless. The next day, however, a discovery of a more intimate nature resolved the mystery! Not only does the desert burn hot but so do passions of a more earthly nature. A signal received at Strike Wing HQ stated that:

Information suggests that the car's commander was caught with his trousers down while 'in flagrante' with a local call girl by the girl's brother, Mohamed Al Ker, who then killed the commander, stole the vehicle and made good his escape, while the car's driver remained hidden behind a bush to await his turn with the girl.

No. 1417 Flight were pleased to include an addendum in the ORB to the effect 'that the HBL liked to observe the niceties of rank'!

The variety of operational sorties undertaken by 1417 Flight eased a little during April, allowing it to concentrate on routine training and aircraft maintenance. Only seventeen operational sorties were flown during the month, including two on RANJI, two to photograph various forts and a further two on post-strike photo-recces over dissident held territory.

For much of April 43 Squadron placed a number of aircraft on standby in readiness to support an SAS troop operating in the Al Anad area. After fifty dissidents had been spotted two miles to the north of the junction formed by Wadis Taym and Bana on the evening of the 3rd, two aircraft were despatched at daybreak on the 4th. Their brief was to fire on the hill on which they had been seen as Wing Commander Chandler observed from an accompanying T.7. Both aircraft fired off their full ammunition loads, but no dissidents were sighted.

Hotter then normal

On the next day, 5 April, exactly a month after his aircraft received a bullet through the tailplane, 43 Squadron pilot Flight Lieutenant Pollock was detailed to carry out an air test on FGA.9 XE609, following rectification and engine maintenance in ASF. Very soon after getting airborne, fire broke-out in the rear fuselage but he was

The EO and airmen inspect the damage sustained by 8/43 Squadron FGA.9 XE609 following a fire that ignited in the rear section of the aircraft shortly after take-off from Khormaksar on 5 April 1966 (Alan Pollock).

The town of Shibam in the Eastern Aden Protectorate is the location (above) for this view of an FR.10 on a long-range photo recce (Ken Simpson). 8/43 Squadron FGA.9 XJ680 pictured (below) on the pan at Masirah (Aviation Bookshop).

able to keep the aircraft airworthy long enough to complete a circuit and make an emergency landing at Khormaksar where the Fire Section was ready to extinguish the blaze. The damage was initially assessed as Category 4 but a more thorough inspection revealed that the damage was more severe and the aircraft was stuck off charge.

Fifty Years Young!

As part of the lead up to the 43 Squadron 50th anniversary celebrations, simulated strikes, combat and close formation sorties provided an excellent platform for the inevitable adrenaline rush. Among the 250 guests who attended a squadron cocktail party on 14 April were His Excellency the High Commissioner, Sir Richard Turnbull and Lady Turnbull. Squadron Leader Davidson and Flying Officers White and Lawton made their broadcasting debuts by enthusing on the squadron's fifty years of service over British Forces Broadcasting Service (BFBS) airwaves. Flying Officers Hughes-Lewis, Screen and Willman participated in a 'Brains of Aden' quiz but were eliminated in round one. Too many cocktails perhaps!

On the day itself, 15 April, three runs were made across the airfield: the first, a figure '43' formation flown with eighteen aircraft included a pair of 1417 Flight FR.10s. Further flybys consisted of a diamond sixteen followed by four boxes of four. Four FR.10s then joined up for the finale, an impressive twenty-ship run-in and break. The 1417 Flight ORB noted that 'It is not often that 1417 have the chance to fly as numbers 17 to 20 in a mass formation'.

Supporting the SAS

May was a more active month with Strike Wing Hunters more heavily involved in providing air cover for operations being carried out by the SAS. A firepower demonstration, followed by a strike on a house and several flagwaves, were also flown to discourage inter-tribal disputes from escalating into open warfare.

Two strikes performed on the 4th by 8 Squadron aircraft were to relieve an SAS patrol tasked with hunting down a dissident group using Wadi Tiban, part of a ground operation code-named STARVIEWER. Subsequent reports confirmed that five of the sixteen dissidents were killed and three injured. Top cover was provided by pairs of 43 Squadron aircraft which completed their mission with a low-level sweep through the wadi in search of rebels who escaped the skirmish. Although none were spotted, a pair remained on station until it became too dark.

When tribesmen living in an area to the north of Nisab in Wadi Markham were found to be allowing smuggled arms to pass through their territory, an FRA patrol was despatched to remind them of their treaty obligations. On being blocked from entering the wadi, it became clear that, due to an administrative error, the tribes were not signatories to the Federation Treaty. A flagwave flown over the miscreants on the afternoon of the 4th by eight 8 Squadron Hunters persuaded them that a more co-operative attitude was in their best interests.

Four days later, two 43 Squadron aircraft were despatched to perform a flagwave over Yib'ath, close to the Eastern Protectorate border, where the Wahidi and Quati tribes had resorted to shooting at each other in a dispute over water and grazing rights. Yib'ath formed the dividing line between them. In an attempt to prevent the dispute from escalating, a pair of 8 Squadron aircraft was despatched on the 10th to perform a flagwave along the line. As the tribesmen ignored the threat and continued to fire at each other, 43 Squadron carried out a further flagwave two days later which appeared to have the desired effect.

Early May saw the departure for the UK of Deputy OC Strike Wing, Squadron Leader Bowie, and a welcome return to Aden of Squadron Leader Trowern, an experienced FR pilot who had previously flown Meteor FR.9s with the APRF and Hunter FR.10s with 8 Squadron between 1959 and 1961.

'Vulture Strike'

Acknowledged perils of flying at high speed and at low level through steep-sided wadis of the Aden hinterland included the shaking of hands with a mountain and being at the focal point of a rebel gunsight. The explosive impact on Flight Lieutenant Ken Simpson's Hunter on 9 May was something else. A huge bird, believed to be a griffin vulture (or 'shitehawk' as this ugly creature was more commonly known), tore into his FR.10 (XE589) while flying at high speed over Lawdar. Considerable damage was sustained in the area around the starboard air intake as the massive bird tore its way through the upper skin of the wing. A large part of the bird was ingested by the engine, causing it to surge but as the rpm stabilised in mid range, the pilot left the throttle where it was. Having jettisoned the four underwing tanks, he succeeded in nursing the aircraft up to 10,000 feet on a heading back to Khormaksar and an emergency landing. Initially assessed as Category 4, subsequent inspection revealed that the aircraft was too badly damaged for it to be repaired on site and was shipped back to the UK for rebuilding by Hawker Siddeley.

The air defence role for 1417 Flight had been given a lower priority over the previous few months, due to the high volume of reconnaissance and searches needed to obtain intelligence on dissident activity. Fortunately, the three remaining FR.10s retained high serviceability levels and, as at least two were available most mornings, long-range recces were flown as a pair.

Reports of two houses being used to store military supplies in the village of Al Mazabah triggered a combined action by 8 and 43 Squadrons. One house belonged to the leader of the Lower Yaffa Front, Ali Melholhar, and the other by his second-in-command, Aquil Quasim Rageh. Two nearby caves were also known to contain large caches of arms. On 11 May seven strikes were targeted at both the buildings and the caves. A post-strike summary reported the attack as being very effective, both houses

The full extent of the damage sustained by 1417 Flight FR.10 XE589 from the bird-strike on 9 May 1966 is not evident in this view but the size of the Griffin Vulture can be gauged by the dent in the Sabrina (Ken Simpson).

sustaining severe damage as had the caves, the roof of one collapsing when the hidden ammunition exploded. No casualties were reported and no other buildings damaged. A herd of cows, however, was reduced in number by four.

To signal the end of a ground operation codenamed VONIP, a firepower demonstration was carried out in the Jebel Maqbill area, twenty miles south-west of Meifa, on the 14th. The operation had been contrived for the FRA to present a show of strength to coincide with the return of the local sultan. The proceedings were completed when five aircraft from 8 Squadron and a pair of 43 Squadron aircraft fired off their Aden cannon into a nearby hillside and performed a formation flypast over the troops and inhabitants of the village.

In line with the ever deteriorating unrest in the Protectorates, the frequency of Strike Wing flagwaves began to intensify. Wadi Ruqub was the location on 18 May for one such mission, followed a day later by another at Khawrah to dissuade 'contestants' from intensifying their inter-tribal dispute. A further two flagwaves were called for

Bearing the initials for Richard Johns, 1417 Flight FR.10 XE614 hugs the mountainside during a recce sortie through the Radfan mountains (Ken Simpson).

on the 26th at Khora and north-east of Shabwah on the 27th, where a large mob was threatening to attack a fort at Bir Asakit.

The accent on training was for simulated strikes by formations of four aircraft while being harassed by a pair posing as an enemy, and on two-on-two combat on the flight back to base. Low-level cine-weave was incorporated into the simulated strike phase. Five days were also devoted to improving the skill levels of FACs, the emphasis being on live firing at the Danaba Basin, Ballbutton and Am Riga ranges.

One of the more unusual requests for photographic intelligence came when Flight Lieutenant Grimshaw was chosen to take vertical and oblique photographs of the oil tank farm at Little Aden to assist the authorities with their security planning.

With the loss of XE589 through the bird strike, the FR.10 flying hours' target was reduced to seventy-five for the month of June. The timing could not have been more vexing as the intensity of FR training was increasing in advance of an exercise, designed to simulate 'war' conditions, about to get underway. To enable its pilots to achieve a full month's flying, 1417 Flight was allocated twenty-five hours on the FGA.9. Under the direction of the training officer, a scenario was devised to test the pilots' navigation skills to the extreme.

June was an unusually quiet month for the Hunter squadrons, only one house strike and three flagwaves being recorded for 43 Squadron. The first flagwave was performed

Looking down on XF436, another 1417 Flight FR.10 as it soars across the Radfan landscape (Ralph Chambers).

on the 4th when two 43 Squadron FGA.9s flew low over the Yibath area in an attempt to calm a dispute between the Wahidi and Quati tribes over grazing rights. Three days later 8 Squadron aircraft were despatched to perform flagwaves in the Awabil and Jebel Harir areas to prevent dissident unrest from getting out of hand.

In making the most of the operational inactivity, 8 Squadron implemented an intensive training programme, composed of five days' concentrated air-to-ground firing on the Khormaksar range, combined with practice diversions to Djibouti. On 20 June the squadron departed on a ten-day detachment to Masirah, releasing space for 208 Squadron to send a flight of aircraft down to Khormaksar to acquaint its pilots with operations in Aden. During its stay at Masirah 8 Squadron continued with its training programme, the main concentration being on high-level battle formations at 40,000 feet at Mach 0.9. During the second week sections of four aircraft were detailed to carry out simulated strikes on targets along the north coast of Muscat, followed by landings at Sharjah. Enemy opposition was provided by Hunters of 208 Squadron operating out of Muharraq.

Back at Khormaksar the lull in operational flying came to an end at 04:55 on 28 June, when Squadron Leader Davidson and Flying Officer Tite (208 Squadron detachment) headed for Wadi Hadramaut, an area only occasionally visited by Strike Wing Hunters. On arrival, they proceeded to perform flagwaves over the towns of Quadfa, Henin, Quatn, Shibam, Saywun and Ghuraf in the forlorn hope of flushing out thirty-six gunrunning rebels. Later the same day, a second pair was despatched to flagwave the Mithaf area in support of an FNG operation in the search for a band of dissidents, but none were spotted.

Prison bust!

Released from the training programme on the last day of the month, 1417 Flight's Flight Lieutenant Johns (XE599) was detailed to search for and photograph a dissident arms dump in Wadi Bana. The recce was carried out following reports that a group of dissidents had stashed a supply of arms in the wadi while preparing to free political prisoners from the nearby Jaar Prison. Having identified a small clump of trees as concealing the likely hiding place, Squadron Leader Davidson led a section of four 43 Squadron aircraft to the junction of Wadis Taym and Bana. Armed with twelve HE rockets and full gunpacks, they dived down from 20,000 feet to force home their attack, catching everyone in the target area off guard. Thirty minutes later a second wave of four aircraft, one from 43 Squadron and three from 208 Squadron, carried out strikes on the same target. Post-strike photographs taken by Flight Lieutenant Chambers revealed substantial damage and a deserted hideout. Needless to say the prison breakout did not materialise.

The ubiquitous Beverley, without which the various land forces would not have been able to meet their obligations, illustrates its ability to operate from rough airstrips such as here at Habilayn (Richard Grevatte-Ball).

When Uniform Radar detected an unidentified aircraft crossing the Yemen border, 8 Squadron scrambled two aircraft, XF456 (Flight Lieutenant Taylor) and XF435 (Flight Lieutenant Langrill), on an air defence mission. Adrenaline levels soon returned to normal, however, when the aircraft was identified as an Aden Airways DC-3 on a scheduled service. Good practice though!

No operational sorties were flown by 43 Squadron in July, much of the early part of the month being dedicated to refresher training at Khormaksar. On the 18th the squadron departed for a twelve-day detachment to Masirah where there was greater freedom to embark on a more adventurous training programme. The majority of the time was spent attacking targets that had been erected along the Trucial Coast by HQ RAFPG personnel, while avoiding pairs of 208 Squadron 'enemy' aircraft attempting to intercept them. Although 43 Squadron claimed a number of targets destroyed, several of its aircraft were caught during their run-outs, resulting in a number of kill claims by the 'defenders of Muharraq'.

This left 8 Squadron at Khormaksar to undertake the twenty-five operational sorties called for during July, the largest monthly total since September the previous year. Based on uncorroborated reports that the pro-British Sharif of Nuqub was using British aid money to train Royalist Army troops in Yemen, the government decided to sever his financial lifeline. Unable to continue with his hidden agenda, the sharif came under increasing pressure from the north to change his allegiance and support the Egyptian ambition, but he refused to acquiesce. In response two MiG fighters were despatched on 30 July to destroy his house. To deter further incursions, fourteen border patrols were flown by 8 Squadron in the Beihan area over the next two days.

Speedy prints!

With two pilots on the 43 Squadron detachment at Masirah and a further two on boards of inquiries, 1417 Flight once again found itself short of pilots. Fortunately, Flight Lieutenant Whitman had just become operational and he, together with Flight Lieutenant Simpson, was briefed for four operational sorties. One of these involved experimenting with a faster method of delivering photographs to up-country Army units. Having taken photographs of a defined area in Wadi Makhran, Flight Lieuteant Simpson flew back to Khormaksar at high speed and, on arrival, remained in his cockpit, engine running, to await the processed prints. These were packed into a container attached to a small parachute. The package was then slipped inside the airbrake and dropped on the Army base at Habilayn, enabling the expedition of an operation currently in plan. Improvisation at its best!

As the security situation in Aden State continued to worsen, two airmen from the Strike Wing Photographic Section sustained superficial injuries from a grenade attack while walking in Tawahi, just one example of a string of terrorist incidents that were

Parked alongside Canberra B.16 WT374 of the Akrotiri Strike Wing, 208 Squadron FGA.9 XG292 is pictured at Sharjah while on one of the Squadron's regular Armament Practice Camps (Aviation Bookshop).

engulfing the State. Fortunately, their wounds were not too serious and, following a short spell in Steamer Point Hospital, they were soon back at work.

One of the grounds for stationing Hunters at Muharraq was to provide a quick response should Iraq decide to have another go at annexing Kuwait. Local defences were continually exercised and reviewed and, following the acquisition of a mobile radar convoy, 208 Squadron was tasked to check it out. Two aircraft sent to test it on 1 August had limited success due to radio failure and ground radar unserviceability. A second pair had more success, the new radar making two intercepts later in the day.

Beihan Runway Extended

Despite the prospect of being intercepted by patrolling Hunters, Egyptian MiGs continued to sneak across the border to attack villages in the Protectorate. To reassure the local population and retain their confidence in Britain's intention to defend them, a much quicker method of getting the Hunters to the border was needed, and urgently. As the only way to do that was to shorten the flying time, the decision was taken to extend the runway at Beihan to 1,800 yards, long enough for cannon-armed Hunters to be able to take off and avoid the surrounding mountains. OC Strike Wing, Wing Commander Chandler, carried out the first of two test landings and take offs on the

OC Strike Wing, Martin Chandler, has just made the first landing of a Hunter at Beihan and the aircraft is immediately surrounded by armed guards. The photograph was taken on 5 August 1966 from an accompanying FR.10 flown by Ken Simpson (Ken Simpson).

The extension of the runway at Beihan enabled the more experienced pilots to undertake border patrols much closer in. This view captures a Hunter taking off during the first few days of operation from the unsurfaced airstrip in August 1966 (Alan Pollock).

8/43 Squadron FGA.9 XJ632 whisks the sand as it performs a touch-and-go at Beihan in front of an audience of British troops and the crew of an 84 Squadron Beverley (Ken Simpson).

rough compacted-sand surface using FGA.9 XF431 on 5 August. Aerial photographs of the event were taken by an FR.10 piloted by Flight Lieutenant Simpson, who escorted the wing commander's aircraft back to Khormaksar.

Operation KIMAR ZAYN

Under the codename Operation KIMAR ZAYN ('take a chance'), the first operational use of Beihan by Strike Wing Hunters took place on 15 August, when Wing Commander Chandler (XF388) and Flight Lieutenant Taylor (XF440) landed on the extended runway at 08:45. The pair remained there at five-minute readiness for three hours until relieved by a second pair for the afternoon standby. A routine was subsequently established whereby the pair finishing the dawn patrol landed at Beihan, refuelled and remained on five-minute standby, until relieved by the pair ending their patrol at around midday. The first pair then departed and completed a further patrol along the border before heading back to Khormaksar. The second pair, meanwhile, remained at Beihan until the late afternoon before completing a dusk patrol on their way back to Khormaksar.

The haste in which the runway extension plan had been created led to the omission of a crucial element, food and liquid refreshment for pilots and groundcrew. Needless to say, this important oversight was soon remedied. Aircraft at Beihan on standby were maintained by a small team of Strike Wing groundcrew who were ferried to and from the airfield in either the 21 Squadron Dakota or a Twin Pioneer on a daily basis, along with the necessary tools, equipment and limited spares.

Whiskey Radar

A newly-installed and much improved UPS 1-type radar system, codenamed 'Whiskey', replaced the original installation at Mukeiras and, following calibration checks using border-patrolling Hunters as targets, went live in early August. The new system enabled the controllers to take over responsibility for scrambling Hunters held on standby at Beihan. Adrenaline levels were high when the first intruder was detected. The standby pair was scrambled and undoubtedly disappointed to find an Aden Airways Viscount en route from Yemen to Khormaksar, but the system proved its effectiveness.

An exceptionally high total of 202 operational sorties was flown by the two ground-attack squadrons during August, the majority on Beihan border patrols, interspersed with flagwaves and a firepower demonstration at Musaymir. These were performed by four 43 Squadron aircraft on the 24th in response to a request from a political officer following the return from self-exile in the Yemen of a sizeable group of particularly hostile tribesmen. Eight flagwave sorties were flown over the Lawdar Plain to reassure resident tribes who had become unsettled at hearing of the dissidents return.

The penultimate day of August marked a changing of the guard on 1417 Flight when Officer Commanding Flight Lieutenant Ralph Chambers departed to take up a staff appointment at RAF Henlow in the UK. His year in charge had seen the flight reach its highest number of operational sorties since the Radfan campaign. He was succeeded in post by Flight Lieutenant Derek Whitman.

As the security situation in Aden State continued to deteriorate, the busy shopping area encompassing The Crescent and Steamer Point was declared out-of-bounds to service personnel and their families. In addition, a worrying rise in the number of grenade incidents in the Ma'alla district reminded everyone of the need to remain vigilant.

An intelligence report dated 13 August confirmed that dissidents were gathering in large groups in Wadis Bana and Yahar, their intention being to terrorise the local population into revealing the whereabouts of their arms stores. In a pre-emptive action, five sections of four Hunters were briefed to carry out strikes on the rebel gatherings. At 07:10 on 13 September Wing Commander Chandler (XE552), accompanied by Flight Lieutenants Malin (XJ632) and Waters (XF388) and Flying Officer McKeon (XJ646), led the first wave of 43 Squadron aircraft on a mission to scatter the Wadi Bana group. Later that morning the squadron directed a further two four-ship strikes at the Wadi Yahar group. Led by Wing Commander Chandler (XJ680), the first of these comprised Flight Lieutenants Pollock (XJ684) and Jennings (XJ692) together with Flying Officer Screen (XJ689). Less then an hour later, Flight Lieutenant Malin (XF388) led Flying Officers Griffiths (XE552), Ashley (XJ646) and Lawton (XF435) on the final 43 Squadron attack of the day.

At midday a four-ship strike by 8 Squadron aircraft on the Wadi Bana dissidents was led by Squadron Leader Melaniphy (XJ680) with the Strike Wing Training Officer, Squadron Leader Trowern (XJ689) as his number two and Flight Lieutenant Webb (XJ684) and Flying Officer James (XF431) at three and four. Aircraft for a second strike, which took place late in the evening, were flown by Flight Lieutenants Taylor (XE552), Kemball (XF431) and Etheridge (XJ684), and Flying Officer Johnson (XF435). On the following day, post-strike recces were flown over the wadis by 1417 Flight FR.10s and photographs taken of the damage inflicted for use in intelligence debriefs.

The heavy operational commitment continued through September with a total of 153 operational sorties being flown by Strike Wing Hunters. Of these, the majority, ninety-six, comprised Beihan and Mukeiras border patrols. The remaining high-profile operations for the month included a two-pronged operation on the 7th, designed to:

a)   deter dissidents from attacking FRA troops during a cordon and search operation and

b)   raise the morale of the occupants of a remote fort that was being fired on by dissidents.

Six flagwave sorties were flown by 8 and 43 Squadron aircraft in the Am Kirsh and Awabill areas, followed by a further two in the Wadi Hadramaut by 8 Squadron aircraft following a shooting incident. Four more flagwaves were flown by 8 Squadron in the Yibath area where the Wahidi and Quaiti tribes were feuding over grazing rights. Following a grenade incident in Mukallah later in the month, an air mobility exercise was mounted in which four 8 Squadron aircraft were briefed to escort an 84 Squadron Beverley as far as Riyan.

Ooops!

An embarrassing 'own-goal' that probably cost the guilty party a round or three in the bar occurred when two 43 Squadron FGA.9s were scrambled to intercept an unidentified aircraft flying close to the Yemen border. It was much to everyone's relief when the intruder was identified as a 1417 Flight T.7 on a training sortie. More good practice!

No. 1417 Flight's main focus during September was on a joint exercise with the Army on Perim Island, codenamed MICHAEL. The flight was tasked to take photographs of a target area, return to Khormaksar and wait for the prints, before returning to the island to drop them onto the designated HQ using the parachuted-package technique.

The flight's flying commitment was not helped by the short-term loss of an FR.10 in an incident on 3 September. While landing slightly overweight and (unknown to the pilot) with dodgy brakes, XE614 overran the runway. At low speed, the pilot deliberately avoided the net by letting the aircraft drift off the runway into the sand, hoping that all would be well. Unfortunately it hit a buried concrete block, ripping off the port undercarriage leg in the process. The flight was left with just two serviceable aircraft for the rest of the month.

Beihan and Mukeiras patrols occupied many Strike Wing flying hours during October with more pilots authorised to make their first landings at Beihan. Several top-cover sorties were flown in support of an SAS operation codenamed CAST IRON, and its objective of placing observation posts along key routes used by dissidents infiltrating from the Yemen. The most hazardous period of this operation occurred when SAS troopers were being flown into and out of the operating areas by helicopter.

The first operational task of the month for 1417 Flight involved a photo-recce on 6 October by Flight Lieutenant Whitman (XF436), who was tasked to gather intelligence for a forthcoming operation along a section of coast in the Eastern Aden Protectorate (EAP). He was escorted by Flight Lieutenant Johns flying a 'loan' FGA.9. Having landed at Masirah to refuel, the pair performed a further recce over the same stretch of coast line on the return flight to Khormaksar.

Another Adeni tribe which had at sometime defected to the Yemen and since returned began to stir up trouble among the inhabitants of Jabirah and nearby villages in Wadis Ruqub and Hatib. Four flagwaves were flown over the area on the 16th by

43 Squadron aircraft as a prelude to a sweep by FRA forces intent on curbing the rebels aggressive behaviour.

Operation FATE

On 27 October a 105 Squadron Argosy departed Khormaksar carrying a contingent of Strike Wing groundcrew on a heading for Salalah. Absolute secrecy was maintained as to the reason, to the extent that the detachment OC, Flying Officer Hawken, was not aware of the destination or objective of the mission. At 04:20 on the following morning, Wing Commander Chandler (XJ646) accompanied by OC 43 Squadron, Squadron Leader Davidson (XF435) and Flight Lieutenant Etheridge (XJ692) of 8 Squadron flew three FGA.9s up to Salalah to join them. Based on photographs and intelligence on the EAP coast line gathered earlier in the month, Operation FATE was about to commence.

Shortly before dawn on 29 October Wessex helicopters of 78 Squadron landed troops of the 1st Battalion Irish Guards within striking distance of the village of Hawf. On the nearby beaches reinforcements were landed from HMS *Fearless*, their objective being to cordon off the village. Search parties were then sent in to arrest a number of tribesmen who had been identified as operating well inside Muscat and Oman territory. Twenty-two rebels were arrested, one of them a well-known rebel leader who had managed to avoid capture for more than three years.

The two 43 Squadron aircraft provided top cover for the landings and searches, leaving Flight Lieutenant Etheridge to wait on standby in readiness to replace the other two as their fuel began to run low. No shots were fired and no injuries reported during the operation which, having achieved its objectives, was deemed a complete success.

Back in the WAP, Flight Lieutenant Johns (XE599) was busy photographing areas of Wadi Milah and Jebel Radfan in preparation for an impending ground operation. As the photographs were needed for the briefing, the aircraft returned to Khormaksar at high speed and waited on the tarmac, engine running, before flying back and para-dropping the prints onto the Army HQ at Habilayn. As the large distances involved, which together with the time allocated for the operation, bordered on the impossible, Flight Lieutenant Johns was flown up to Habilayn to brief 43 Commando RM on the operating window and limitations of the FR.10 in the photographic reconnaissance role.

With three serviceable FR.10s available, the outlook for 1417 Flight for November was looking good, a target of ninety flying hours seemingly well within its grasp. The positive outlook, however, was destined not to last as all three aircraft became unserviceable at the same time. As the month drew on, the flight was declared non-operational on two occasions. Only four operational sorties could be flown, the most interesting being on the 28th when Flight Lieutenant Whitman (XE599) was briefed to mark a target in Wadi Bana for a four-ship strike by 43 Squadron and to remain on station to take post-strike photographs. By this time, the flight's manpower was back to full strength with a complement of six pilots, one SNCO, four corporals and nine airmen.

Continuation Training

The Beihan and Mukeiras patrols continued to occupy the ground-attack squadrons during November, the total of 144 being split evenly between the two. In addition to operational commitments, it is interesting to note that 8 Squadron also managed to complete an extensive training programme. Of the 249 training sorties, ninety-

8/43 Squadron FGA.9s captured on an FR.10's Vinten camera as the pilots practice their diamond-nine formation over desert scrub to the north of Khormaksar (Ken Simpson).

seven comprised rocket and gun attacks on the range, plus a further fifty-eight on up-country targets selected at random by 1417 Flight pilots. Ten of these consisted of four-ship strikes with simulated air opposition. Fifty combat interceptions were also flown, nine of them in co-operation with the Royal Navy, and eighteen sorties using the T.7s for FAC training. Two Kenyan Air Force pilots on short-term attachment to the squadron and two students on a FAC course were given air experience rides in the T.7s and, to round things off, a nine-ship formation flypast was flown for the departing station commander. The combined operational and non-operational flying hours for 8 Squadron for November exceeded 337.

DC-3 downed!

On 22 November Aden Airways DC-3 VR-AAN was operating on a scheduled service from Meifah to Aden when it crashed near Hasn Valide, two miles inland, killing all twenty-seven passengers and crew of three. Subsequent investigations revealed that the aircraft had been blown apart by an explosive device when passing through 6,000 feet. The bomb was believed to have been carried onboard in a passenger's hand baggage. The FRA was dispatched to prevent local inhabitants looting the wreckage as 43 Squadron aircraft provided top cover.

Four days later, Whiskey Radar detected a hostile aircraft heading towards the border and issued an air defence scramble. By the time the two 43 Squadron Hunters

The ill-fated Aden Airways DC-3 VR-AAN seen in earlier times taxiing onto the Visitors pan at Khormaksar (author).

arrived in the area the intruder had nipped back into the Yemen. On 28 November Wing Commander Chandler led a four-ship rocket and cannon strike on a wooded area in Wadi Bana following a report from a rebel informer that dissidents were gathering beneath the foliage to plan their next skirmish. Post-strike photographs confirmed that his former comrades would be of no further concern for the authorities.

Airborne Direction

On the same day two close air-support sorties were flown by 8 Squadron pilots, Flight Lieutenant Webb (XJ692) and Flying Officer Loftus (XJ646), to counter a mortar and light-machine-gun attack by dissidents on an FRA fort at Awabil. In spite of fading daylight, and coming under direct fire himself, a FAC controller from the Irish Guards, who was airborne in a Sioux helicopter, competently directed the Hunters as they ran in for their attack. The pilot of the Sioux, Lieutenant Michael Barnes of the Welsh Guards, was reported as saying that:

> both his helicopter and the Hunters came under heavy AA fire from three different positions – the tracer straddling both jets as they lined themselves up to attack their targets. Undaunted, they pressed home their attack and were able to silence the dissidents guns, destroying an anti-aircraft gun emplacement in the process.

Although the intensity of operations diminished in December, only twenty-six border patrols being flown, Strike Wing remained on high alert. When a Beverley came under fire on finals into Dhala airstrip, the 8 Squadron air defence pair scrambled but by the time they arrived, as was often the case, the attackers had fled the scene.

A reduced demand for operational support at this time enabled 8 Squadron to return its concentration to the training programme, no fewer than 303 sorties and 288 hours being reported in the squadron records for the month.

No. 43 Squadron records also reflected a decrease in operational activity, the highlights being three air defence scrambles on the 14th, 19th and 31st. The latter was accomplished in a time of seven minutes from the issuing of the word 'scramble' to calling the radar controller at 5,000 feet. All three scrambles reverted to practice strikes when no intruders were encountered.

SNEB – trials and tribulations

No. 208 Squadron successfully completed tests on the SNEB nose cone over the period 1 to 7 November and a further seven sorties were flown on the Rashid range over the final few days of the month. Despite a number of initial test firings in March, the first full trial of the SNEB rocket system took place on 2 and 3 December during a 208 Squadron APC. The trial was conducted using two FGA.9s, one flown by a 208 Squadron pilot and the second by a pilot from Khormaksar Strike Wing. One aircraft

208 Squadron pilots and groundcrew pictured at Muharraq on the occasion of 50th Anniversary of the Squadron. Seated either side of the OC Sqn Ldr Tony Chaplin are AVM Sir Geoffrey Bromet and Major Draper, the first two Squadron Commanders (Dougie Marr).

was equipped with a Mark 8 centre-spot gunsight, the second with a fixed sighting capability only. Nineteen sorties were flown on the Rashid range at distances of 800, 900 and 1,000 yards and at dive angles of 10 and 25 degrees. The main conclusion reached was that the hollow-charge rocket was an accurate weapon that should be fired at a range of 900 yards and at a dive angle of 10 degrees, to enable the aircraft to clear the debris zone when firing a full pod of rockets and to reduce the exposure of the aircraft to enemy ground fire.

    Although an extremely effective weapon, its use in the heat of the Middle East raised a number of questions. In one serious incident, a rocket exploded inside a SNEB pod while the aircraft was parked on the pan, causing severe damage to the airframe. The pods were withdrawn from use until the cause could be established. The inquiry concluded that the detonation was triggered due to the extremely high temperatures experienced in Bahrain during the peak summer months. Strict limitations were placed on its future use; a maximum temperature of 35 C on the aircraft pan and a maximum speed of 450 knots at 30 C when airborne.

Lost Sioux

On 6 December a Sioux helicopter (XT125) based at Habilayn with the Army Air Corps was reported missing while in transit from Musaymir. Flight Lieutenant Nicholls and the crew of a 37 Squadron Shackleton were diverted from the Khormaksar bombing range to carry out a visual search until darkness fell. Two further searches were flown by Shackleton aircraft on the next day, along with several AAC helicopters and Beaver aircraft.

At 17:30 on the 7th the wreckage of the helicopter was located, it having crashed into the side of a mountain. Using 4.5-inch recce flares, Flight Lieutenant Davies and the crew of his Shackleton remained on station to provide illumination for an Army helicopter flying out of the crash site and heading towards Habilayn. The Shackleton remained overhead for a further four hours using 1.75-inch flares to illuminate the terrain over which a party of FRA soldiers was attempting to reach the crash scene. The pilot and two passengers were sadly confirmed dead at the scene.

On 10 December, the following message was received at Strike Wing HQ from OC 13 Flight, AAC, Habilayn:

From all of us at Habilayn Garrison, please accept our most sincere thanks for the truly marvellous and instantaneous assistance afforded us in the search and rescue operation. We will long remember the unstinted work of the pilots and ground staffs.

Inter-tribal feuds in the Ar Rubat and Am Madinah areas were pacified following a leaflet drop by a 105 Squadron Argosy and flagwaves by a pair of 43 Squadron aircraft on the 12th of the month. To discourage the inhabitants of Al Khabr, Hada and Al Mithaf from harbouring political prisoners who had escaped from nearby Meifa jail, a pair of Hunters was sent to perform a flagwave over the three villages on the 28th. Among the escapees was the dissident responsible for the assassination of the commander of the Hadramaut Bedouin Legion, Colonel Grey, and number of people from the assassin's tribe who had been imprisoned in an effort to curb its recalcitrance.

Otherwise 43 Squadron pilots began to experiment with a new training curriculum in which the more experienced pilots flew together on four-ship simulated strikes with two-ship bounces, concluding with four-*vs*-two combat down to 2,000 feet. An innovative programme of FAC training on the Khab Khab range gave pilots from both Hunter squadrons the opportunity to perform in the role of airborne controllers. Considering that Hunter pilots had not tried this before, the standard was found to be remarkably high.

In what transpired to be the final Santa Claus delivery in Aden, Flight Lieutenants Taylor and Hayward flew their Hunters on the annual round of Christmas card drops on up-country Army garrisons at Beihan, Mukeiras, Dhala and Habilayn on 24 December.

In addition to the festivities and celebrations, 1417 Flight had enjoyed a rewarding December. With four aircraft available for most of the month, its flying task was

A rare photograph of a 105 Squadron Argosy dropping warning leaflets on feuding tribesmen near Ar Rubat (Roger Wilkins).

achieved with ease. Two of its more challenging sorties were flown in support of an SAS operation which required accurate navigation and exact positioning in order to align their cameras on the target. And when it was reported that dissidents were preparing to launch mortar attacks on Khormaksar airfield, Flight Lieutenant Neal (XF436) was detailed to take photographs of any suspicious-looking objects or activities in the area of a cluster of shacks on the north side of the airfield.

Christmas passed pleasantly enough with the usual muster of mess and private functions and it was reassuring to report that none were marred by terrorist activity. One of the main highlights for Strike Wing was the arrival of Squadron Leader R. Barraclough to assume command of 1417 Flight from Flight Lieutenant Whitman.

The year had begun under the threat of increased terrorist activity in Aden State and that is precisely what happened. Terror-related incidents rose at an alarming rate, 50 per cent per quarter, with casualty figures approaching 500.

Mortar attack

The daunting prospect of Khormaksar coming under direct attack became reality when dissidents managed to encroach on the airfield boundary from the Sheikh Othman direction and get close enough to fire a salvo of mortar bombs onto the station. Fortunately, no damage was sustained by aircraft parked on the open pans nor were injuries caused to personnel in close proximity. To reduce their exposure to splinter and shrapnel damage should any future attacks occur, waterfilled oil drums were stacked in rows between aircraft lined up on the pans. A permanent guard composed of Army and RAF Regiment personnel, and airmen from the station, was established around the airfield perimeter. A downside of this was that as airmen were rostered for guard duty every six days, aircraft maintenance difficulties arose as serviceability levels declined.

All in all, a precarious situation and one that did not bode well for the year ahead.

Chapter 12

1967 – Farewell to Aden

The British Government's announcement that its military forces would be withdrawn from Aden much earlier than expected was issued at the same time as the acknowledgement that the Federation would gain its independence. The effect on the population was far reaching, not only for the morale of Federal government ministers but, and perhaps of more significance, the local police force. As the terrorists intensified their attacks on security and service personnel, the more the authorities felt exposed and betrayed. Fierce fighting between rival nationalist factions jockeying for power, the NLF and FLOSY in particular, resulted in fifty-one people killed and 240 wounded in the first two months of the year alone. Attacks on British servicemen and their families intensified and came to a head following the killing of several British citizens, including a child of five. Service personnel were constantly reminded of the need to remain alert and vigilant at all times, and to stay away from known troublespots.

As far as Strike Wing was concerned, the year began in much the same way as the preceding years, albeit with fewer Beihan patrols, flagwaves and strikes on dissident targets. Three scrambles were flown by 43 Squadron to provide top cover for cordon and search operations in the Jebel Mishwarah area on 7 January, and at Al Khubayrah on the 8th and 9th.

The first strike of the year occurred on 12 January when OC 8 Squadron, Squadron Leader Melaniphy, led the first of two four-ship sections to Wadi Bana, to destroy a suspected rebel arms dump. Wing Commander Chandler led the second some thirty minutes later, accompanied by a pair of 1417 Flight FR.10s, whose pilots, Flight Lieutenants Simpson (XF436) and Neal (XE599), were tasked to photograph the resulting damage.

In an attempt to resolve a feud between the head of Hilyan and a brother whose rebel group had captured an FNG wireless operator, two flagwaves were flown over the town by 43 Squadron aircraft on the 19th. Although the captive was released, continuing skirmishes between the two persisted until a four-ship flagwave was performed over the village a week later.

January was one of those rare months when 1417 Flight was credited with the bulk of Strike Wing operational sorties. One of these was flown by the flight's new OC, Squadron Leader Barraclough (XF436) who, together with Flight Lieutenant Whitman (XF460), performed a two-hour search for tracks that may have recently been made by arms smugglers in the Shabwash area of the EAP. Later in the day a pair of FR.10s performed a flagwave over the area to encourage two warring parties to settle their differences over the location of a boundary.

3D images

Following a request from the SAS, two areas to the west and north-west of Habilayn became the focal point for the Vinten cameras on a pair of FR.10s flown by Flight Lieutenants Neal (XE599) and Johns (XF460) on 25 January, in preparation for an operation still in the final stages of planning. Using a technique known as 'stereo-pair', two photographs were taken of the same target microseconds apart. When viewed through a twin-lens frame, the processed prints give the appearance of a 3D image. An object such as a camouflaged tank, for example, would stand out from the background, providing an invaluable tool for the photographic interpreter and a more accurate aid for front-line troop commanders.

A general strike by members of the banned political party, the National Liberation Front (NLF), in early February reduced the quantity of fuel being delivered to Khormaksar. Flying by Strike Wing aircraft was limited to operational needs only, a total of 106 sorties being recorded for the month. To make matters worse, the strike was being used as a front to trigger an increase in terrorist violence across the State. Nighttime curfews and movement restrictions during daylight hours for service families made their lives extremely unpleasant.

To add a little spice to the diet of border patrols, Hunter pilots were given the opportunity to carry out practice approaches and overshoots at Beihan airfield. On the 2nd of the month, two 43 Squadron aircraft were scrambled from Khormaksar when an unidentified aircraft appeared on a radar trace flying in the vicinity of Perim Island. An RAF VIP Andover was spotted flying close by; otherwise nothing untoward was seen.

Groundfire – an ever-present danger

The village of Tawr Al Bahah was unusual in that the border with Yemen passed right through it. It was also unique in having two sheikhs, one on each side of the border. Their opposing views often led to conflict, requiring the intervention of FRA troops based in the area to settle things down. On one occasion 1417 Flight was detailed to send an aircraft to photograph the village and surrounding area together with that of Al Ghurayq, a neighbouring village 300 yards farther along the border. Flight Lieutenant Whitman duly departed Khormaksar in his FR.10 (XE614) and headed towards the border, some fifty miles north-west of Aden. Having fulfilled his task, he noticed a stream of fuel venting from the top of the starboard wing, close to the air intake. On landing back at Khormaksar, a quick inspection confirmed his suspicion that his aircraft had been hit by small-arms fire. Intelligence sources ascertained that the culprit was a Yemeni army sergeant assigned to the border post near Al Ghurayq.

He was stripped of his rank and, to dissuade any of his colleagues from copying his reckless deed, 8 Squadron despatched a pair of aircraft to perform a flagwave as three 43 Squadron FGA.9s performed a firepower demonstration on a hillside overlooking the area.

Hunter ejection

In a separate incident on 20 February two 43 Squadron aircraft were performing a flagwave over the village of Dhi Surrah, when Flying Officer Sowler began to suspect that his FGA.9 (XF440) had been hit by groundfire. One by one, the aircraft's hydraulics, turret drive and ASI services began to close down. Groundfire had ruptured hydraulic lines which then caught fire, destroying the radio bay in the process. Flying Officer Lawton (XJ684), flying as his No. 2, used hand signals to try and get him to eject as he could see the seriousness of the fire. Eventually, with no radio contact, Flying Officer Sowler switched from power to manual control but, with a strong smell of burning, he reluctantly decided to eject near Al Ittihad, about ten miles short of Khormaksar. As he floated down on his parachute, he watched his aircraft dive into the ground some three miles ahead. Having landed safely, he only had a few minutes to wait for a SAR Flight Whirlwind to pick him up. This was the first ejection involving a 43 Squadron pilot for two-and-a-half years.

At 06:00 on the 24th the first of six pairs of 43 Squadron aircraft took off to carry out a strike on a target in Wadi Bana, an area notorious for dissident activity. Pairs were despatched at hourly intervals to attack specific targets with cannon and rocket fire. Post-strike photographs were taken by a pair of 1417 Flight FR.10s by Flight Lieutenants Neal (XE599) and Johns (XF460) for damage assessment.

The final operation for the month of February occurred on the 26th when two 8 Squadron FGA.9s were scrambled to provide cover for an SAS patrol attempting to extricate itself from a dissident group it had stumbled across in Wadi Tiban.

Aden State, meanwhile, remained in the grip of a general strike and a rapidly deteriorating security situation. When attempts to increase the reserve stock of fuel held on Khormaksar airfield to 280,000 gallons failed, a limit of seventy-seven operational sorties was placed on the FGA squadrons for the month of March. Fortunately, most were border patrols in the Beihan and Mukeiras areas.

When a feud between two tribes in Wahidi State erupted into open warfare with surrounding tribes on 2 March, the FRA moved into Al Mithaf to separate the warring factions as two 43 Squadron Hunters maintained top cover. In another incident, six days later, a feud between members of the Audhali tribe was sufficient to trigger a leaflet drop over Wadi Ruqub by a pair of 43 Squadron Hunters.

When reports were received that the fortified hilltop village of Hilyan, in Upper Yaffa, had been attacked and destroyed by dissident tribesmen, Flight Lieutenant

With Tim Lawton at the controls, FGA.9 XE546 was photographed in 8/43 Squadron markings while en-route to the Hadramaut (Rod Harrison).

Farquhar-Smith was despatched in an FR.10 (XE599) on the 7th to try and establish what had actually occurred. The resulting photographs confirmed that extensive damage had been inflicted on buildings in the village which appeared to be deserted. The aggressors were long gone and were never identified. A subsequent recce confirmed that every building had been razed to the ground. Sadly, episodes such as this were but a microcosm of the depths to which feuding tribes were delighted to stoop and typical of many incidents across this region.

No. 8 Squadron – new Standard

Sunday 12 March 1967 was a significant day for 8 Squadron when it laid up its old Standard at St Clement Dane's church in London. Squadron Leader Melaniphy, Flight Lieutenant Webb and Flying Officer Heather-Hayes formed the Colour party, the honour of standard bearer being fulfilled by Flying Officer Bain. Many distinguished former members of the squadron were invited to attend the ceremony.

Floods!

Not the headline one might expect to see in Adeni media headlines! The month of April was, like the curate's egg, only good in parts. Aden was never an attractive place to live and work, even at the best of times, but it could hardly have appeared less inviting when, on April Fool's Day, the worst storms in living memory caused severe flooding of the townships nestling below Mount Shamsan. Matters were made worse as it occurred on the first day of yet another general strike, the intention this time being to demonstrate the solidarity of various political factions during a United Nations mission visit to South Arabia. The torrential rain also caused extensive flooding at Khormaksar, leading to a breakdown in electrical services. Inevitably, restoration of power was delayed due to electricity workers being on strike. The majority of the 376 reported security incidents during the month occurred during the period of the strike.

Patrol profile changed

As the established border patrol profile offered little prospect of catching Yemeni jets and helicopter gunships crossing into South Arabia, the decision was taken to restructure the model in an attempt to effect an illusion of a greater presence of Hunters on Yemeni radar screens than was actually the case. This was achieved by dividing the border between Perim Island and Beihan into four sectors and allocating a pair of aircraft to each sector. Different profiles were flown by each pair, one at high level at 30,000 feet at mach 0.9, and the second at low level at a speed of either 360 or 540 knots. The speed and height could be varied to avoid uniformity. Patrols were flown at a frequency of three per week, per sector and a standby pair retained at fifteen-minute readiness during daylight hours. Both 8 and 43 Squadrons committed to rostering sixteen pilots at two-hour readiness, twenty-four hours a day, the pilots rotating on an 'on call' rota during off-duty periods. As anticipated, the tempo of operational sorties began to pick up, a total of 117 being flown by the wing during April.

When the British government announced that the withdrawal of its forces from Aden would be brought forward to the end of 1967, the various political groups vying for power decided the time had come to eliminate each other using a significant increase in terrorist activities as a cover. A peaceful handover of power by the British authorities appeared extremely unlikely.

False alarm!

Up at Muharraq 208 Squadron was placed on a high readiness state to reinforce Strike Wing at Khormaksar should the need arise. To ensure they were prepared and ready to go at any time of day, a programme of long-range, cross-country nightflights was flown from Muharraq to Masirah and back. The culmination was a practice exercise on 18 April, in which the squadron took off from Muharraq with the intention of continuing all the way down to Khormaksar. The aircraft had been airborne for a short period when they were recalled to Muharraq following reports that an Iraqi Army patrol had crossed the border with Kuwait. The squadron remained on immediate readiness as

Strip of film from a 1417 Flight FR.10 Vinten camera illustrates the clarity and detail presented to the Photographic Interpreters and intelligence gathering staff (Roger Pyrah).

men of the Parachute Regiment killed time while waiting for the call to board the Beverleys of 30 Squadron. Nothing further was reported until early the following day when Iraq conceded that its troops had made a navigational error.

Hunter loss

After a short break, on the 26th and 27th a further two nighttime missions were flown from Muharraq to Masirah, each composed of six aircraft. On the return flight on the second night, Flying Officer Howick-Baker was killed when his Hunter (XJ691) crashed into the sea, eighteen miles short of Muharraq. His aircraft had been picked up on the airfield radar but it disappeared from view soon after. No cause for the accident was established.

A flagwave over the border town of Tawr Al Bahah on 2 April should have comprised a standard pair of 43 Squadron aircraft but, when one failed to start, the pilot of the second aircraft, Flight Lieutenant Waters, flew the mission solo. After thirty minutes over the target area, he was compelled to leave when he came under fire from rebels on the Yemen side of the border. In a separate incident two days later, a pair of 8 Squadron Hunters was despatched to perform a flagwave over Am Shatt to quell tribal unrest there, but when that failed to convey the 'cut-it-out' message, a firepower demonstration was carried out nearby on the next day. As the Sharif of Beihan was not convinced that order had been restored, a further firepower demonstration was carried out at his behest by four 8 Squadron aircraft on 24 April.

Based on surveillance reports describing a notable increase in dissident activity to the south-west of Habilayn, Strike Wing was committed to flying top-cover sorties over Army convoys moving along the Dhala Road between Little Aden and Habilayn. Visual and radio contact was made between aircraft and convoy as the latter passed Nobat Dakiam, the escort being maintained until the convoy reached Habilayn. Any thoughts dissidents may have harboured on attacking the mix of trucks and armoured

Much of the re-supply of up-country Army garrisons was fulfilled by the Twin Pioneers of 78 Squadron and latterly, 21 Squadron, and the Beverleys of 84 Squadron, using rough unsurfaced airstrips similar to the one above or compacted sand as seen in the picture below. Other dangers facing the air crews were the uncomfortably close proximity of the mountains and sniper fire from dissidents hiding among the rocks (Richard Grevatte-Ball).

cars were dampened by the sight and sound of Hunters performing dummy attacks under the direction of a FAC flying in a 78 Squadron Wessex ahead of the convoy. Top-cover sorties were also flown in support of cordon-and-search operations being carried out by SAS troopers working in close co-operation with 78 Squadron.

In spite of having one aircraft out of action through groundfire sustained in February and another due to a birdstrike, 1417 Flight completed twelve operational sorties in April. Sheikh Othman was the subject for the cameras of one of its serviceable FR.10s, the photographs being required for a planned cordon and search of the township by Army units. A further three missions were flown over Habilayn and Radfan to provide photographic coverage of areas in which 1st Battalion Irish Guards were preparing a series of ambushes. The flight was also tasked with locating and photographing a Russian cargo vessel out at sea at the request of Naval Intelligence.

Formations and Balbos

By contrast to April, the merry month of May produced a veritable kaleidoscope of activities for 1417 Flight after it accepted a challenge to photograph a number of large mixed formations of aircraft from the RAF and RN. Flight Lieutenant Simpson led

Three Buccaneer S.2s from 809 Squadron HMS Hermes fly passed Crater prior to landing ashore at Khormaksar on 6 May 1967. The photograph was taken by RAF exchange and former 8 Squadron Hunter pilot Peter Sturt who was flying a fourth Buccaneer (Peter Sturt).

the way on 1 May, when he took photographs of a diamond-nine formation performed by 8 Squadron to mark the departure of the GOC, Middle East Command. A more challenging assignment twelve days later was to capture a mixed formation comprising sixteen Strike Wing Hunters and eight Sea Vixens and six Buccaneers from HMS *Hermes*. It was Flight Lieutenant Whitman's opportunity to demonstrate his prowess in the FR.10 on the 16th when he was entrusted to photograph a Strike Wing diamond-sixteen formation, flown to mark the departure of the retiring High Commissioner for Aden, His Excellency Sir Richard Turnbull.

Last, but certainly by no means least, in a show of strength designed to impress the local population, a huge balbo consisting of fifty-five aircraft was flown low over Aden State and a large part of the Western Aden Protectorate on 17 May. With the sixteen Sea Vixen FAW.2s and twelve Buccaneer S.2s from HMS *Victorious* and HMS *Hermes* leading the way, a combined force of thirty-one 8, 43 and 208 Squadron Hunter FGA.9s from Khormaksar and Muharraq brought up the rear. As this was one of the rare occasions on which two Royal Navy carriers were in the Aden area at the same time, the opportunity was taken by Strike Wing to indulge in co-operation exercises with the carrier-based squadrons. No. 208 Squadron then flew up to Masirah for an overnight stop before completing the final leg back to Muharraq.

On the morning of the 19th six 208 Squadron aircraft took off to practise for a firepower demonstration scheduled for the afternoon. All six fired full loads of 30mm HE cannon at the three targets, with four aircraft firing twelve 60lb hollow-head rockets, leaving the remaining pair to discharge full loads of SNEB rockets.

When Lord Shackleton paid a visit to Aden, 1417 Flight pilot Flight Lieutenant Farquhar-Smith was selected to chauffeur Khormaksar's esteemed guest around the WAP in a Hunter T.7. Shortly after getting airborne, however, the aircraft developed a pressurisation fault and had to return to base. A second attempt was more successful and Lord Shackleton was reported as having been extremely pleased at having been able to see large parts of the Federation from a pilot's perspective.

For the ground-attack squadrons, the number of operational sorties recorded in May was double that for April, the majority being flown on Army convoy protection duties along the Dhala Road. The first operational sorties by 8 Squadron's Hunters occurred on 9 May. Following an attack on an AAC helicopter in Wadi Matlah, its two standby FGA.9s were scrambled on a Topcat call out (the term Topcat is understood to be the reference used for top cover sorties for helicopters). No dissident casualties were reported and a follow-up recce revealed signs of their having left in a great hurry.

Later in the month a large band of dissidents ambushed a party of Royal Engineers engaged in road repair work with small-arms fire and anti-tank rocket launchers, known as 'blindicides'. Several troops were badly injured in the attack. The 8 Squadron

Perfect timing! A Buccaneer is about to land on the deck of HMS Hermes as 8/43 Squadron perform a diamond-nine formation overhead. Ken Simpson took the photograph on 1 May 1967 taking full advantage of his FR.10's Vinten cameras (Ken Simpson).

The combined formation of RAF and RN aircraft (above) comprising sixteen Hunters leading eight Sea Vixens and six Buccaneers from HMS Hermes, photographed by a 1417 Flight FR.10 on 12 May 1967 (Ken Simpson). The largest formation to overfly Aden (below) consisted of fifty-five aircraft from 892 and 893 Squadrons (Sea Vixen FAW.2), 801 and 809 Squadrons (Buccaneer S.2) and Strike Wing Hunters from all four units, 17 May 1967 (Peter Sturt).

standby pair was scrambled and, under the direction of a helicopter-borne FAC, scored direct RP hits on the entrance to the cave into which the attackers had fled. A number of dissidents managed to escape and, despite further bursts of gunfire from the Hunters, were able to make good their escape along a well-protected ridge. Even so, five dissidents were reported killed and several more wounded. A further seven top-cover sorties were flown to protect the engineers as they continued with their work on the road.

The first of three scrambles called in support of a Topcat operation in an area bounded by Habilayn and Dhala was flown by Flying Officers McKeon and Loveday of 43 Squadron. They arrived at Dhi Hurran, to the north-east of Dhala, as troops manning a FRA cordon, part of a combined SAS/FRA search operation, were being fired on by dissident tribesmen. As a supporting Wessex developed a radio problem, the Hunter pilots were forced to hold their fire and return to Khormaksar.

When intelligence channels reported that a well-known dissident leader was about to receive a shipment of arms smuggled into the country from Yemen, 43 Squadron pilots were briefed to intercept it with a dawn strike as it passed through the Jebel Al Urays area on 15 May. No. 78 Squadron Wessex and AAC Scout helicopters would then drop FRA troops into the area in the hope of capturing any rebels who may have escaped the Hunter strike. However, when Squadron Leader Davidson and Flight Lieutenant Waters arrived they found a large gathering of Bedouin in the target area, forcing them to hold off while maintaining top cover. This did not prevent the helicopters from coming under dissident fire, the airframe of one Wessex receiving direct hits and bullet wounds to three soldiers. Due to the nature of the terrain, the dissidents were able to make good their escape and were never traced.

On 22 May a Wessex helicopter on a supply operation to the Special Guard in Wadi Taym, was fired on while unloading stores intended to replace those stolen by three members of the Guard who had deserted the night before. In its haste to leave the area, the helicopter left a soldier behind, but he was able to reach cover in a nearby fort and await rescue later in the day.

Towards the end of what had been a busy month, a number of firepower demonstrations were performed near Beihan and to the north of Dhala. Fourteen strikes were also carried out on 24 May by 8 Squadron aircraft with the intention of destroying dissident arms dumps in Wadi Bana. In the Eastern Aden Protectorate, the threat of a mutiny by a company of the Hadramaut Bedouin Legion at Markaz as Hajar, diminished after Strike Wing carried out a flagwave.

Preparing for withdrawal

The continuing failure of Her Majesty's Government to confirm a date on which the last British forces would leave Aden and the garrison close caused a great deal of frustration among those charged with planning an orderly exit. Several acknowledged that the prospect of handing over to a stable Federal Government, supported by a faithful South Arabian Army, was highly unlikely. If Britain was to withdraw its forces in good order and without sustaining a high number of casualties, the date needed to be established as quickly as possible. Originally proposed for sometime during the early months of 1968, ambiguous pronouncements issued by Downing Street were not clarified until May 1967, when the C.-in-C. was informed that 20 November 1967 would be the final day. At least twenty-eight days' notice would be given should the need arise for the date to be changed.

Decisions could now be taken regarding the destiny of the Khormaksar squadrons and the order in which they would move out or disband. With 30 Squadron (Beverley), 208 Squadron (Hunter FGA.9) and 152 Squadron (Pembroke/Twin Pioneer) already at Muharraq, the initial plan stipulated that a balanced and relevant force of modern aircraft should be retained for operations in the Gulf. The hastily developed plan was distributed on 23 May and the main points relating to the flying wings are outlined below:

- **8 Squadron (Hunter FGA.9).** To move to Muharraq and form a fighter/ground attack wing with 208 Squadron.
- **43 Squadron (Hunter FGA.9).** To remain at Khormaksar until the last days of the withdrawal and then disband, its aircraft being re-allocated to 8 and 208 Squadrons or returned to the UK.
- **1417 Flight (Hunter FR.10).** To disband, its aircraft and fighter reconnaissance mission being absorbed by 8 Squadron.
- **37 Squadron (Shackleton).** To disband at Khormaksar and its aircraft returned to the UK.
- **21 Squadron (Andover/Twin Pioneer/Dakota).** To disband at Khormaksar, its aircraft being re-allocated to other squadrons or returned to the UK.
- **84 Squadron (Beverley).** To move to Sharjah and to re-equip with Andovers in due course.
- **105 Squadron (Argosy).** To move to Muharraq and to disband once 84 Squadron had completed its Andover re-equippment programme.
- **78 Squadron (Wessex).** To move to Sharjah on completion of the withdrawal.

It was estimated that twenty-four passenger and six freighter sorties, with assistance from the command's own transport force, would be required to make the final lift of personnel and equipment from Khormaksar over a three-day period.

The Six-Day War

The outbreak of hostilities between Israel and the neighbouring Arab countries on 5 June relieved the pressure on Strike Wing as the number of operational sorties began to subside. Due to Britain's support for the Israeli position, anti-British feeling in the Federation increased notably and fuel supplies to the airfield were severely curtailed once again. The re-introduction of fuel rationing limited the majority of Strike Wing sorties to border patrols by single aircraft and top-cover patrols over the Wadi Matlah area along Dhala Road as this remained a favoured location for dissident ambushes on Army convoys. A slight easing in the fuel quota saw the Strike Wing allocation increase to 4,000 gallons per day; well below the quantity needed, considering that a fully-fuelled Hunter required 1,050 gallons. However, the situation improved after restrictions were lifted on the 13th.

Unrest in the east

With unrest also on the increase in the Eastern Aden Protectorate, two FGA.9s were fitted with 100-gallon drop tanks on the outboard pylons and placed on 15-minute standby on 10 June, ready to respond to requests for aerial support, as they would

A pile of rubble at the foot of the building on the right of this up-country estate would suggest it had been subjected to Strike Wing attention in the recent past (Ken Simpson).

undoubtedly arise. Nothing untoward occurred until the 15th when reports of dissident tribesmen having stolen a Land Rover from the South Arabian Army were received at Strike Wing HQ. Two 8 Squadron pilots, Flight Lieutenant Webb (XK151) and Flying Officer Mathie (XJ680), were ordered to scramble and head for Musaynaah, eighty miles east of Riyan. A flagwave was flown over the local Hadramaut Bedouin Legion fort and several villages and encampments suspected of sheltering the culprits.

Two days later, and by way of reassurance for the local Sultan and HBL forces, OC 8 Squadron elect, Squadron Leader Trowern (XF431), led a section of four aircraft on a firepower demonstration near the town of Saywun. The other three aircraft were flown by Flight Lieutenants Taylor (XE655) and Webb (XG298) and Flying Officer Pym (XF456). Despite severe storms and blowing sand, all aircraft managed to hit their intended targets. The return leg to Khormaksar was disrupted by the turbulent weather, the leader and his number three losing some of their instrumentation as they made their way back to base.

On 19 June the 8 Squadron standby pair was scrambled on a Topcat call out, following receipt of a radio message concerning an AAC Scout that had been fired on by dissident tribesmen in Wadi Misrah. Fifteen dissidents had been spotted by the helicopter's crew but, by the time the Hunters arrived, they had taken refuge in a nearby mosque. The Hunters performed a flagwave low over the building and its surroundings to issue the warning.

Police mutiny

A marked increased in terrorist activity during the latter part of June culminated with a mutiny by both the South Arabian Police in Crater and factions of the recently-formed South Arabian Army in Champion Lines. In one incident the Strike Wing Servicing hangar was struck by machine-gun fire from the direction of the SAA Lines.

Having officially taken over command of 8 Squadron, Squadron Leader Trowern was in action once again on 21 June when he led four 8 Squadron Hunters and a pair from 43 Squadron on an operation codenamed KNIT. Using a cocktail of HE cannon and HE rockets, the operation's objective was to destroy a pair of houses deep inside Wadi Bana, following intelligence reports that they were being used to store dissident arms. Such strikes were commonly referred to as 'knocking them over' and 'slum clearance'. No. 1417 Flight pilot Flight Lieutenant Farquhar-Smith was tasked with taking action photographs of the strike as it was pressed home and of the resulting damage. On their way back to Khormaksar, Squadron Leader Trowern was instructed to divert the six Hunters and perform a low, fast and noisy flagwave over the police barracks in the centre of Crater, following a murderous attack on British troops by rebellious South Arabian policemen the previous day. One aircraft received six hits from a Russian 7.62mm light machine gun but managed to land safely back at Khormaksar.

Despite its rather drab paintwork, the markings of all three Hunter units are evident in this view of 1417 Flight T.7 XL566 taken at Khormaksar in 1967 (author's collection). The T.7s were coded in the range TW to TZ ('T' for trainer) during their final few years of service in Aden.

Growing unrest in the SAA and the associated riots were just the latest in a series of crises to confront the British authorities in Aden. To deter copycat actions by FRA troops, four flagwave sorties were flown over camps at Museimir, Dhala and Habilayn by 8 Squadron aircraft. The number of Strike Wing FGA.9s held at five-minute readiness was increased from four to eight to cover further incidents should they occur.

Perfecting the paradrop

Meanwhile, the Vinten cameras on a pair of 1417 Flight FR.10s had been busy photographing potential targets in the Habilayn area at the request of 1st Battalion Irish Guards. On landing back at Khormaksar, one of the pair waited, engine running, for the processed prints which were flown back at high speed and para-dropped over the Habilayn HQ. Similar photographic and para-drop missions were flown by the FR.10s in the Habilayn area later in the month in support of operations in plan by the SAS and 45 Royal Marine Commando. OC 1417 Flight, Squadron Leader Barraclough, was also detailed to photograph targets in Wadis Lusm and Danis and para-drop the processed prints at the Habilayn camp.

In spite of continued tension throughout southern Arabia, a detachment of seven 8 Squadron and four 43 Squadron pilots, plus the wing weapons officer, were detached to Sharjah for an APC on 20 June together with seven FGA.9s and a T.7. Additional pilots and sufficient members of the groundcrew followed up in a 105 Squadron Argosy. A total of fifty-six cannon and forty-three RP strike sorties were flown on the Jeb-a-Jib range over the duration of the detachment.

The impact of terrorism

An analysis of terrorist incidents in Aden State during the first part of 1967 and an assessment as to the effect they were having on the population in general sent shockwaves through British government circles. The alarming figure of 492 had already exceeded the total for the whole of the previous year. Sixty-one people had been killed, including twenty-eight servicemen, and 113 people injured, thirty-nine of them servicemen. For the first time in its history, Khormaksar airfield had to be closed for two hours when RAF Regiment patrols guarding the perimeter fence came under sustained attack from terrorist groups. To make matters worse, the Federal Government was rapidly losing what little control it retained, as the NLF engaged in pitched street battles with its political counterparts in Sheikh Othman.

Sabotage at Aden Airport

Having been taken out of service for an engine change, Aden Airways Viscount VR-AAV was isolated on the civil airport apron for twenty-four hours, just in case a bomb

Engines running, Aden Airways Viscount VR-AAV prepares to depart the Civil Airport in March 1964, shortly after entering service with the airline (author).

had been placed on board during its time in the hangar. Lax security at the airport enabled the terrorists to do exactly that. At 15:30 on 30 June a bomb exploded and the aircraft caught fire, damaging it beyond repair. Large fragments from the aircraft landed on the Hunter pan less than thirty yards away but, fortunately, no aircraft were damaged or personnel injured. Much too close for comfort though!

Jail break!

On the last day of June Squadron Leader Davidson (XF431), Flight Lieutenant Hayward (XJ646) and Flying Officers Dean (XG296) and Lawton (XF440) were detailed to carry out a 43 Squadron strike on a large group of dissidents spotted at the junction of Wadis Bana and Taym as they prepared to storm Jaar Prison and free political prisoners. Diving down from 20,000 feet to maintain the element of surprise, the Hunters unleashed full loads of rocket and cannon fire at the unsuspecting rebels. Thirty minutes later Flight Lieutenant Taylor (XG205) led a second wave of four aircraft to effect a similar attack on the dishevelled remnants below. The remaining three aircraft were flown by Flight Lieutenants Thornton (XJ632), Tite (XE530) and Davis (XF388), who were on detachment from 208 Squadron.

At the end of his tour, OC 43 Squadron, Squadron Leader Davidson, returned to the UK to take up a post at the RAFC Bracknell. To succeed him, OC 208 Squadron, Squadron Leader T. Thornton, moved down from Muharraq to assume command of 43 Squadron.

All but ten of the seventy-four operational sorties recorded for July were flown by 8 Squadron pilots, the majority on border patrols. Twelve 43 Squadron pilots had, meanwhile, relieved those on the Strike Wing APC at Sharjah, leaving eight at Khormaksar as back-up for 8 Squadron. Border patrols were flown without the assistance of Whiskey Radar between 11 and 17 July, while it was uprooted and moved from Mukeiras to Fort Morbut, high above RAF Steamer Point.

Another bout of tribal warfare in Wadi Rihab was responded to when three top-cover sorties were flown by 8 Squadron aircraft on the 15th to protect a 78 Squadron 'casevac' Wessex evacuating a wounded local national from Huen Suffa. As the fighting persisted, further of flagwaves were flown on the 19th and 20th and a firepower demonstration on the 21st.

For some time the inhabitants of a small village near Al Khabr had been causing serious problems for the local constabulary, in spite of the close proximity of a company of SAA. The infighting continued until a pair of Hunters appeared overhead. On the 25th the standby pair was scrambled to the Aqqan area following reports that dissidents had stolen a Land Rover from an SAA camp at Museimir. On arrival, the pilots found no trace of the vehicle, nor were there any signs of troops having been in the area. With no offensive action required, the pilots resorted to performing a flagwave over Aqqan before heading back to Khormaksar.

Automatic exposure

No operational tasks were detailed for 1417 Flight during July, most of its flying time being devoted to pre- and post-recce training. The flight's sixty-minute standby commitment remained in force, however, requiring two pilots and two FR.10s to be at the readiness state between 05:30 to 17:30 each day. The most engrossing topic of conversation on the flight at this time concerned the installation of automatic iris aperture controls on the F.95 cameras fitted to FR.10 XF460. Its infinitely-variable, automatically-controlled lens aperture enabled the flight to provide 'customers' with top-quality photographs irrespective of the prevailing daytime light conditions.

Towards the end of the month, the photographic processing caravans were removed from the Strike Wing complex and prepared for transfer to Muharraq. The AFME Processing Centre assumed responsibility for 1417 Flight's film processing requirements, while the Strike Wing Processing Centre retained the less demanding task of processing GGSR and G.90 cine film. As July drew to a close, it was confirmed that 1417 Flight would disband in September and its FR.10s reallocated to 8 Squadron. The intention had been to leave the four aircraft behind to form the nucleus of a fledgeling South Arabian Air Force, but this was changed when an FR element was considered to be a necessary requirement in Bahrain.

Bearing its master's initials on its fin, 1417 Flight FR.10 XF460 flies low and fast through a fertile valley while on a mission to catch sight of dissident activities that could warrant the attention of the FGA.9s (Ken Simpson).

Beginning of the end

The reducing demand for medium-sized transport aircraft in Aden enabled 105 Squadron to begin the process of moving some of its fleet of Argosys up to Muharraq. Six were flown up during July leaving a flight of four aircraft at Khormaksar's disposal. Likewise, there no longer being a need to retain a heavylift capability in Aden, three 84 Squadron Beverleys were flown to the UK, leaving the remaining three to move up to Sharjah and await their call to assist with the big airlift out of Khormaksar. As events transpired, they were recalled to Aden on several occasions to participate in various operations.

In early August, a small band of terrorists managed to evade security patrols and fire mortar bombs at the aircraft aprons. The improvised revetments, comprising oil drums filled with water, absorbed most of the blast damage but two Shackletons sustained minor damage from splinters and flying debris. They were quickly repaired.

Hunter rundown – 8 Squadron

With the rundown of British forces in Aden gaining momentum, the time had come to reduce the size of the strike force at Khormaksar. With 1417 Flight's disbandment scheduled for September and that of 43 Squadron in November, 8 Squadron was instructed to prepare to move to Muharraq. Operational flying for the squadron in August amounted to just nine patrols along the Yemen border, the honour of flying the Squadron's final sortie in Aden being credited to OC, Squadron Leader Fred Trowern in FGA.9 XJ692 on the 7th.

On the following day, after forty years of almost unbroken service in Aden, emotions were running high as eight 8 Squadron FGA.9s departed Khormaksar for the last time and headed north for Masirah. To ensure sufficient aircraft and pilots were retained at Khormaksar, four aircraft were handed over to 43 Squadron, together with four 8 Squadron pilots – Squadron Leader Taylor, Flight Lieutenant Langrill and Flying Officers Bain and Heather-Hayes.

No. 8 Squadron remained on detachment at Masirah until the end of the month in case it should be needed to reinforce the final days of the withdrawal from Aden. Flying consisted initially of sector recces deep into Muscat and Oman to familiarise pilots with the area, followed by visual reconnaissance competitions run along the lines of the 'Royal Flush' events held in 2nd Tactical Air Force (2 TAF).

With internal unrest on the rise in the Persian Gulf, pairs of 42 and 206 Squadron Shackleton MR.3s were flown out from the UK to form the Sharjah Maritime Detachment. Its principal role was to intensify surveillance of the Gulf region with the objective of stopping, or at least reducing, an alarming increase in arms shipments being smuggled to insurgents through the coastal states.

(above) A farewell formation tour of the Aden hinterland by nine 8 Squadron FGA.9s led by OC the Squadron Des Melaniphy (Chris Bain). With their shadows trailing behind, eight 8 Squadron FGA.9s leave Aden for the last time on a heading for Masirah and a new chapter in the Squadron's impressive history, 8 August 1967 (Ken Simpson).

XF701, one of four UK-based MR.3/3s allocated to the Sharjah Maritime Detachment in September 1967 (Aviation Bookshop).

Anyone hoping for a smooth rundown in Aden was in for a rude awakening as the pace of Hunter operations accelerated through August. No. 43 Squadron found itself flying top cover, flagwaves and border patrols with increasing regularity as a counter to inter-tribal feuding in the Ruseis, Sur and Museinah areas. An SAA push to eject a band of dissidents from Al Kirsh saw the squadron flying top cover as a 1417 Flight FR.10 provided a radio link between the various units engaged in the operation. In response to reports of a large infiltration of NLF sponsored dissidents crossing from the Yemen, a loose low-level formation of six Hunters was flown along the border between Mukeiras and Am Mijea on an intelligence-gathering exercise. Large numbers of tents were spotted but none of the occupants.

To cover an SAA advance into the Al Kirsh area, a firepower demonstration by four aircraft on the evening of the 16th was followed by a second comprising three pairs of aircraft early the next morning. Three days later an intelligence message received late in the evening reported large numbers of NLF supporters crossing the border into the WAP. At first light on the 20th two FR.10s flew reconnaissance sorties over Wadis Bana and Yahar, leaving a second pair to make visual and photographic recces of suspect dissident encampments in Wadi Milh area. Meanwhile, six 43 Squadron aircraft departed Khormaksar at 05:50 to carry out armed recces over the suspected access routes but, apart from a large number of tents, nothing suspicious was sighted.

Knocking down a fort!

The most elating operation of the month occurred on 24 August at Shurjan Fort, close to the Yemen border.

After Flight Lieutenant Bagshaw (FR.10) and Flight Lieutenant Willman (in a 43 Squadron FGA.9) had obtained visual and photographic evidence on the previous day that NLF sympathisers had taken over the fort, eight FGA.9s, each armed with twelve HE rockets and full HE gunpacks, were despatched with instructions to destroy the structure. Led by Flight Lieutenant Malin, the first section of four aircraft lifted off at 16:40. At 17:05 the second section, led by Flight Lieutenant Willman in T.7 XL612, with GLO Major Lees seated alongside in the role of observer, took off and headed in the same direction. The explosive impact of ninety-two rockets and 2,940 rounds of 30mm cannon-fire proved too much for the solid stone-built structure. Post-strike photographs taken by Squadron Leader Barraclough and Flight Lieutenant Simpson confirmed that it was completely destroyed. This was the first time that a 'live' target had been attacked in a pre-planned strike for some time and gave recent arrivals first-hand experience in how to knock over a defended fort.

Despite sixteen operational sorties being flown in as many days, 1417 Flight was also involved in extra-curricular activities. Flight Lieutenant Farquhar-Smith had the distinction of flying His Excellency The High Commissioner, Sir Humphrey Trevelyan, on a tour of the South Arabian Federation in a Hunter T.7, while Flight Lieutenant Simpson was busy taking photographs of the 8 Squadron farewell formation flypast as it departed Khormaksar for the last time.

As initial plans foresaw the handing over of the four 1417 Flight FR.10s to a newly-formed South Arabian Air Force (SAAF) at some point before the final pull out, the 8 Squadron T.7 remained at Khormaksar to fly supervisory and familiarisation checks on five prospective SAAF pilots. With this completed, it departed for Masirah on 27 August. Whether the SAAF pilots were sufficiently competent to fly the Hunter was not disclosed in the ORB.

Confirmation that 1417 Flight would disband on 8 September and its aircraft and personnel be absorbed into 8 Squadron as its B Flight was received in the final few days of August. Two FR.10 pilots and their aircraft would remain at Khormaksar after the disbandment, as the 8 Squadron (FR) detachment, to provide a photo-recce function for 43 Squadron. Squadron Leader Barraclough would be re-assigned as Deputy Officer Commanding Flying Wing.

The flight continued to utilise its aircraft intensively through the first week of September, an average of two operational sorties being flown per day. Several photographic sorties were flown to complete a photographic survey of every town and village within a fifteen-mile radius of Khormaksar.

To mark its impending disbandment, two parties were held, one for airmen in 'The Hair of the Dog' (the RAF Police Club), and a luncheon for the pilots and distinguished RAF officers. A state of 'poor photographic light' was declared for the afternoon to allow members to continue their festivities until well after darkness had fallen.

No. 37 Squadron disbands

To the surprise of many, 37 Squadron was disbanded on 5 September. The last Shackleton sortie was a SAR scramble on the 4th when one of the aircraft's Griffon engines was struck by a bullet! Together with a 1417 Flight FR.10, it had been tasked to find an AAC Scout that had gone missing on a flight from Ataq to Mayfa'ah on the previous day.

No. 37 Squadron had been at the forefront of operations throughout its ten-year tenure in Aden and had served the command well. Air-to-air photographs of a solitary Shackleton MR.2 as it performed a farewell flypast over the disbandment parade on 5 September were taken by Flight Lieutenant Simpson in his FR.10. All four aircraft were flown back to RAF Shawbury in the UK on the 8th and 9th.

No. 1417 Flight disbands

Between 4 and 7 September a number of sorties were mounted by 1417 Flight to try to locate an AAC Scout helicopter which had gone missing on a flight from Ataq to Mayfa'ah. On the 7th Flight Lieutenant Whitman reported seeing a suspicious dark patch in the sand, about twelve feet in diameter, in a wadi east of Mayfa'ah. With Flight Lieutenant Whitman for company in a 43 Squadron FGA.9 (XF431), Squadron Leader Barraclough flew FR.10 XF429 on a low-level sortie over the area to capture close-range images of the patch. A subsequent search by Army personnel verified that it was indeed a crash site and that the Scout had been burnt-out and its two occupants murdered. This gruesome find was the last sortie flown by a Hunter bearing 1417 Flight markings.

On 8 September, a signal was received from SASO on behalf of the AOC who was absent in the UK. It read, 'Thank you on behalf of the AOC for the excellent work done by your pilots and groundcrews during your time in AFME. Your skill and knowledge remain in theatre – good luck for the future.' No. 1417 Flight was disbanded on 9 September.

The flight's nose flashes having been painted over and 8 Squadron markings and tail codes (W-Z) applied, one FR.10 (XE599), together with a 43 Squadron FGA.9, were flown up to Masirah late in the day, there to join the rest of the squadron. FR.10 XE614 had already flown up to Muharraq to undergo a primary service. Having completed its four-week detachment on the island, 8 Squadron moved north to take up permanent residence at its new home at Muharraq. Flight Lieutenants Whitman and Bagshaw remained at Khormaksar to fulfil local requirements and provide a photo-recce function for 43 Squadron as the 8 Squadron (FR) detachment, along with the

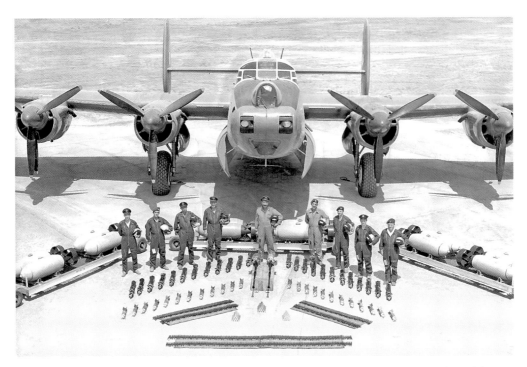

(above) A 37 Squadron crew poses in front of one of its Shackletons and a display of munitions at Khormaksar in August 1967, shortly before the Squadron's disbandment (Alan Taylor). The end is also nigh for 1417 Flight (below) as it parades for the final AOC's inspection, the photograph being taken from one of its FR.10s (Ken Simpson).

two remaining FR.10s (XF429 and XF460). Both pilots were kept on their toes, a total of eighty-eight hours operational flying being recorded between them for the month.

Operation FALDETTA

A fair proportion of these missions were flown in support of an operation named FALDETTA, its objective being to monitor the movement of British troops, vehicles and weapons, 25-pounder guns in particular, Saladins and Ferret cars in the Beihan, Ataq, Mukeiras, Dhala and Kursah areas. FALDETTA would form an increasing proportion of the FR detachment's flying commitment during its final months in Aden. One mission, flown on the 17th in support of FALDETTA, saw Flight Lieutenants Whitman (XF429) and Bagshaw (FGA.9 XJ645) taking off at dusk to perform a recce over Harib village and the nearby fort, and completing the return leg in the dark.

No. 21 Squadron disbands

The next squadron to disband was 21 Squadron on 15 September. While a few of its Twin-Pioneers were re-issued to 152 Squadron at Muharraq, the majority were flown back to MUs in the UK. Just two squadrons, 43 (Hunter FGA.9) and 78 (Wessex), plus the pair of 8 Squadron FR.10s and a flight of 105 Argosy transports were all that remained at Khormaksar to fulfil the air defence, strike, transport and search and rescue commitments.

Exchanging its Twin Pioneers for Wessex helicopters enabled 78 Squadron to work much closer with the troops on the ground. Here we see XS676 lifting off from the Habilayn Army garrison (Richard Grevatte-Ball).

For 43 Squadron, the first few weeks of September had begun well enough with a daily quota of border patrols and an occasional scramble. Dissident tribesmen, meanwhile, had turned their focus of attention to shooting at RAF transports and AAC aircraft using up-country airstrips to re-supply SAA units. To counter these attacks, a variation in the top-cover role was adopted. As it could take anything up to an hour to unload and reload a large transport aircraft, pairs of Hunters were directed to arrive low and noisy at these strips to make their presence known, then climb to a higher level to continue their surveillance while avoiding being shot at and to conserve fuel.

This rather monotonous routine was relieved on the 24th when the Hadramaut Bedouin Legion transmitted a request for firepower demonstrations to be carried out in the proximity of three forts located in Wadi Hadramaut, 300 miles north-east of Aden. Accurate planning and timing were essential due to the limitations on fuel. Three pairs were despatched, each to their designated area, and the demonstrations executed as requested. A GLO had departed earlier in a Beverley to act as an airborne FAC. Everything went as planned for the first two demonstrations but by the time the final pair arrived the light was fading fast and the FAC had difficulty in pinpointing the target area. It was eventually located and the Hunter gunpacks emptied at it. By the time they headed for home, their fuel levels were borderline and it was almost dark when they touched down at Khormaksar.

A further nine sorties were flown on up-country reconnaissance later in the month, two as escorts to Canberra PR.9s on photographic missions. All told, 159 operational sorties were flown during September, only sixteen short of the squadron maximum achieved during one month of the Radfan campaign. Whereas the average sortie length back then was fifty-five minutes, the total number of operational hours for this month was 265. This gave an average sortie duration of 1 hour 40 minutes, the difference being due to the nature of the sortie, flying at endurance speed and at high level.

Operation HISTORIC

Despite in-depth preparations for a trouble-free exit by military planners, the prospect of a firefight formed part of their planning. Under the codename Operation HISTORIC, seven 8 Squadron FGA.9s at Muharraq were permanently configured with long-range underwing tanks and gunpacks fully armed with HE cannon, and placed on sixty-minute readiness to fly down to Khormaksar should their assistance be required. The aircraft were otherwise utilised on the squadron's training programme with the armament safety break under the port wing disconnected.

Operational flying for the two FR.10s at Khormaksar during October consisted mainly of sixty-one surveillance and top-cover sorties for an SAA supply convoy heading for Beihan and a South Arabian Police convoy moving between Lawdar and Mayfa'ah. Operation FALDETTA also kept 43 Squadron's aircraft fully employed. Although very little in-house training was carried out, three jet-conversion training flights for SAAF pilots were conducted in the T.7 over the first three days of the month. On the 5th OC Flying Wing, Wing Commander 'Pancho' Ramirez, flew the C.-in-C. MEC, Admiral Sir Michael Le Fanu around the standard South Arabian 'tourist route' in the T.7, escorted by Squadron Leader Barraclough in an FR.10.

On 10 October Wing Commander Ramirez, Flying Officer Bain (8 Squadron) and Flight Lieutenant Willman (43 Squadron), ferried three 'redundant' FGA.9s, (XG255, XG298 and XE645) to Amman, gifts to the Royal Jordanian Air Force as replacements for Hunters lost in the six-day war. Each aircraft was repainted in Jordanian markings, including Arabic serial numbers, before departure.

DC-3 hijack?

Between 14 and 18 October several recces were discreetly mounted by 43 Squadron FGA.9s and 8 Squadron FR.10s to track an Air Djibouti DC-3 (nicknamed the 'Phantom Dakota') that had been chartered to fly the HBL payroll to the former RAF airfield at Riyan, now under the control of the SAA. No preventive measures were taken when the DC-3 was hijacked by the NLF although, as suspected, the perpetrators were planning to use it to run guns for their supporters. The crew was ordered at gunpoint to fly several trips between an airstrip near Ataq and another undiscovered location. With the final shipment unloaded, the crew was released and the aircraft allowed to fly on to Khormaksar where it arrived on the 18th. The authorities were unable to verify that the aircraft had been used for gun-running.

No. 43 Squadron disbands

Although 43 Squadron would continue to honour its operational commitments until the final few days of occupation, its disbandment parade was brought forward to 14 October to avoid conflicting with the anticipated high rate of aircraft and personnel movements during the latter stages. The ceremonial parade was reviewed by the AOC, Air Vice-Marshal A.H. Humphrey CB OBE DFC AFC RAF, but operational commitments restricted the farewell flypast to just five aircraft, three FGA.9s, a T.7 and an FR.10. The latter was flown by Flight Lieutenant Whitman who subsequently broke away to photograph the squadron's aircraft flying in box formation. Flight Lieutenants Derek Whitman and David Bagshaw attended the formal disbandment celebrations which followed, as did OC 8 Squadron, Squadron Leader Fred Trowern, and his A Flight commander, Flight Lieutenant Mike Webb, both of whom had flown down from the Gulf in an FGA.9 and an FR.10.

As the squadron was no longer operational no further entries were recorded in the 43 Squadron ORB for the period following its disbandment but its Hunters continued to fly on operations until the end of November. The final few paragraphs for this period are, therefore, based on information gathered from alternative sources.

The last two Hunter FR.10s to operate in Aden, XF429-X and XF460-Y, had discarded their former 1417 Flight markings in favour of those of 8 Squadron when photographed over the Aden hinterland in late 1967 ('Noddy' Hawkins).

During the afternoon of 18 October an SAA convoy was spotted by 8 Squadron (FR) pilot Flight Lieutenant Bagshaw unexpectedly heading in an easterly direction from Lawdar. From then until the 26th a regular pattern of twice-daily surveillance sorties was flown by 8 and 43 Squadron aircraft, until the convoy reached Mayfa'ah, its destination. SAA units comprised primarily NLF supporters and it was subsequently learned from intelligence sources that the purpose of the convoy was to introduce an NLF presence into the FLOSY-dominated Aulaqi sultanate. The two parties had been responsible for executing terrorist activities in Aden State and were staunch opponents in the battle to govern South Arabia after the British withdrawal. Subsequent reports appeared to confirm that the NLF achieved its aim as the ruling sultan was spirited away from his palace in As Said into Saudi Arabia. The SAA commander designate resigned the following day.

It was perhaps fitting that the penultimate month of Hunter operations in Aden should produce one of the highest number of operational sorties, over 160 by 43 Squadron and eighty by 1417 Flight. Comprising mainly top-cover sorties for RAF and AAC aircraft operating from up-country airstrips, the Hunters were also employed on search-and-rescue missions for convoys and aircraft.

The departure to Bahrain on 27 October of the AOC, Air Vice-Marshal Humphrey, was marked by a co-ordinated flypast of twelve 43 Squadron Hunters, six 78 Squadron

Water-filled oil drums provided improvised revetments to protect the Hunters and Beverleys from mortar attacks in the autumn of 1967 (author's collection).

Wessex, plus three Beverleys and a Dakota from 84 Squadron. The three elements of the formation were timed to pass over the airfield as the AOC was about to board his VIP Andover. Flight Lieutenants Whitman and Bagshaw flew their FR.10s as airborne spares, allowing the former to take photographs of the formation as it flew across the airfield.

Dates for withdrawal

Due to the multiplicity of perplexing statements issued earlier by the British government, there remained a high degree of uncertainty as to the actual date for the final withdrawal. Having originally stated that it would take place 'shortly after independence, at the beginning of 1968', the date was changed to 20 November in May 1967 and this remained the departure date target. Such was the indecision that the withdrawal date was changed yet again on 2 November, when it was deferred by ten days to 30 November. Thirteen days later, as the major airlift of personnel and equipment was getting underway, the decision was taken to bring the departure forward twenty-four hours to 29 November, in the hope of avoiding a terror attack on the final day.

Naval handover

Air defence patrols by 43 Squadron were discontinued on 7 November when HMS *Eagle* joined the large naval task force gathering in the Gulf of Aden in readiness to cover the final phase of the withdrawal. On the following day, the air defence commitment was handed over to the Sea Vixen and Buccaneer squadrons operating from the carrier.

Having flown ashore from HMS Eagle, 800 Squadron Buccaneer S.2 XV337 stands on the Visitor's pan at Khormaksar in readiness to take over the air defence role from 43 Squadron (author's collection).

The last Hunter strikes were flown on 9 November, against dissident targets near Kirch, following a special request from the SAA. The squadron's Hunter allocation had by this time been trimmed to ten FGA.9s: XE546, XE550, XE618, XE620, XF456, XG154, XG256, XG296, XJ645 and XJ692. In addition to providing a standby facility, they were occasionally utilised on recce sorties by the two FR pilots. The last sortie flown by a 43 Squadron Hunter was recorded in the 8 Squadron (FR) ORB, as a FALDETTA recce by Flight Lieutenant Whitman in XG154 on 24 November.

Hunter fatality

On 20 November Flight Lieutenant Patterson was leading a section of four 8 Squadron FGA.9s flying from Sharjah for a practice session on the range. On approaching the target, he called 'pulling-up' at the correct point, followed by 'contact target' as he rolled into the attack but his aircraft (XE654) continued rolling until it crashed into the ground, killing the pilot.

The two 8 Squadron (FR) FR.10s continued to perform in the role for which they had proved so invaluable in Aden since their introduction in 1961. The difference in these final weeks was that up-country sorties were flown in company with pairs of Buccaneers. The latter had the added advantage of two pairs of eyes, the pilot concentrating on tracking the FR.10 and the observer on visual intelligence gathering. The two aircraft completed eighty-four hours flying on mixed operations during November, the majority on Operation FALDETTA related sorties, tracking the movement of military vehicles, weapons and 25-pounder guns, in areas around Beihan, Ataq, Mukeiras, Dhala and Kursah, while keeping a watchful eye on the movements of friend and foe.

Operation JACOBIN TWO

Operation JACOBIN TWO, the largest logistics operation to be mounted by the RAF since the Berlin Airlift of 1948, had been in plan for some months and was about to be put into action. At its core was a plan to evacuate no fewer than 3,700 people and tons of military equipment from Khormaksar over a seven-day period. Due to the limited availability of civil aircraft, the main lift was carried out by AFME Argosys and Beverleys, plus three RAF and three BUA VC10s, fourteen RAF Britannias, fifteen Hercules and two Belfasts of Air Support Command.

To ease the administrative burden, servicemen were assigned to groups comprising twenty-five men, all of whom were fully customs-cleared before departure. Having disembarked at Muharraq, their aircraft returned to Khormaksar to collect the next group, and this was then repeated until all had left. At Muharraq personnel were fed and watered before being embarked on RAF VC10 and Britannia aircraft for the flight to RAF Lyneham. The procedure was quick and efficient and worked like clockwork.

On 28 November, with Flight Lieutenants Whitman and Bagshaw at the controls, the two 8 Squadron (FR) FR.10s, XF429 and XF460, were detailed to escort the High Commissioner's RAF Britannia away from Khormaksar and continue north to Masirah, there to rejoin the squadron which remained on standby should it be needed to cover the withdrawal. No. 8 Squadron had proudly lived up to its nickname, 'Aden's own', but after forty years of dedicated service in South Arabia, its tenure at Khormaksar was finally at an end.

The withdrawal from Aden was a master class in inter-service co-operation. At 15:00 on 29 November 1967, as the last RAF transport disappeared from view, Royal Marines of 42 Commando climbed aboard the Wessex helicopters of 78 Squadron and squadrons from the Royal Navy waiting on the golf course to the north of the airfield and headed out to HM Ships *Albion*, *Intrepid* and *Fearless*, anchored in the Gulf of Aden.

After 128 years British rule in South Arabia experienced an unseemly and abrupt conclusion. Aden was an uncomfortable and exhausting place in which to live and the work was difficult and challenging to say the least. When asked if there were any positive aspects of their time in the heat, an overriding sense of camaraderie, experience and a feeling of satisfaction for a job well done were the most common responses from former servicemen fortunate to fly and maintain the wide variety of aircraft that once graced the desert skies above Southern Arabia.

Pastures new!

The story of Hunter operations in the Middle East did not end with the closure of Khormaksar, however, as they continued to serve in the Persian Gulf for a further four years and this is the subject for the final chapter.

The ceremonial parade marking the departure of the last High Commissioner of Aden, Sir Humphrey Trevelyan, captured as he climbs the steps leading to Britannia, XM518, on 28 November 1967 (John Severne).

Chapter 13

1968-1971 – Gulf pursuits

Background review

A steady secure supply of oil was and still is of vital importance to a British economy which will continue to rely on this crucial source of energy for the foreseeable future. The government's determination to protected both its production and the oceans through which it is shipped has been demonstrated on many occasions. As we have seen in Chapter 6, the first real postwar threat to the supply occurred in June 1961 when the Iraqi leader, General Kassim, laid claim to Kuwait and proceeded to mobilise his forces in preparation for an invasion of the tiny oil-rich state. Fortunately, Britain was able to respond in time to prevent this happening but it was a close-run thing.

In spite of Iraq's continued threat to other countries in the region, the Ruler of Bahrain, Sheikh Sir Salman II bin Hamad al-Khalifa, steadfastly refused to allow Britain to locate an offensive strike force in Bahrain, as he believed this would be interpreted as a weakness by other Arab States. The communications and transport aircraft operated by 152 Squadron – Pembrokes and Twin-Pioneers – were the only military aircraft granted permanent status on Bahraini soil.

In recognising the detrimental effect of an Iraqi invasion on the supply of oil from other Gulf states, while not wishing to be caught off-guard a second time, Britain, through its political officer in Bahrain, attempted to persuade the late Ruler's successor, Isa bin Salman al-Khalifa, that it was in his and his country's interests to overturn his forebear's resistance. Reluctantly, he conceded and agreed for one Hunter and one heavylift transport squadron to be stationed at RAF Bahrain but only on short-term detachments.

A programme of rotating aircraft and personnel from the two Khormaksar-based Hunter squadrons, 8 and 208, together with the Eastleigh- and Khormaksar-based Beverley squadrons, 30 and 84 respectively, to Bahrain every two months was seen as the best solution, at least for the time being. In addition, pairs of Canberra PR.9s from 13 Squadron were detached from RAF Akrotiri, Cyprus, to maintain surveillance on troop and aircraft movements to the north of the Iraq border. Daily photographic sweeps over the country became routine for the squadron whose aircraft and crews were rotated every few weeks.

The practice of rotating the Hunters and Beverleys continued for nearly three years, when agreement was reached with the Ruler for the restraining order to be lifted. As Khormaksar had insufficient space to house three Hunter squadrons simultaneously,

Once the Sea Vixen and Buccaneer squadrons had become accustomed to operating out of Khormaksar, 43 Squadron flew its last FGA.9s up to Masirah where XJ645 awaits its next allocation (author's collection).

the decision was taken to redeploy 208 Squadron to RAF Muharraq (the new name for RAF Bahrain from 1 December 1963) on a permanent basis, the move taking place in June 1964. It was joined there by the remaining 30 Squadron Beverleys a few months later. The 13 Squadron Canberra detachment, however, continued to function on a rotating detachment basis.

No further deployments were sanctioned until 1967 when, with the impending closure of Khormaksar, 105 Squadron moved a flight of Argosys up to Muharraq, followed by the remaining aircraft during the final days of the occupation of Aden. At the same time, 43 Squadron flew its Hunters up to Masirah where they remained to await their next unit allocations. One or two joined the Gulf squadrons but the majority were flown to back 19 MU in the UK.

No. 8 Squadron settles in

Following its departure from Khormaksar and four weeks on standby at Masirah, 8 Squadron moved north to Muharraq on 3 September 1967 and began the process of settling in to a less intense pace of life alongside 208 Squadron. Gone was the daily diet of border patrols, strikes and flagwaves over hostile terrain, and the inherent risk of being shot down by a lucky strike from a dissident rifle, a sentiment echoed in the ORB. Whereas very little of consequence relating to the squadron's social life was

To accommodate a second Hunter squadron at Muharraq, the apron had to be extended at an angle due to the proximity of the runaway, as can be seen in this view of 8 Squadron aircraft parked round the apex of the corner (Ken Parry).

noted during its time in Aden, a special section was reserved for the subject after the move to Muharraq.

Nonetheless, there remained an ever-present threat of terrorist activity in neighbouring states on the mainland to the south of Bahrain. A worrying increase in arms cache discoveries in the Trucial States during 1963 had culminated in a series of incidents involving dissidents near RAF Salalah. In the most serious the RAF driver of a supply truck was killed by a landmine that exploded under his vehicle as he travelled from the port to the airfield. The Sultan of Oman decided not to request the assistance of the RAF at this time as he believed the Piston Provosts and Beavers of his diminutive air force were capable of maintaining control. Even so, to ensure that it was prepared to counter any dissident threat, RAF Persian Gulf Command (RAFPG) maintained discreet surveillance across the whole of the northern region, keeping an eye on the movement of nationals considered to be a danger in particular.

Revised Defence Strategy
Shortly before 8 Squadron moved to Muharraq, the British government published a supplementary statement to the effect that it was considering withdrawing British forces from bases in the Far East, the decision being ratified in 1968. Although there were no direct references to RAF bases in the Gulf, the implication was that their retention would probably not form part of the government's long-term defence strategy.

For much of November 1967, both 8 and 208 Squadrons were detached to Sharjah to free up sufficient space at Muharraq for the high volume of transport aircraft expected to make use of the airfield during the final weeks of the withdrawal from Aden. The squadrons remained there until early December when the last passengers staging through from Khormaksar had departed for the UK.

Gulf Command

To cater for the influx of squadrons, a re-organisation of the command was put in hand. The two Hunter squadrons, 8 and 208, were incorporated into a new wing known as the Offensive Support Wing (OSW), leaving the transport squadrons at

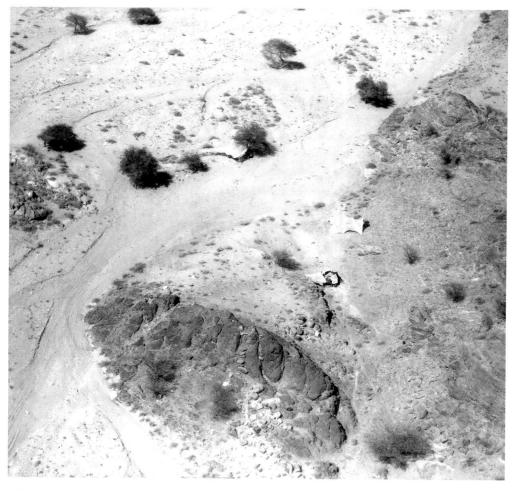

Above and opposite: The ability of SAS troops to merge into their surroundings was key to their success and to help hone their skills, patrols were regularly flown out to the Oman hinterland from the UK for exercises with the RAF. These two photographs were taken by 8 Squadron FR.10 pilot Tim Thorn once he had spotted the tents on the left and Land Rovers on the right (Tim Thorn).

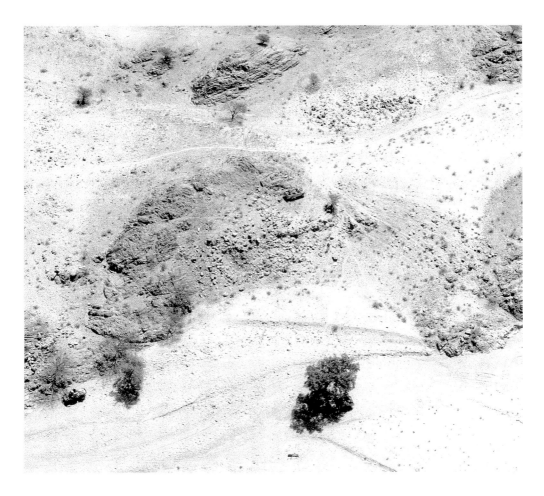

Muharraq, 30, 105 and 152, plus 78 and 84 at Sharjah, to reform under the Operations and Transport Wing umbrella. Middle East Command was disbanded and in its place, a new command, Gulf Command, was established.

Following the arrival of replacement Andover C.1s at Sharjah, 84 Squadron waved goodbye to the last of its Beverley transports as the year drew to a close. The questionable disbandment of 105 Squadron on 31 January 1968 and loss of the Argosy in theatre was quickly acknowledged and resolved by rotating flights of Argosys every three months from RAF Benson in the UK.

No sooner had the newly-composed force settled down than thoughts turned to establishing closer working relationships between the three service elements. From an RAF perspective, the policy was initiated with a series of exercises with Army units operating in the mountainous Jebel Akhdar region of Oman. A degree of authenticity was added by flying members of the SAS out from the UK to take on a role of evasive insurgents. OSW Hunters were then despatched to locate them and direct the defending force to their hideouts.

Squadron composition

Whereas 208 Squadron comprised two flights each of six FGA.9s – A and B Flights, 8 Squadron consisted of one flight of eight FGA.9s – A Flight – and a second with four FR.10s – B Flight. By March 1968 No. 8 Squadron was heavily involved in ground-attack training, which consisted primarily of strikes, cine-weave and tactical FR. Both flights were engaged in an exercise codenamed GOLDLEAF, the objective being to locate small groups of SAS troopers scattered around the foothills near Jebel Akhdar. Despite limited success, the exercise exposed shortcomings that could only be resolved by working more closely with Army units on the ground. Accordingly, 8 Squadron produced a paper outlining the limitations and capabilities of fighter-recce aircraft in a desert environment. In spite of there being no call for offensive flying, the intensity of operational training remained high, the squadron returning a total of 177 hours for March. At 369 hours, the figure for April was more than double.

When, on 9 April, the Ruler of Bahrain, Sheikh Sir Salman II bin Hamad al-Khalifa, paid a visit to RAF Muharraq, the Hunter wing flew sixteen aircraft in formation over the saluting dais at the moment he climbed the steps. Two weeks later the Ruler was treated to a firepower demonstration on the southern tip of Bahrain island, by eight 8 Squadron aircraft armed with twelve rockets and full gunpacks. Two FR.10s then paradropped packages of photographs they had taken during the Ruler's arrival, close to his enclosure.

New weaponry

Although no offensive strikes had been flown by either squadron since their departure from Aden, they continued to maintain their strike capability at a high standard by

A 208 Squadron FGA.9 releases a pair of water-filled 100-gallon drop tanks over the Jeb-a-Jib range in a simulation of a Napalm attack (208 Squadron Association via Graham Pitchfork).

Armed with SNEB rocket pods on the outboard pylons, 208 Squadron FGA.9 XG205 is seen on the pan at Sharjah in March 1968 during a Squadron APC (208 Association via Graham Pitchfork).

allocating sufficient time on the ranges. While operating out of Sharjah, for example, 8 Squadron spent the whole of the first week of May on the range at Rashid. As well as the 30mm cannon and 3-inch rockets that they were well accustomed to, the choice of weapons for training exercises was broadened following the introduction of the 25lb practice bomb, simulated napalm and the SNEB rocket system, recently introduced into RAF service by 208 Squadron. Modification of some of the FGA.9s to carry the SNEB pod on the outer pylons gave pilots the opportunity to gain experience in the use of the new weapon by firing at old Army vehicles on Yas Island under guidance from students on an FAC training School.

Double ejection!

On 6 May Flight Lieutenant Taylor completed his turn on the range and decided to fly low and fast over the range officer's hut. Unfortunately, his aircraft (XE532) struck the HF aerial mast in the process, causing the engine to lose power and, unable to reach Dubai airport nearby, he decided to eject. He was picked up from the sea by the Muharraq Wessex SAR helicopter and flown back to Sharjah, leaving the remnants of his aircraft at the bottom of the ocean.

No sooner had talk of the incident begun to wane than a second ejection grabbed the attention. No. 8 Squadron pilot Flight Lieutenant Pym had completed a series of aerobatic manoeuvres over the desert some fifty miles south-east of Dubai and was tracking back to Muharraq at 3,000 feet. The engine rpm and jpt on his aircraft, FGA.9

One of the many 208 Squadron APCs held at Sharjah in 1968 captures FGA.9 XJ687 (above) with a pair of SNEB pods on board and T.7 XL613 with practice bomb carriers on the outboard pylons (both, author's collection).

8 Squadron FGA.9 XJ680 undergoing undercarriage checks at Muharraq in July 1968 following its return from refurbishment in the UK (Aviation Bookshop).

XF388, suddenly began to fluctuate until the engine eventually flamed out. When down to 1,000 feet, and all attempts to relight the engine having failed, he decided to eject over the sea. He was quickly spotted by other Hunter pilots operating in the area and picked up by the Muharraq rescue helicopter.

In January 1969 No. 8 Squadron pilot Flight Lieutenant Widowson was attached to the Sultan of Oman's Air Force in his capacity as PAI to give instruction on gunsight handling in advance of the arrival of the force's first Strikemasters. While there he flew in a Beaver and Piston Provost and took the opportunity to fire Surs rockets from the latter. On his return to Muharraq he obstinately refused to release his scores to his inquisitive colleagues.

Premature SNEB discharge
During a live SNEB firing exercise on Rashid range on 30 January Wing Commander Hewitt's 208 Squadron FGA.9 received shrapnel damage when a SNEB rocket exploded immediately on exiting the pod. He flew his aircraft back to Sharjah where damage to the pressure cabin was provisionally assessed as Category 3. As a result, SNEB rocket firing was suspended until authorisation was received from HQ RAFPG for a new batch of rockets to be used.

Ferry record?
As has been referred to in earlier chapters, ferrying Hunters to and from MUs in the UK was cause for many a tale of woe and delay at exotic-sounding places,

Pilots and airmen on an 8 Squadron APC at Sharjah relax for the camera around one of their FR.10s. A Jambiya on the nosewheel door is an interesting innovation having first appeared for a short period in 1960 (Brian Hersee).

A rare photograph depicting all four 8 Squadron FR.10s, XF436–W, XF460–Y, XE614–Z and XF429–X flying in formation over the Persian Gulf ('Noddie' Hawkins).

with pilots happy to be awarded the record for the longest trip. The record for the shortest trip, however, probably belongs to 208 Squadron pilots Flight Lieutenant Metcalfe and Flying Officer Griffiths. Having departed Sharjah in FGA.9s XE649 and XG135 at 07:40 on 24 June 1969, they arrived at St Athan at 14:00 the next day. After a further day-and-a-half recuperating, they left Lyneham at 07:00 on the 27th in a pair of refurbished aircraft, XF445 and XJ687, and arrived back at Muharraq at 12:45 on the 28th. The entry in the ORB states: 'This unusual two-way ferry, taking only four-and-a-half days, will be difficult to better.' Both pilots expressed appreciation for the expeditious handling of their aircraft by 56 Squadron groundcrews at RAF Akrotiri.

The majority of exercises carried out by the Hunter squadrons in the Gulf were either between themselves or with one or more elements of the Army and Navy. A naval co-operation exercise with Tribal-class frigate HMS *Zulu* on 25 July was held in an ECM environment presented by Canberras of 360 Squadron. Of the five attacks carried out by a pair of 208 Squadron Hunters, only one succeeded in closing to within 3,000 yards of the ship due to poor visibility and insufficient liaison between the Hunters and Canberras. The remaining four attacks were acquired by the ship's gunnery radar at between five and seven miles range.

Dropping bombs!

The opportunity to employ the Hunter in a bombing role had not been pursued in Aden but had become a standard part of armament practice camps at Sharjah. In October 1969 it was 8 Squadron's turn to explore the aircraft's capability as a bomber, using redundant Army 3-ton trucks as targets. With drop tanks fitted to the outer pylons to simulate bombs, two techniques were employed; skip-bombing at an angle of 3 degrees and level delivery at 50 feet. Due to a local water shortage, permission was granted for the tanks to be filled with fuel. At the completion of the exercise, the largest remaining part of the former military vehicles were the rear axles.

On 13 November a full complement of 208 Squadron aircraft departed Muharraq for an APC at Sharjah. On the whole the range programme went very well with above average gunfiring scores being recorded. The SNEB-firing phase of the programme, however, was curtailed following two incidents of rockets exploding prematurely. No damage was inflicted on the aircraft involved. Problems were also encountered during the bombing phase, with the 25lb practice bombs either hanging up or suffering double release.

Hunter loss

Following an invitation from Kenya for a Hunter squadron to give staff officers a demonstration of close air support (CAS), 8 Squadron flew two FGA.9s and a pair of

FR.10s to Nairobi on 21 November. Members of the groundcrew and spares pack-ups followed on in an ArDet (Argosy Detachment) transport and an 84 Squadron Andover. During the return flight on the 28th, one of the Mark 9s (XF462), was badly damaged while landing at Jeddah. Having selected undercarriage down, the pilot received no indication that it had lowered, although the flaps lowered normally. The pilot of a second Hunter noticed copious amounts of hydraulic fluid pouring from the underside of the aircraft. An attempt to blow the undercarriage down using the emergency air system succeeded in lowering the nose and starboard main wheel but the port wheel remained in the up position. Running low on fuel, the pilot attempted a landing on the right side of the runway but could not prevent the aircraft from veering across the runway and over rough ground into a ditch. The badly damaged aircraft was retrieved by personnel from 71 MU and returned to the UK.

Refining SNEB

Despite having been available for use on the Hunter since 1966 very little testing had been carried out to ascertain the best firing angle for the weapon. In attempting to resolve this part of the brief, 208 Squadron undertook a series of trial firings at Sharjah on 16 and 17 February 1970, the objective being to determine whether the recommended angle of 10 to 15 degrees achieved the most accurate results or if one at 25 degrees was better. It was found that accuracy did not necessarily improve with an increase in dive angle. In fact, it was found that in instances of large wind shears, the shallower dive produced more accurate results. The trial report concluded that the best approach to improving accuracy when using SNEB was to decrease the firing range. As this would incur an increase in 'debris hemisphere height', further advice was sought from the MoD.

To enable Hamala Radar to practise full control of an air defence scenario and keep the Hunter squadrons on their toes, an air defence exercise was conducted on 7 March 1970. No. 208 Squadron was detailed to defend Jebel Dhukan, forty miles south of Bahrain, against an attacking force composed of 8 Squadron Hunters and Vulcan bombers flying out of Masirah. Despite devoting a lot of time preparing for the event, 208 Squadron reported it was disappointed with Hamala Radar as it only offered two intercepts, one a Vulcan and the other a Hunter, leaving the rest of the attacking force free to 'destroy' the target.

Having been flown out to Bahrain in an RAF VC10, Squadron Leader George Ord assumed command of 208 Squadron from Squadron Leader Taylor on 25 May.

Oil!

In 1969 oil began to flow from an isolated wellhead known as Liwa Hollows on the Saudi Arabia/Abu Dhabi border, an area that had been the subject of an ownership

OC 8 Squadron, Sqn Ldr 'Jock' McVie, his pilots and airmen take a break during an APC at Sharjah in 1970 (Ken Parry).

battle between the two states for some time. The discovery of oil had finally brought the matter to a head. In early May 1970 Saudi Arabia issued an ultimatum for Abu Dhabi to remove the installation and disperse the workforce from the area by 19 May. Based on Saudi Arabia's past record, RAFPG decided to place the Hunter Wing on alert and move 208 Squadron on detachment to Sharjah. A schedule was produced for each squadron to carry out visual recces along the border on alternate days, once in the morning and again in the afternoon. Patrols were flown continuously from dawn to dusk over the period between 21 and 31 May and no incidents were reported.

Social activities!
Reference was made earlier of the ability of the squadrons to let their hair down once the aircraft had been secured for the night. This extract from the 8 Squadron ORB dated August 1970 is but one of many similar entries:

Social activity at Sharjah was mainly centred around the consumption of alcohol, paid for by various members of the Squadron. Ken Parry celebrated the arrival of his twins and Keith Grumbley the arrival of his promotion to Flight Lieutenant. The Squadron also threw a beer call for the Mess and had a successful aircrew/groundcrew party. For once, the Boss, Squadron Leader 'Jock' McVie, managed to avoid getting beer thrown at him. On 29 August, having returned to Muharraq, the Squadron took advantage of 208 Squadron's hospitality at a first class pool party.

Fresh from refurbishment in the UK, 8 Squadron FR.10 XJ714 was bereft of Squadron markings when photographed on the line at Sharjah in October 1970 (Ken Parry).

Exercise HOT ROD

In addition to run-of-the-mill exercises the Hunter squadrons were kept on constant alert to ensure that they were ready to respond to any unforeseen incidents. An exercise codenamed HOT ROD was devised to test the wing's ability to prepare a maximum number of fully-armed aircraft within a twelve-hour window, without prior warning, and then to fly them at maximum intensity. The exercise was held on 5 September and became the first of a series. At the end of the twelve-hour window, the aircraft departed on a scramble take off and headed south-east towards the mainland for a live firing session on the Jeb-a-Jib range. A practice air defence of Muharraq was performed on the return leg.

Skills dilemma

Unlike Aden where an unaccompanied tour for airmen was two years, the equivalent at Muharraq was just thirteen months. The largest turnover of Hunter groundcrew since the wing was formed in 1967 occurred in September 1970 when more than 50 per cent of airmen were posted out over a period of seven weeks. The situation was exacerbated further when it was discovered that few of their replacements had experience of working on the Hunter. A HOT ROD exercise exposed the problem when the wing failed to maintain the required sortie rate of three to four sorties per aircraft per day. The airmen did their best and learned very quickly but it was a trying time for everyone on the wing. This state of affairs would not have arisen a decade earlier as the Hunter was in extensive use by several squadrons but, by 1970, 229 OCU was the sole operator and skills resource in the UK.

His tour completed, OC 8 Squadron, Squadron Leader McVie was dined out at a mess function attended by his successor, Squadron Leader Stoker on 16 October.

Iranian challenge

Perhaps the most challenging of exercises undertaken by 8 Squadron was to absorb its attention for the seven days beginning 12 November. With the Imperial Iranian Air Force and Navy mimicking an 'enemy' force, its Hunters were tasked to perform simulated strikes against Iranian shipping each day, but it was the mouthwatering prospect of air combat with Iranian F.5 fighters that was most eagerly anticipated. Sections of four aircraft were launched on intercept sorties but, to everyone's dismay, the F.5s failed to appear 'due to their pilots not being cleared for close combat'.

Exercise AIDEX

Jebel Dhukan was the target for a simulated attack by six Vulcan bombers on 8 December as they made their way at predetermined heights and speeds from Masirah to Cyprus. Exercise AIDEX was devised to give the OSW squadrons the opportunity to intercept them. Five pairs of Hunters were despatched by Hamala Radar, two from 8 Squadron and three from 208 Squadron, and all six bombers were intercepted before reaching their respective targets.

Operation INTRADON

When a report came in that a band of dissidents, indeterminate in number and armed with a heavy machine gun and automatic weapons, had infiltrated an area near Khasab, north-east of Sharjah, four 208 Squadron FGA.9s and an 8 Squadron FR.10 were flown down to Sharjah on 14 December, in readiness to provide close air support for an Army 'clean-up' operation. At first light on the 17th soldiers of the Trucial Oman Scouts were landed at Bukha and Ghumla by 78 Squadron Wessex helicopters. At Ghumla the troops rushed a house in which the rebels were believed to be hiding only to discover that it was a mosque. A mistake by a cartographer had led to the landing being made near the wrong village! When the correct house was eventually located in the right village, it was found to have been recently evacuated. The Hunters maintained a dawn-to-dusk, fifteen-minute readiness state for two days but, as no rebels were spotted, they returned to Muharraq on the 19th.

Exercise ARABIAN NIGHTS

An appropriate name for a training exercise held jointly with the fledgeling Abu Dhabi Defence Force (ADDF) in which both forces were required to employ their respective

The attractive colour scheme borne by Abu Dhabi Defence Force Hunter 701 belies a background of six years service with 8 Squadron and 1417 Flight as FR.10 XE589. Having sustained Cat 4 damage from a bird strike, it was sold back to Hawker Siddeley, rebuilt to FGA.Mk.76 standard and delivered to its new owner on 9 March 1970 (Hawker Siddeley).

air and ground units. Sponsored jointly by HQ RAFPG and the ADDF, the RAF component comprised three 8 Squadron FGA.9s and an FR.10 operating out of Sharjah over a five-day period beginning 25 January 1971. At the time the ADDF comprised 15,000 men, an artillery battery and had recently received eight out of an order for twelve Hawker Hunter F.Mk.76/FR.76A aircraft. These were flown by former RAF pilots on contract and were found to be no mean opponents, their obvious experience leading to a very interesting and constructive exercise.

Goodwill visit to Pakistan

On 1 March 1971 OC 208 Squadron, Squadron Leader Ord, led a flight of four Hunters on a week-long goodwill visit to Pakistan Air Force (PAF) units based at Peshawar, the North West Frontier, Maseer and Karachi. Additional pilots, the ground crew, plus servicing equipment and spares followed in an ArDet Argosy. The purpose of the visit was to:

- Evaluate current squadron tactics against different aircraft
- Gain experience of operating over 'foreign' terrain with unfamiliar procedures
- Examine the problems of support at airfields not suitably equipped for Hunter operations

The flying programme produced by PAF showed little ambition, pitting two pairs of Hunters against F.86 Sabres, MiG-19s and Mirage IIIs on consecutive days. The Mirage session was unfortunately cancelled due to poor 'English-type' weather, but

Sharing the Sharjah pan with a pair of Mark 3 Shackletons, 208 Squadron FGA.9 XK140 is probably awaiting attention from an engine fitter, judging by the panels hanging loose (author's collection).

the Hunters scored a 1-1 draw against the Sabres and a valiant 1-0 victory over the MiG-19s, thanks to Flying Officer Dean. Nine months later, PAF pilots came up against the Hunter for real in a war with neighbouring India.

The clock ticked on!

In the early spring of 1971 a statement confirming that British forces would withdraw from the RAF stations at Muharraq and Sharjah by 31 December 1971 was published by the British government. Both Hunter squadrons would disband, 208 Squadron by late summer and 8 Squadron in December. Making the most of the time remaining, Offensive Support Wing decided to pool all resources to give its pilots experience in leading large formations in combat and bounced simulated strike situations.

In the event the rundown commenced in early April 1971. Having only recently been brought to a peak level of efficiency, the withdrawal plan envisaged that 208 Squadron would gradually diminish in strength over a period of months. Having been associated with the Hunter in the Middle East for the previous eleven years, it now faced the prospect of a slow contraction in the lead up to disbandment.

Before the effects were felt, however, OSW crews became engulfed in another Exercise HOT ROD. The alert was raised at 02:00 on 26 April. Six hours later, following an outstanding effort by the ground crews, fifteen armed and serviceable Hunters were ready to go. The number had increased to twenty-one by the time the flying phase kicked off on the morning of the 27th. The objective for this exercise was for the pilots to fire 120 rounds of HE cannon at obsolete Army vehicles dispersed around the Jeb-a-Jib range, under FAC control.

The departure of three 208 Squadron FGA.9s from Muharraq to the UK marked the beginning of the rundown. Aircraft unserviceability marooned all three aircraft and pilots on an island (unnamed in the ORB) in the Mediterranean for several days and, with a further three pilots on courses in the UK, the squadron had only eight pilots for much of the month. On 24 May, Squadron Leader Ord handed over command of 208 Squadron to newly promoted Squadron Leader Ian Dick AFC.

With the closure of the last land-based radar unit (3 ACC), the frigate HMS *Zulu* became the sole provider of an air defence radar system in the Persian Gulf. As a consequence, co-operation exercises between the Hunter squadrons and various ships of the Royal Navy were intensified.

The 208 Squadron rundown gained momentum on 7 June with the departure of a further four FGA.9s to 5 MU in the UK. One aircraft went AOG at Malta, stranding the pilot, Flying Officer Barrow, for eighteen days. Squadron strength now stood at six aircraft, eleven pilots and forty-two groundcrew. As the month drew to a close, more details of 208 Squadron's demise became known. Plans were put in place for an open day and a low-profile flying display to be held on 21 August,

Three 208 Squadron FGA.9s airborne from Muharraq with XJ688-E and XF431-M closest to the camera (Aviation Bookshop).

attended by a large gathering of former members. The official disbandment would take place on 10 September.

Navy Days

The largest RAF and Royal Navy joint exercise in the Gulf for some time took place some fifty miles north-east of Muharraq on 19 July. Aircraft from both Hunter squadrons were tasked to perform simulated strikes against seven warships – HM Ships *Zulu*, *Wiston*, *Puncheston*, *Gavinton*, *Beachampton*, *Brinton* and *Brereton* – in the morning and firepower demonstrations in the afternoon. The target for the live strike was an obsolete Marine Craft Unit air-sea-rescue launch which was no match for 30mm HE cannon shells and 68mm SNEB rockets.

On 20 July, to mark the twentieth anniversary of the first flight of the Hawker Hunter, Offensive Strike Wing aircraft mounted two flypasts over the station, one composed of a large diamond formation and the second depicting the figure twenty.

From this point on, the majority of Hunter sorties comprised co-operation exercises with Royal Navy warships operating in the Persian Gulf. Opportunities to fire dummy SNEB 30mm ball ammunition at splash targets were taken at regular intervals and a number of 208 Squadron pilots were given the opportunity to fly the FR.10 on low-level recce sorties through the Trucial States and mountainous regions

8 Squadron FGA.9 XF442 undergoing maintenance in the servicing hangar at Muharraq in 1970. In April 1968, XF442 achieved notoriety as the aircraft that flew under Tower Bridge (Aviation Bookshop).

(above) Eleven of 8 Squadron's compliment of thirteen aircraft are present in this 1970 view of the Hunter line at Sharjah, taken during an APC detachment. From right to left, the first four aircraft are; FR.10s XJ714-V and XF441-Y, plus FGA.9s XG252 and XE552-A. (below) A nicely captured photograph of 8 Squadron FGA.9 XE552-A during a sortie from Sharjah (both, David Ainge).

Looking across the 208 Squadron line towards the Argosy detachment (ArDet) pan and the large servicing hangar at Muharraq in August 1970. A pair of 84 Squadron Andovers can also be seen in the background (Ken Parry).

of Muscat and Oman. For the majority, this was their first chance to engage in an FR-type mission and was judged to have been of considerable value.

Bahrain independence
As Iran had laid claim to Bahrain for many years, the government held a referendum to decide the island's future in early 1970. Two options were offered to the population: independence from Britain; or submit to Iranian rule. Not unexpectedly, the overwhelming majority voted for a fully-independent and sovereign state. Iran renounced its claim and Bahrain became an independent nation on 14 August 1971.

No. 208 Squadron disbandment
In order not to raise tensions on the island, the decision was taken to limit the 208 Squadron disbandment to a parade and a reception. The former took place on the squadron apron at 18:00 on 21 August and was reviewed by the Queen's representative in the Persian Gulf, Sir Geoffrey King KCMG. As members of the squadron marched past, a formation of Hunters led by Flying Officer Dean passed overhead in diamond-nine formation. Seven aircraft and pilots were provided by 8 Squadron. The proceedings were rounded off with an all-ranks reception in the Moonrocket Club and an informal dance in the Officers' Mess.

A mixed formation of 8 and 208 Squadron Hunters captured from an FR.10 F.95 on 19 August 1971 while practicing for the 208 disbandment flypast (David Ainge).

Rod Dean leads a combined formation of nine Hunters over the dais during the 208 Squadron disbandment parade held at Muharraq on 21 August 1971. The parade was reviewed by the Queen's representative in the Persian Gulf, Sir Geoffrey King KCMG (Aviation Bookshop).

OC 208 Squadron, Squadron Leader Dick, returned to the UK to take over as leader of the Red Arrows aerobatic team, as two of his fellow officers also returned to take on new appointments, leaving the seven remaining pilots to join 8 Squadron along with four FGA.9s. Apart from a number of airmen who were transferred to other sections and squadrons on the station, the 208 Squadron groundcrew returned to new postings in the UK. On the official disbandment date, 10 September 1971, the following entry was recorded in the 208 Squadron ORB:

> After fifty-one years associated with the Middle East, 208 Squadron is disbanded. This historical end of an era was marked in the tradition and style that has made 208 a great and respected fighter squadron. The very best of luck to whoever next contributes to this fine and splendid history and may the Squadron reform in the spirit with which it disbanded.

Expelled!

On 3 September the British government was informed that the Ruler of the newly independent Bahrain no longer wished for the continued presence of an offensive strike-fighter force on his island. The station commander advised Squadron Leader Stoker that he had three weeks to prepare to move 8 Squadron away from Muharraq. As the T.7 was due to return to the UK, a concerted effort was made to ensure the instrument ratings for every pilot would remain current until the end of the year. This had been achieved by mid-September, the two-seater departing for the UK on the 14th in company with a pair of FGA.9s.

A pair of 8 Squadron FR.10s, XF460-X and XF441-Y, taxi out from Muharraq for the last time on 24 September 1971 on the first stage of their ferry flight back to the UK (David Ainge).

The quota of pilots now needed was achieved by short-touring four of the remaining seven 208 Squadron pilots. Having bade their farewells, they flew the two remaining FR.10s (XF441 and XF460) and a pair of FGA.9s to the UK on 24 September. Despite slow recognition of the type's value to MEC during its early years at Khormaksar, the FR.10 went on to distinguish itself in a role for which it was intended in an environment for which it was not. It made an invaluable contribution in the war against insurgency and deserved all the plaudits belatedly acknowledged. Intelligence gathering from now on would depend on the Mark 1 eyeball!

As preparations for a smart evacuation were being completed, the squadron was dined out by RAF Muharraq on the 24th. A traditional farewell party concluded with members serenading the mess with a reworked rendition of the squadron song. Having said their goodbyes to members returning to the UK, an advance party was flown down to Sharjah on 27 September. Two days later, the eight remaining FGA.9s arrived in an impressive arrowhead formation. The equipment and spares packs were flown down by ArDet Argosys over the following few days. With just twelve pilots and an adequate allocation of airmen, the squadron had become a shadow of its former years but with an important job still to do.

Exercise HIGH POINT

Having barely had time to settle in at Sharjah, the squadron became immersed in a complex, week-long exercise, codenamed HIGH POINT, on 4 October. For the purpose of the exercise, the Trucial Oman Scouts assumed the role of an enemy attempting to advance on villages along the western side of Wadi Shimal, fifty miles east of Sharjah. The villages were defended by members of the 1st Battalion Staffordshire Regiment, who had been flown into the area by 78 Squadron Wessex helicopters. No. 8 Squadron was tasked with performing reconnaissance and simulated strikes under guidance from an airborne FAC but, as events transpired, only one pair of Hunters was called to fly in the strike phase. All enemy positions were located and the positions of scouts and an enemy HQ transmitted to the 1st Staffords for them to take follow-up action. For much of the remaining part of October the squadron concentrated its training on simulated strikes against RN ships operating in the Gulf.

The number of flying hours was confined to 133 through November and the early part of December as the date for the squadron's disbandment drew near. Although the emphasis remained on training, 8 Squadron was requested to fly recces over Aba Musa and Tumbs, islands that were possessed by Sharjah and, being located close to the entrance to the Gulf, were of both political and strategic importance. The objective was to ascertain the nationality of their occupants and the quickest way to achieve this was to identify the flags on display.

On 8 November a four-ship simulated strike was flown against HMS *Falmouth*, followed by co-ordinated pairs attacks and low-level flypasts over the ship. Unfortunately,

David Ainge keeps his 8 Squadron FR.10, XF460, low to get a closer view of shipping movements in the Straights of Hormuz on 10 September 1971 (David Ainge).

from this point on, the records in the ORB are rather erratic but would indicate that the final day of operational flying for November took place on the 23rd when four pairs of Hunters were flown on FAC training sorties with the 1st Staffords.

Independence and the UAE

When the treaty between Britain and the Trucial Sheikhdoms expired on 1 December 1971, the sheikhdoms within the Trucial States became fully independent. A further four states – Ajman, Fujairah, Sharjah and Umm Al Quwain – had decided to join with Abu Dhabi and Dubai in signing the United Arab Emirates founding treaty which came into effect on 2 December 1971.

No. 8 Squadron disbands

No flying was undertaken by 8 Squadron during the final week of November and the period covered by the signing of the treaty. The final series of sorties to be flown by 8 Squadron Hunters comprised a co-ordinated attack by four aircraft flying as two pairs on an inland target. The same target was subsequently attacked by Flight Lieutenants Ainge (XF376) and Goodall. On 30 November the squadron received confirmation that its aircraft and personnel would return to the UK on 7 December. On that momentous day, in company with an Air Support Command Hercules transport, the eight Hunters departed Sharjah in two waves of four and headed for Tehran. On approaching the airport, Squadron Leader Stoker decided to arrive in style with a straight-in approach from high level followed by a high-speed break into the circuit. The break and landing were uneventful but as soon as the aircraft were parked on the apron, they were surrounded by armoured vehicles, with guns pointing at them. When a long line of staff cars arrived, the OC was informed in very stark language that they had nearly been shot down by anti-aircraft fire, the country being on full alert as a result of the India/Pakistan crisis. The rest of the trip home was less eventful and, having staged through Akrotiri, Luqa and Istres, they arrived at Kemble on 11 December.

The curtain had finally come down on the last RAF squadron to operate the Hawker Hunter in front-line service. Due to the prevailing circumstances in the region, unlike other units in the Middle Eastern theatre, there had been no disbandment parade, the official disbandment date for 8 Squadron being recorded as 21 December 1971.

Probably the last RAF Hunter related photograph from the Middle East! Seven of the 8 Squadron pilots detailed to fly the last eight Hunters back to the UK taken at Akrotiri on the ferry back to Kemble, 11 December 1971. l to r, 'Rocky' Goodall, Dave Ainge, John White, Bill Stoker (OC), Ron Elder, Roger Hyde and Mick Herberts. The missing pilot, Peter Griffiths, took the photograph (David Ainge).

All that remained were for the official closures of RAF Stations Muharraq and Sharjah to proceed. A simple ceremony involving the lowering of the Ensign in the presence of Sir Geoffrey Arthur brought an end to the RAF's tenure at Sharjah on 14 December 1971. During the afternoon of the following day, the Ensign was lowered at Muharraq, shortly before the last aircraft, a Belfast heavylift transport, departed for the UK. Control of the two remaining RAF stations at Masirah and Salalah thereafter came under the command of the Near East Air Force.

A moment of reflection

Acknowledged by many as the 'Queen of the Skies', the Hawker Hunter was a beautiful, sleek aeroplane which served the RAF in a variety of roles for forty years. Unlike many of its contemporaries that had quickly fallen by the wayside during the early postwar era, the Hunter's rugged construction, superior performance and formidable firepower secured its subsequent development and evolution into one of the most versatile of ground-attack and reconnaissance aircraft. Without the Hunter the story of the final decade of British rule in the Arabian Peninsula may well have taken a different course. Its success in the ground-attack and reconnaissance roles in the Middle East theatre undoubtedly led to orders for several hundred examples from countries around the world. Many continue to fly in civilian guise under military contracts and on the display circuit, thus ensuring that 'The Legend of the Hunter' lives on.

Hunter sunset! The end of an era is captured in this striking image of an 8 Squadron FGA.9 against the backdrop of a setting sun at Sharjah in November 1971 (David Ainge).

Accidents and incidents

This chapter takes a more in-depth look into reported accidents and incidents involving Hunters during the period covered by the main narrative. They are based on ORB records, compilations from former 8 Squadron armourer Alan Lowe, extracts from Tony Haig-Thomas's biography with kind permission of the author, and Colin Cummings' extensive catalogue of RAF aircraft losses entitled 'Category Five'. Entries are listed in chronological order under the sub-headings Fatal, Major and Minor.

Major incident:
8 Squadron – FGA.Mk.9 XF424
29 March 1960 While flying through 250ft near Sharjah, a large bird, believed to have been a seagull, struck the lower side of the starboard air intake. Although the pilot was able to make a safe landing back at Sharjah, the aircraft was declared Category 5 (Category 5) and Struck Off Charge (SOC).

Fatal accident:
8 Squadron – T.Mk.7 XL615
1 June 1960 (This extract is from Tony Haig-Thomas) 'Andy Devine, who was due to return to a ground job in the UK, kindly asked John Volkers and me if we would join him and his wife April for dinner. I had had a good day and at last flown two sorties in our twin-seat Hunter with John Morris, so we much looked forward to a social evening with April and Andy. John and I arrived at 19:30 but Andy had not turned up as the Squadron had been night flying, so April gave us a couple of drinks and we waited. Suddenly there was a knock on the door and the Station Commander appeared; he said nothing to us, but John and I, realising that this was not a social call, left at once. Andy was dead.

'One of the new pilots, Mike Walley, had been having a dual night check and both he and Andy were used to flying the much higher performance Hunter FGA.9. They had climbed to what would have normally been 20,000 feet in the Mark 9 but in reality, was only 10,000 feet in a T.7. The skies above Aden at night are extremely dark and altitude can only be determined by reference to an altimeter. Misreading of altimeters by 10,000 feet was very common indeed in the Hunter era and came about due to the mismatch of power between the single-seaters, which were flown all the time, and the trainer with the smaller 100-series Avon, flown very seldom.

The standard let-down in those days was to home overhead at 20,000 feet, be given an out-bound heading which was then followed by a steep descent to half the start height plus 2,000 feet. Their T.7 started its descent and called 'Turning left in-bound at 12,000'. A few seconds later there was a big flash in the desert as the aircraft buried itself in the sand and exploded. It had actually been at 2,000 feet when it started its turn, not 12,000 feet.'

Fatal accident:

8 Squadron – FGA.Mk.9 XG128

13 January 1961 (A second extract from Tony Haig-Thomas) 'Les Swain was the pilot of Hunter FGA.9, XG128, flying as No. 2 to Flight Lieutenant 'Porky' Munro on a pairs recce in the Upper Yaffa district of the Western Aden Protectorate. The pair were flying at 500 kts to minimise the risk of small-arms fire, when his aircraft hit the ground. It was probably an accident but could have been the first of many runaway tailplanes or a lucky rifle shot from a dissident gun. The accident was particularly tragic as Flight Lieutenant Swain's wife had arrived in Aden only the previous evening by troopship.'

A second account of this tragedy is recalled by Roy Hollow, an airman working on the Hunter line at the time:

> We were on the early shift from 05:00 when two pilots walked out to their aircraft. Les was in one of his usual jovial moods as I strapped him in; he was always joking and talked quite a bit. His favourite wind-up was to ask you to check the wing tips for any goblins and gremlins that might be sitting out there. The start-up was normal, and I checked underneath for any sign of a fire, shut the starter bay door, pulled chock away and off he went.
>
> I can't recall how much time had gone by but we knew something was wrong when the Station and Wing Commanders arrived and went straight into the office on the pan. They then informed us that one of the aircraft had hit rising ground in the Wadi Yahar; it was only when the other aircraft landed that we knew it was Les Swain.
>
> When the wreckage was located the next day, it was found that although he managed to eject from his aircraft, he died from loss of blood, having sustained a serious leg injury during the ejection sequence.

Fatal accident:

208 Squadron – FGA.Mk.9 XG134

11 July 1961 While carrying out simulated rocket attacks in poor visibility on British Army positions over Mutla Ridge during the Kuwait crisis, the aircraft struck the ground during the recovery, killing Flying Officer F. Hennessy.

Fatal accident:
8 Squadron – FR.Mk.10 XE579
8 August 1961 Flying Officer John Volkers was on his first tour after gaining his wings at RAF College Cranwell and was thought to have a bright career in front of him. His aircraft flew into the ground while approaching a gunnery range, six miles east of Zinjibar, Aden.

Minor incident:
208 Squadron – FGA.Mk.9 XE647
12 September 1961 After a normal start-up, the pilot started to taxi out of the dispersal area. This involved moving forward approximately 20ft, followed by a 90° turn to starboard. The brake-check proved uneventful and three green lights were indicated, but when the starboard brake was applied, the starboard undercarriage leg collapsed. The drop tank split, flooding the dispersal with fuel.

The investigation found that a bolt securing the starboard undercarriage forward pivot bearing cap had stripped its threads. Although nothing was recorded to indicate a recent heavy or short landing, the cause was deemed to have been caused by a heavy landing in the undershoot or by the wheel striking the lip of the runway.

Fatal accident:
8 Squadron – FGA.Mk.9 XE581
22 November 1961 While the Squadron was on detachment at Bahrain, Flying Officer Dick Gaiger was detailed by his Flight Commander to lead a section of four Hunters to practise high-level battle formation, followed by a pairs tail chase over the Qatar Peninsula. The Flight Commander briefed the leader on the exercises and the leader subsequently briefed the pilots on his section. Due to radio unserviceability, only three aircraft departed Bahrain; one of these returned shortly afterwards, also with a radio problem. The remaining pair continued with the exercise, Flying Officer Gaiger still in the lead. After completing battle practice off the west coast of Qatar, the leader instructed his number two to take up position 800 yards line astern for a tail chase before making a gentle wing-over to port at about 30,000 feet and commencing a straight 30/40° dive. Number two followed and noticed nothing unusual except that he had some slight difficulty in depressing his gunsight pipper to bear on the leader as the dive developed. Between 15,000 and 20,000 feet and at mach 0.94, the leader suddenly transmitted; 'Blue leader ejecting – now!!', in a clear and unexcited voice. Number two broke away to avoid the path of the ejection seat and climbed to make a 'Mayday' call. When smoke and flames were spotted on the ground, he descended to where the aircraft had crashed but could see no sign of a parachute. A search and rescue operation was launched from Bahrain and some 3½ hours later, the fatally injured pilot, ejection seat and parachute were recovered from the desert. The

parachute canopy was found to have detached from the parachute harness, which was still attached to the pilot's body.

Further investigation proved difficult due to the remote location of the crash, the vagueness of eyewitnesses and the destruction and disappearance of many key components from the aircraft. From the sparse material recovered, it was found that the tailplane was probably in the fully nosedown position when the aircraft struck the ground, symptomatic of a runaway tail trim. There was no other evidence to suggest that any other emergency existed at the time of ejection to cause the pilot to abandon his aircraft.

The ejection

There was also no evidence to show at what altitude the pilot ejected or the aircraft's attitude at the time. However, since the aircraft canopy, ejection seat, pilot's body and personal equipment were found one mile from the wreckage, back along the final approach path of the aircraft, it was concluded that the ejection took place after the aircraft had turned onto an approximate heading of 280°. For some reason, therefore, the actual ejection was delayed after the pilot transmitted that he was ejecting immediately. A possible cause is that the effect of negative 'g' caused by full nose down trim, made it difficult for the pilot to operate either ejection seat handle.

The ejection seat pan of the Mark 2H seat had collapsed, leading to the conclusion that the seat pan collapsed at the start of ejection. The sequence of events is thought to be as follows: After pulling the blind, the canopy blew off and one second later the seat cartridges fired and the seat started moving up the guide rails. At this point the seat pan collapsed, shearing off the snubbing units and tearing the metal thigh guards. The bottom of the seat pan also cut the lower half of a leg restraining line as it was found in the aircraft wreckage. At this stage, with the seat pan collapsing, the pilot fell back into his seat thus pulling the parachute out of the seat container. As the seat entered the airstream, air-blast pulled out the parachute pack pins and started to stream the parachute. The black seat apron was torn off at this point and was never found. The parachute rigging lines broke under the tension induced by the instant air-blast. A short while later, the barometric time release operated and the scissor shackle opened, allowing the drogues, which had deployed normally, to detach from the seat and fall away along with the parachute canopy. At the same instant as the barometric time release unlocked, the pilot, who was still attached to the parachute harness, its broken rigging lines and the seat, fell towards the ground. The seat landed about 40 yards from the pilot and the left thigh guard was torn off when the seat first entered the airstream. The main attachment to the right-hand side of the Mae West was severed and, as the pilot did not have the two side attachments connected to the Mae West, the dinghy pack came out of the harness at some stage and fell away independently.

Investigation revealed that Mod 1129 (Strengthening of the Seat Pan) was not embodied on this seat. At the time of the accident, the Mod had not been introduced and was not, therefore, awaiting embodiment.

Mod 907 (Standby Trim Switch Cover) to the tailplane standby system was not embodied on this aircraft either and this may well be the reason why the pilot was unable to recover from the emergency. Under negative 'g' it is extremely difficult to reach the tailplane main actuator circuit breaker. Mod 907 kits arrived shortly after and were applied to all aircraft in the Command.

Minor incident
208 Squadron – FGA.Mk.9 XE643
9 December 1961 When the aircraft lost power during its take-off run at Mombassa, the pilot abandoned the take off and raised the undercarriage in the hope of preventing the aircraft from overshooting. The aircraft continued beyond the end of the runway, sustaining Category 5 damage in the process. It was subsequently SOC.

Major incident:
This incident bears a remarkable similarity to the fatal accident involving FR.10 XE581 on 22 November 1961.

At first glance the damage to 208 Squadron FGA.9 XE643 would appear to be superficial following its aborted take-off from Mombasa but subsequent inspection found it to be more serious and the aircraft was SOC (author's collection).

8 Squadron – FGA.Mk.9 XE620

12 December 1961 Flying Officer Peter Webbon took off from Bahrain for a battle, close formation and tail-chase exercise. While following the leader during the tail-chase sequence in a nose-down attitude, at a height of 28,000 feet and at an estimated speed of mach 0.7, the pilot felt the aircraft become nose heavy. As pulling the control column back had no effect, he throttled back. The tail-trim needle showed 2° nose-down and continued to move in a downward direction as the aircraft entered a steep dive. Confirming that the flaps were up, he selected standby nose-up trim for around two seconds. This had no apparent effect. In a near vertical dive at 20,000 feet and approaching mach 0.9 while under strong negative 'g', the pilot tried to pull the control column back with both hands but it had no effect on the aircraft's attitude. Having had no response from a distress call, the pilot attempted to eject but was unable to reach the ejection seat handle. With both hands and feet pushing forward on the control column the aircraft adopted a horizontal inverted position at about 4,000 feet. He then rolled the aircraft and attained a gentle climbing attitude which he was able to maintain.

A quick test of the standby trim found it to be in perfect working order and he was able to return to base without further incident. Apart from being exposed to +4½ g and in excess of –5 g, minimal damage was sustained by the aircraft.

The pilot stated that the aircraft started a diving manoeuvre with no conscious assistance from himself and that the tail trim indication needle was moving in the nose-down direction. This led to the conclusion that the diving manoeuvre was initiated by movement of the variable incidence tailplane.

Technical investigation

Accidental trim selection by the pilot was discounted in view of the continued movement of the indicator needle after he had taken action to regain control. A subsequent technical investigation did reveal, however, that tailplane runaway was most likely triggered by the initial trim selection.

The investigation eliminated practically every component of the tailplane variable incidence assembly except for the reversing contactor, which showed evidence of a momentary tack weld. Although it was possible to unstick a tack weld, the pilot had not attempted to trim back on the main trim as part of his actions to correct the dive.

It was also discovered that the limit switches shorted out when welding of the reversing contactor occurred, allowing the tailplane to overrun the normal nose-down limit set by these switches. It was established that this overrun amounted to some twenty-three minutes of angular movement or 1.6 divisions on the trim indicator, sufficient to induce a very strong nose-down movement at high IAS, making recovery virtually impossible through backward movement of the control column.

The investigation concluded that a full technical investigation be initiated to establish whether the reversing contactor could be modified to eliminate tack welding and a further modification to prevent the tail-plane from overrunning the limit set by the limit switches.

Fatal accident:

8 Squadron – FGA.Mk.9 XE607

30 March 1962 The main RAF contribution to Aden Forces Week was an Open Day held at Khormaksar on 30 March 1962. The flying display was scheduled to start at 15:15 with a sonic boom followed by a high-speed, low-level flypast.

Three Hunters took off in formation at 15:04 and separated once they were out of sight. Number three was to perform a flypast from West to East on the South side of the runway. Numbers one and two were to aim sonic booms at the centre of the airfield, throttle back to subsonic speed and steepen their dive before pulling out to fly across the airfield from East to West on the North side of the runway. The three aircraft were to cross in front of the control tower at the same time and at 250 feet.

A delay of one minute in getting off the ground gave one and two a slightly lower entry speed from that used in practice but the timing was perfect. The pair dived at mach 0.98, reduced speed and increased the angle of dive as planned before starting their pull-out from the 45° dive at 7,000 feet. Flying as number two in XE607, Flying Officer Blackgrove never fully recovered from the dive, the aircraft striking the ground at an angle of about 25° and exploding on impact. Half the wreckage was buried in the sides and bottom of the resulting 20-foot crater and the remainder in small fragments carried forward along the line of flight for 3,000 feet.

Although 60,000 spectators witnessed the crash, comparatively few realised what had happened. HMS *Centaur* was in Aden at the time and some people thought the RAF had borrowed the 'Atomic Explosion' pyrotechnics from the Royal Navy. Corporal Technician Edmondson of 37 Squadron came forward with an 8mm film that showed the final seconds of the dive. This confirmed the angle of impact and that the aircraft had made an appreciable recovery from the dive. The force of the explosion destroyed the majority of the evidence that might have proved the cause of the accident. However, the tailplane actuator ram was recovered intact and indicated that the aircraft had a 2° 15' nose-down trim at the time of impact. The recovery of an elevator hydraulic jack showed that the main hydraulic supply had not failed.

The briefing was that the tailplane interconnection should be ON. Subsequent flight tests along a similar profile with the interconnection ON, confirmed that during a pull-out the tail trim was between zero and ½° nose up. Tests also showed that at mach 0.95 with full nose-down trim, an aircraft remained in the dive with the control column held fully back and that at mach 0.95 with 2¼° nose-down trim, a slow recovery was possible.

The Board examined a number of possible causes of the crash, ranging from structural failure to hyperventilation. The only theory consistent with the facts was that the tail trim ran fully nose-down during the dive and that this would become apparent to the pilot at or about the time the pull-out commenced (7,000 feet). The pilot would find that he could not trim back on the main trim and would use the standby trim. Due to its slower motoring rate insufficient nose-up change of trim could be made to effect the pull-out, but sufficient recovery would be made to lead the pilot to think that he might make it, hence no attempt at ejection. An estimate of the flight profile suggests that another 300 feet of height might have been sufficient.

An investigation into the causes of and cures for 'runaway' trim on the Hunter was instigated by the Air Ministry, following the Board's conclusion that a short circuit in electric wiring or plug welding of contacts were the cause of the trim tail control failure.

Major incident:
8 Squadron – FR.Mk.10 XF436
20 June 1962 Flying Officer Barry Stott was briefed to carry out interceptions and simulated attacks from the rear quarter on a section of four Hunters, the objective being to exercise the lookout capabilities of the four pilots. The attacks were to be gentle with no evasive action and a break-off distance of 500 yards.

The pilot planned his first attack for shortly after the four had taken off; he was airborne five minutes before them and had climbed in a gentle left-hand orbit to 6,000 feet to a point south-east of the airfield. Strengthening struts were fitted to the 230-gallon drop tanks, each less than half full, and there were no other external stores. The limitation in this configuration is 7g with half lateral movement of the stick and level ailerons. The pilot in his wisdom resolved to keep well inside this limit.

On spotting the four Hunters on their take-off runs, he eased gently into a dive towards them with engine at 6,500 rpm and allowed the speed to build up to 450 knots. XF436 was spotted by the other pilots as they passed through 1,000 feet and were horrified to see its port tank break away and hurtle towards them as the aircraft pulled up. Fortunately it missed and fell harmlessly into the sea off the end of the runway.

The equally horrified FR.10 pilot saw that not only the tank, but its pylon and part of the wing tip were missing. The remaining tank was jettisoned at 250 knots into a clear area, and a low speed check carried out at 140 knots IAS with 40° flap and undercarriage down. Everything appeared normal, but all precautions were taken during the subsequent uneventful landing.

Inspection showed that the threads on eleven of the twelve anchoring pylon nuts had stripped and the twelfth bolt sheared. Modifications 964 and 965 introduced thicker nuts and longer bolts. Although these were easy to fit and the Mod kits were

The damage wing and salvaged drop tank from the incident involving 8 Squadron FR.10 XF436 at Khormaksar on 20 June 1962 (author).

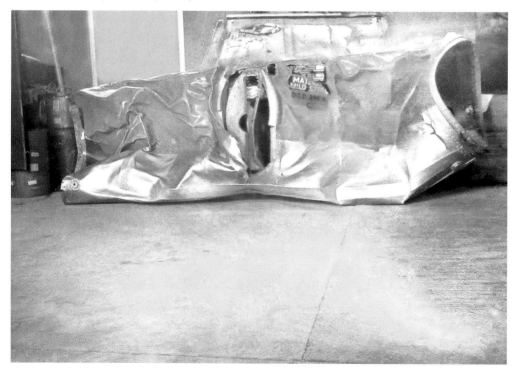

soon available, Mod 964, on the other hand, required 130 man-hours per aircraft. Hunters without Mod 964 were limited to 4g when fuel was being carried in the 230-gallon tanks.

The pilot was in no way to blame for this incident; on the contrary, he was congratulated for the cool and correct way in which he handled an unpleasant situation.

Major incident:
208 Squadron – FGA.Mk.9 XJ688
22 June 1962 The pilot of XJ688 was firing concrete-headed rockets on the recently-opened range at Jeb-a-Jib, near Sharjah. The first five rockets fired without incident, although two were noticeably late in releasing from the rails. The sixth failed to fire and the normal hang-up procedure taken. 'Ripple' was selected for the last dive and the button held pressed from before to after the normal firing point. The rocket still appeared to hang up and the pilot, having dipped below his safety height, eased gently out of the dive. During the initial part of the recovery, the rocket fired and the rocket head or other debris was thrown up and struck the aircraft causing extensive damage to the starboard leading edge.

The range at Jeb-a-Jib comprised undulating sand with some scrub and isolated well-buried rock. The depth of the sand cover varied according to the degree of drifting, but from the surface grading aspect it was considered the Command's best range. The pilot was entirely to blame for this incident due to him dropping below his safety height and for not recovering from his dive more quickly.

Fatal accident:
8 Squadron – FGA.Mk.9 XE600
25 June 1962 Flying Officer Webbon was flying XE600 as number two on an RP cine and live air-to-ground firing exercise at Khormaksar range. Number one completed firing first and returned home to base. The pilot of XE600, having received two low warnings, was sent home by the Range Safety Officer (RSO). Instead, he asked for and was given permission by the RSO to perform a further safety height check. Instead, the aircraft was flown towards the RSO at a height estimated at five feet with undercarriage and flaps fully extended and at an estimated speed of 150 knots. On reaching the RSO's position, the throttle was opened and the aircraft climbed steeply. At around 150 feet it stalled, turned over and nosed into the ground, killing the pilot.

A Board investigation presumed the attack on the RSO was a fit of pique and the configuration selected intended to produce the greatest disturbance of sand in giving discomfort to him. The engine would have been throttled well back during the reduction in height and speed. The slow engine acceleration below 4,500 rpm and the configuration selected produced control difficulties which this inexperienced pilot was unable to cope with.

Ill-fated 8 Squadron FGA.9 XE600 on the line at Khormaksar on 25 May 1962, one month before it crashed on the range killing the pilot (author).

Major incident:
8 Squadron – FGA.Mk.9 XE649

17 August 1962 The RN exchange pilot was undergoing conversion training in XE649 and was taking off in the maximum all-up weight configuration with an experienced Hunter pilot on the port side as his number two. Half way along the 8,000-foot runway, with no airspeed indication, number one abandoned his take off, engine stop-cocked and braking-chute deployed. Number two's aircraft was indicating 145 knots at this time and completed his take off.

The emergency stopping capability of the Hunter in maximum configuration at near take-off speed is not good, being estimated as about 5,000 feet. Knowing that the barrier was being serviced and out of use and to avoid the possibility of running into the sea, the pilot swung his aircraft to port. It struck the partially erected barrier and came to rest with undercarriage leg collapsed.

The cause of the accident was the pilot's decision to abandon his take off, contributed to by a poor pre-flight inspection – he had forgotten to remove the pitot head cover!!

There was no warning flag attached to the cover when the aircraft came to rest. It had been taxied for 2,000 yards; both the number two and the runway controller were on the pitot-head side of the aircraft but neither had noticed a flag. Without the four full drop tanks, the aircraft could probably have been stopped within the 4,000 feet available.

FGA.9 XE649 was pictured in 8/43 Squadron markings at Khormaksar, some four years after the aborted take-off incident (Aviation Bookshop).

Major incident:
208 Squadron – FGA.Mk.9 XE544
17 September 1962 The pilot abandoned take off at Embakasi after a fire warning light came on. When a tyre then burst the undercarriage was raised and the aircraft swung off the runway. Category 5 damage was sustained by the aircraft which was SOC.

Major incident:
1 Squadron – FGA.Mk.9 XG253
28 October 1962 During a squadron detachment from the UK to the Middle East, Flight Lieutenant B. Scotford safely ejected from XG253 when the engine flamed out due to loss of oil, thirty-seven miles north-east of Khormaksar.

Fatal accident:
43 Squadron – FGA.Mk.9 XG136
17 April 1964 This account of an accident involving XG136 was written by Flight Lieutenant John Batty and contributed by Roger Wilkins. John Batty was flying as number two to Flying Officer Martin Herring on a four-ship practice ground-attack mission.

Lost on 28 October 1962 during a detachment to Khormaksar, 1 Squadron FGA.9 XG253 was photographed during the week before the crash (author).

The briefing was for four of us (Flying Officer Martin Herring in the lead, Flight Lieutenant John Batty as number two, Flying Officer John Thomson as number three and Flight Lieutenant Glyn Chapman at number four) to perform a low-level navex and practice RP strike on a target about 120 miles east-north-east of Khormaksar. The briefing was to use a conventional Initial Point for the turn in and then attempt a new manoeuvre. This involved flying directly over the target at low level, in low-level battle formation, continue for approximately 1 minute and 30 seconds before pulling up into a loop and spacing out to around 1,000 yards. Then, continue the roll-out and dive back on a reciprocal heading towards the target. The height above ground level at the top of the manoeuvre would be approximately 5,000 feet.

I commenced filming on lifting the RP switch on the control column and the bottom diamond in the vicinity of the target. The exercise went as planned until Martin commenced his pull out, at which stage I was about 1,200 yards behind him. As Martin pulled out, his aircraft rolled very rapidly to the right and crashed into the ground. I noticed what appeared to be smoke (probably fuel vapour) coming from the right wing during this time and saw no sign of Martin ejecting.

As I flew over the crash site, debris from the aircraft was flying forward, covering a sizeable area. I then climbed up and, on Glyn's instruction, put out a 'Mayday' call to Operations in Khormaksar. The other two aircraft circled the

Photographed at Khormaksar in March 1964, 43 Squadron FGA.9 XG136 crashed into a mountainside when a drop tank broke away during a high g pull-out, killing the pilot (author).

crash site whilst I relayed messages from about 12,000 feet or maybe higher. I vividly remember one of the questions I was asked by operations being were there any survivors, to which I replied it was most unlikely.

On Glyn's instructions I then returned to base independently to be met by OC the Squadron, Squadron Leader Phil Champniss and the Station Commander Group Captain Blythe. Subsequent to the crash my cine film was developed and I believe that the film was of great help to the investigators in establishing the cause of the crash.

The aircraft were fitted with 230-gallon drop tanks and calculations revealed that we would not have burned off sufficient fuel to empty the drop tanks. There were no baffles in the tanks at that time to prevent the fuel sloshing forward in the dive. It would appear that the fuel had moved forward and that in the pull-out, Martin put such a load on the tanks that one broke away from the pylon. It then flew up, hitting the right aileron, forcing it to the fully-up position in the process, and causing the aircraft to roll violently to the right. At a height of less than 500 feet above the ground, the aircraft was placed in an irrecoverable position with no time or height to eject.

Fatal accident:
208 Squadron – FGA.Mk.9s XE647 and XK139
30 June 1964 Two FGA.9s were part of a four-aircraft formation on a Hi-Low-Hi sortie that was due to be followed by a practice air-to-ground strike on a disused lightship near Dasa Island in the Persian Gulf.

During the attack, the pilot of XK139 did not see the target initially but on having acquired it, turned into the attack out of sequence. Despite the efforts of the pilot of XE647, the two aircraft collided. XK139 flew on for about 1,000 yards before crashing.

Flight Lieutenant Mike Gibson, who was flying XE647, ejected at 6,000 feet and at an IAS of 290 kts with the aircraft in level flight. As he could not reach the overhead ejection handle (with its protective face blind), his bone-dome being in contact with the canopy, and with insufficient time to lower his seat, Flight Lieutenant Gibson used the seat pan handle to initiate the ejection sequence. Under these circumstances there would have been no facial protection on entering the airstream.

Ken Parry, who joined 8 Squadron after the move to Muharraq and knew both pilots, recalled that:

The other pilot was Flying Officer Tony Willcocks. Both he, Mike Gibson and I were all on the same Vampire course at 4 FTS, Valley, in 1962-63. My understanding of the collision (from a subsequent meeting with Mike) was that for some reason the two aircraft were on converging headings onto the target, both pilots head-down on their gunsights, and neither saw the other. XK139 also crashed and Tony Willcocks was killed. Whether he attempted to eject no one knows, but my recollection from talking to Mike is that he probably did not.

Refurbished 208 Squadron FGA.9 XE647 had yet to receive its markings when photographed at Bahrain in 1963 (Gordon Macadie).

The second aircraft lost in the mid-air collision was 208 Squadron FGA.9 XK139 seen at Khormaksar in 1963 (author).

Major accident:
8/43 Squadron – FGA.Mk.9 XE623

11 August 1964 Flying Officer Ron Burrows of 43 Squadron was flying as number two in a formation led by Flight Lieutenant John Osborne. After take-off they turned to fly at low level in battle formation up the coast to the north-east of Khormaksar. At about ten miles distant, the engine in XE623 flamed out. The pilot immediately pulled up to 2,500 feet and turned back towards the airfield. Several attempts were made to relight the engine but when these failed, the pilot ejected as the aircraft dropped through 800 feet. The aircraft crashed on the Khormaksar aerial farm and remained remarkably intact after a pilotless landing. The pilot suffered the usual 'Martin-Baker' back but made a quick recovery and was back on flying duty three months later. The cause of the engine failure was subsequently confirmed as being due to a defective fuel pump.

In Roger Wilkins judgement: 'What remained of the wreck and the length of the skid marks across the bondu, it must have hit the ground nigh on straight and level.'

Fatal accident:
8/43 Squadron – FGA.Mk.9 XE592

16 October 1964 Roger Wilkins recalls that:

> There was a short detachment to Masirah Island involving six aircraft of the Khormaksar Strike Wing. The pilots were from both 8 and 43 Squadrons, which was unusual in that they rarely ever flew together. At the end of the detachment,

Station and TacWing officers inspect the partially intact remains of 8/43 Squadron FGA.9 XE623 a few miles the north of Khormaksar (Roger Wilkins).

a six-ship formation took off in pairs and commenced a climbing turn onto the track back to Khormaksar. The weather was fine.

As the first two pairs climbed through 4,000 feet, Flying Officer Ian Stephens flying in XE592 as number 5, passed beneath number 6 and appeared to be attempting to catch up with the other four aircraft when it rolled-out and descended until crashing into the sea.

Major incident:
208 Squadron – FGA.Mk.9 XE617
7 May 1966 The aircraft ran out of fuel and crashed in the undershoot at Muharraq. The pilot safely ejected but the aircraft was SOC.

Major incident:
1417 Flight – FR.Mk.10 XE589
9 May 1966 The aircraft sustained severe damage from a birdstrike with a griffin vulture. The enormous bird entered the starboard intake, part of it smashing its way out through the upper skin of the wing root as the rest entered the engine, causing it to surge. As the rpm stabilised in mid-range, the throttle was left in that position. By dropping the aircraft's external tanks, Flight Lieutenant Ken Simpson was able to keep

Looking in pristine condition at Khormaksar following refurbishment in 1962, 8 Squadron FGA.9 XE592 was lost when it crashed into the sea off Masirah Island, killing the pilot (author).

the aircraft airborne and nurse it up to 10,000 feet on a heading back to Khormaksar where he was able to carry out an emergency landing.

Due to the severe damage sustained by the wing root and air intake, the aircraft was assessed as Category 4 damage and transferred to 131 MU. After several weeks of further investigation, it was shipped back to the UK and rebuilt to FGA.76 standard by Hawker Siddeley for onward sale to the Abu Dhabi Air Force as its number 701.

Major incident:
8/43 Squadron – FGA.Mk.9 XE530
6 February 1967 The aircraft was damaged in a flying incident, the details of which are not recorded but it is known to have run off the runway at Khormaksar, sustaining serious damage to the main undercarriage in the process. Initially assessed as Category 3, the aircraft was transferred to 131 MU for repairs, but on further investigation the damage was re-assessed as Category 4 and the aircraft classified SOC on 31 October 1967.

It was sold back to Hawker Siddeley who rebuilt it to two-seat T.Mk.67 trainer standard for the Kuwait Air Force as its number 220.

A partial view of the extent of the damage sustained by 1417 Flight FR.10 XE589 following the bird-strike (Ken Simpson).

Major incident:
8/43 Squadron – FGA.Mk.9 XF440

20 February 1967 Flying as one of a pair at low level over the village of Dhi Surrah, Flying Officer Sowler's aircraft was believed to have been hit by groundfire, as it began to lose several of its services one after the other. On reaching Al Ittihad, some eight miles from Khormaksar, the pilot decided to eject, the first ejection from a 43 Squadron aircraft for 2½ years. On landing he found himself in a hollow in some sand dunes. Shortly after, an Arab in a white suit clambered over the sand and asked if he could give him a lift. Unbeknown to Flying Officer Sowler, the main road was just beyond the dune he was sitting in. He politely declined the offer by explaining that his rescue helicopter would be arriving in a few minutes.

Looking resplendent with Gordon Lewis's initials on the fin and a Kenyan independence zap on the nose flash, FGA.9 XE530 was photographed at Khormaksar in 1963, four years before sustaining damage in a mysterious incident (author).

Major incident:
8/43 Squadron – FGA.Mk.9 XF421

23 March 1967 The aircraft was badly damaged when, having lost power on the approach to Khormaksar, it overshot the runway and ran into the sea with the engine off. The wreckage was recovered by 131 MU and subsequently declared Category5. SOC.

Fatal accident:
208 Squadron – FGA.Mk.9 XJ691

27 April 1967 The pilot took off for a nighttime cross-country flight from Masirah to Muharraq as one of a section of six aircraft. Radio contact was lost and although his aircraft was picked up by the Muharraq airfield radar, it disappeared from the screen shortly after. Flying Officer Howick- Baker was killed when his Hunter crashed into the sea, eighteen miles short of his destination. No cause for the accident was established.

Fatal accident:
8 Squadron – FGA.Mk.9 XE654

20 November 1967 The pilot was leading a formation of four aircraft on an air-to-ground range sortie over Oman. On pulling up at the correct point, he called 'contact

8 Squadron FGA.9 XF440, seen here at Khormaksar in 1962 following refurbishment in the UK, was believed to have been hit by ground fire forcing the pilot to eject near Al Ittihad on 20 February 1967 (author).

target' and rolled into a simulated attack. The aircraft was still rolling at the pull-up point when it flew into the ground, killing the pilot, Flight Lieutenant Roger Patterson.

Major incident:
8 Squadron – FGA.Mk.9 XE532
6 May 1968 Having completed his turn on the Rashid range, Flight Lieutenant Taylor decided to fly low and fast over the range officer's hut but his aircraft struck the HF aerial mast in the process. The engine began to lose power and, unable to reach the airport at Dubai, the pilot was forced to eject. He was picked up from the sea by helicopter and flown back to Sharjah, leaving what remained of his aircraft at the bottom of the sea.

Major incident
8 Squadron – FGA.Mk.9 XF388
26 June 1968 Having been airborne for around forty minutes, Flight Lieutenant Pym decided to perform a series of aerobatic manoeuvres over the desert, some fifty miles south-east of Dubai, and then descend to 3,000 feet while tracking back to Muharraq. The aircraft's engine rpm and jpt suddenly began to fluctuate until finally the engine flamed out. Attempts to relight the engine having failed, the pilot ejected over the sea when down to 1,000 feet. He was quickly spotted by other Hunter pilots in the area who maintained cover until the Muharraq SAR Wessex helicopter arrived to pick him up.

It is 10 February 1963, the acceptance checks are nearly complete and FGA.9 XE654 will soon depart Khormaksar for an air test. The initials 'LJ' on the fin are those of OC 8 Squadron, Squadron Leader Laurie Jones (author).

Appendix 2

Aircraft Allocation

Appendix 2 contains the aircraft serial numbers, marks and dates allocated to MEC squadrons. It is possible that other Hunters were allocated to the Command but none were noted on the aircraft record cards.

8 Squadron

Serial	Code	Type	From	To	Comments
XE532		FGA.9	20-01-68	06-05-68	Crashed into the sea
XE552		FGA.9	25-03-70	17-06-71	To 208 Sqn
XE579	X	FR.10	11-05-61	08-08-61	Crashed: pilot killed
XE581	D	FGA.9	29-01-60	22-11-61	Crashed: pilot killed
XE589	V	FR.10	28-04-61	26-04-63	To 1417 Flt
XE592	F	FGA.9	26-11-62	01-06-64	Combined 8/43 Sqn
XE599	X	FR.10	03-07-61	09-10-62	Command reserve. To 1417 Flt 26-04-63
XE599	W	FR.10	08-09-67	16-12-67	To 19 MU for refurbishment
XE599		FR.10	15-07-68	01-07-70	To 5 MU at Kemble. Sold to HSA
XE600	G	FGA.9	20-01-60	25-06-62	Crashed: pilot killed
XE607	F	FGA.9	29-03-62	30-03-62	Crashed: pilot killed
XE609	A	FGA.9	26-02-63	01-06-64	Combined 8/43 Sqn
XE611		FGA.9	07-08-67	07-05-68	To 19 MU for refurbishment
XE614	W	FR.10	28-04-61	26-04-63	To 1417 Flt
XE614	Z	FR.10	08-09-67	18-07-68	To 19 MU for refurbishment
XE614		FR.10	05-02-69	19-07-71	Sold to HSA
XE618	D	FGA.9	16-06-62	01-06-64	Combined 8/43 Sqn
XE620	F	FGA.9	15-02-60	24-08-62	To 19 MU for refurbishment
XE620	B	FGA.9	26-06-63	01-06-64	Combined 8/43 Sqn
XE649	S	FGA.9	06-04-60	17-08-62	Category 4/R: to 19 MU St Athan
XE651	M	FGA.9	21-01-60	05-12-62	To 19 MU for refurbishment
XE654	E	FGA.9	25-01-60	29-05-62	To 19 MU for refurbishment
XE654	LJ	FGA.9	02-02-63	30-07-63	Bird strike: to 131 MU then 208 Sqn
XE654		FGA.9	07-08-67	20-11-67	Crashed: pilot killed
XE655	H	FGA.9	30-09-60	24-04-63	To 5 MU for refurbishment

Serial	Code	Type	From	To	Comments
XE655		FGA.9	07-08-67	21-06-68	Sold to Royal Jordanian Air Force
XF321		T.7	08-09-67	14-11-67	To 19 MU for refurbishment
XF376	Q	FGA.9	31-01-61	19-09-61	Category 4/R: to 131 MU then 208 Sqn
XF376	K	FGA.9	01-10-63	01-06-64	To 8/43 Sqn
XF376		FGA.9	07-08-67	29-01-69	To 19 MU for refurbishment
XF376		FGA.9	29-09-69	07-12-71	To 19 MU for refurbishment
XF388		FGA.9	31-03-68	21-06-68	Category 5. SOC
XF421	C	FGA.9	16-06-62	01-06-64	To 8/43 Sqn
XF424	S	FGA.9	18-01-60	29-03-60	Category 5: Bird strike
XF429	X	FR.10	08-09-67	11-08-69	To 19 MU for refurbishment
XF429		FR.10	22-06-70	26-03-71	Sold to HSA
XF431		FGA.9	07-08-67	16-01-68	To 19 MU for refurbishment
XF435	E	FGA.9	15-10-62	01-06-64	Re-coded 'J' 63. To 8/43 Sqn
XF435		FGA.9	07-08-67	07-05-68	To 19 MU for refurbishment
XF436	U	FR.10	28-04-61	26-04-63	To 1417 Flt

Approaching the threshold at Sharjah in November 1963, its paintwork looking jaded, XE620 was one of the first FGA.9s to be allocated to 8 Squadron in February 1960. Following refurbishment in the UK, it was adopted by the OC, Squadron Leader Tam Syme, as his aircraft, denoted by the Squadron colours on the nose-wheel door. It remained in Aden with 8/43 Squadron before eventually moving on to 208 Squadron at Muharraq (author).

Having first served with 208 Squadron at Eastleigh, FGA.9 XE609 was allocated to 8 Squadron on returning from refurbishment in June 1963 and was pictured on the Khormaksar line one month later (author).

Having entered service as an FGA.9 with 208 Squadron in 1960, XF376 spent the next twelve years in the Middle East and was one of the last eight of her type to depart in December 1971. Looking in pristine condition following refurbishment, XF376 was captured on the 8 Squadron line at Bahrain on 19 November 1963 (Gordon Macadie).

8 Squadron

Serial	Code	Type	From	To	Comments
XF436	W	FR.10	21-11-67	28-02-70	Sold to HSA
XF440	S	FGA.9	15-10-62	01-06-64	Re-coded 'L' 63. To 8/43 Sqn
XF441		FR.10	20-05-69	25-09-71	Sold to HSA
XF442	H	FGA.9	nn-nn-69	nn-nn-71	To UK for refurbishment
XF445	O	FGA.9	28-02-63	31-07-63	To 19 MU for refurbishment
XF454		FGA.9	07-08-67	26-01-68	Sold to Royal Jordanian Air Force
XF455	T	FGA.9	15-02-60	05-12-62	To 5 MU for refurbishment
XF460	X	FR.10	16-08-62	09-03-63	To 131 MU. Command reserve
XF460	Y	FR.10	08-09-67	22-01-69	To 19 MU for refurbishment
XF460		FR.10	11-09-69	25-09-71	Sold to HSA
XF462	A	FGA.9	20-01-68	28-02-70	Sold to HSA
XG128	Q	FGA.9	07-05-60	13-01-61	Crashed: pilot killed
XG135	P	FGA.9	18-01-60	31-10-63	To 5 MU for refurbishment
XG135		FGA.9	19-02-70	07-12-71	To 5 MU for refurbishment
XG136	C	FGA.9	21-01-60	19-06-62	To 19 MU for refurbishment
XG154	H	FGA.9	26-02-63	01-06-64	Re-coded 'E' 08-63. To 8/43 Sqn
XG154	G	FGA.9	01-12-67	11-12-68	To 19 MU for refurbishment
XG169	B	FGA.9	24-01-60	16-04-63	To 5 MU for refurbishment
XG169		FGA.9	03-11-63	24-01-64	Uncoded. To 208 Sqn
XG169		FGA.9	21-10-68	06-10-70	To 5 MU for refurbishment
XG228	C	FGA.9	nn-nn-69	nn-nn-71	To UK for refurbishment
XG237	T	FGA.9	15-10-62	01-06-64	Re-coded 'M' 1963. To 8/43 Sqn
XG255	G	FGA.9	13-04-62	30-05-64	To 19 MU for refurbishment
XG256	H	FGA.9	21-08-63	01-06-64	To 8/43 Sqn
XG256	B	FGA.9	08-02-68	29-06-68	To 19 MU for refurbishment
XG256		FGA.9	10-02-69	17-06-71	To 208 Sqn
XG261		FGA.9	19-02-70	19-01-71	To 19 MU for refurbishment
XG292		FGA.9	17-05-68	01-04-70	Sold to HSA
XJ646		FGA.9	07-08-67	29-11-67	To 19 MU at St Athan. Sold to HSA
XJ680		FGA.9	15-07-68	04-12-69	Sold to HSA
XJ684		FGA.9	31-03-68	04-12-69	Sold to HSA
XJ687	E	FGA.9	26-05-62	05-12-62	To 19 MU for refurbishment
XJ687		FGA.9	07-08-67	17-11-68	To 19 MU for refurbishment
XJ688		FGA.9	07-08-67	27-09-67	To 208 Sqn
XJ688		FGA.9	06-11-67	18-03-68	To 19 MU for refurbishment
XJ688		FGA.9	15-05-71	07-12-71	To 19 MU for refurbishment

Serial	Code	Type	From	To	Comments
XJ689		FGA.9	07-08-67	09-10-67	To 19 MU for refurbishment
XJ689		FGA.9	17-05-68	01-04-70	Sold to HSA
XJ692		FGA.9	01-12-67	17-01-68	To 19 MU at St Athan. Sold to HSA
XJ714		FR.10	18-10-70	07-06-71	Sold to HSA
XK150	A	FGA.9	19-01-60	02-02-63	To 5 MU for refurbishment
XK151	X	FGA.9	19-01-60	02-02-63	Re-coded 'P' then 'J'. To 19 MU for refurbishment
XK151		FGA.9	07-08-67	20-01-69	To 19 MU for refurbishment
XL565	Y	T.7	12-12-60	25-06-63	To 1417 Flt
XL565		T.7	08-09-67	06-11-67	To SF West Raynham
XL612	T	T.7	08-09-67	24-07-69	To 5 MU for refurbishment
XL613	Z	T.7	22-09-59	01-06-60	To 208 Sqn
XL613	Z	T.7	29-11-60	26-04-63	To 1417 Flt
XL613	Z	T.7	25-06-63	29-10-63	To 1417 Flt
XL615	Y	T.7	19-09-59	01-06-60	Crashed: both pilots killed

Nick Adamson taxiing 8 Squadron FGA.9 XG154 at Bahrain in November 1963 during Operation Longstop. Having served initially with 43 Squadron and for a brief period with 208 Squadron, XG154 was reallocated to 8 Squadron in February 1963. It formed part of the 8/43 Squadron pool from June 1964 before serving further periods with 8, 43 and 208 Squadrons. It is currently on display at the RAF Museum Hendon (Nick Adamson).

Engine fitters prepare to perform slam checks on 8 Squadron FGA.9 XG237 at Khormaksar in 1963. One of the first ground attack Hunters to be issued to 43 Squadron in 1960, it subsequently saw service with 8 and 208 Squadrons before being sold back to Hawker Siddeley in 1967, having sustained Cat 4 damage (author).

One of two Hunters to participate in the VRET trials in 1958, FGA.9 XK150 was issued to 8 Squadron in January 1960. The aircraft saw further periods of service with 208, 8/43 and 43 Squadrons before being sold back to Hawker Siddeley in 1967 for conversion to FGA.73A standard for the Royal Jordanian Air Force. The photograph was taken during the 8 Squadron detachment to Southern Rhodesia in July 1960 (author's collection).

43 Squadron

Serial	Code	Type	From	To	Comments
XE546	B	FGA.9	28-02-62	01-06-64	To 8/43 Sqn. CO's aircraft
XE546		FGA.9	07-08-67	12-10-67	To 208 Sqn
XE550	C	FGA.9	19-11-61	01-06-64	To 8/43 Sqn
XE550		FGA.9	07-08-67	28-12-67	Sold to Kuwait
XE611	J	FGA.9	07-10-63	01-06-64	Re-coded 'X'. To 8/43 Sqn
XE618		FGA.9	07-08-67	28-12-67	Sold to Kuwait
XE620	R	FGA.9	07-08-67	14-12-67	To 19 MU at St Athan. Sold to HSA
XE623	H	FGA.9	26-06-63	01-06-64	To 8/43 Sqn
XE655	L	FGA.9	28-12-63	01-06-64	To 8/43 Sqn
XF445		FGA.9	07-08-67	17-11-68	To 19 MU for refurbishment
XF456	P	FGA.9	26-06-63	01-06-64	Re-coded 'E' then 'S'. To 8/43 Sqn
XF456	S	FGA.9	07-08-67	10-12-67	To 19 MU for refurbishment
XG136	G	FGA.9	06-05-63	17-04-64	Crashed: pilot killed
XG154		FGA.9	20-06-60	10-06-61	AFME 131 MU at Khormaksar
XG154		FGA.9	07-08-67	01-12-67	To 8 Sqn
XG169		FGA.9	16-09-66	28-11-66	To 208 Squadron
XG255		FGA.9	07-08-67	09-09-67	Donated to Royal Jordanian Air Force
XG256		FGA.9	12-10-67	01-12-67	To 208 Sqn
XG292	H	FGA.9	28-02-62	01-06-64	To the UK for refurbishment
XG296	A	FGA.9	16-12-61	01-06-64	To 8/43 Sqn
XG296		FGA.9	07-08-67	14-12-67	To 19 MU for refurbishment
XG298	E	FGA.9	05-12-61	28-01-64	To 208 Sqn
XG298		FGA.9	07-08-67	09-09-67	Donated to Royal Jordanian Air Force
XJ645	N	FGA.9	07-08-67	10-12-67	To 19 MU for refurbishment
XJ680	F	FGA.9	05-12-61	01-06-64	To 8/43 Sqn
XJ680		FGA.9	07-08-67	14-11-67	To 19 MU for refurbishment
XJ683	L	FGA.9	15-01-62	12-07-63	To the UK for refurbishment
XJ684	D	FGA.9	16-12-61	01-06-64	To 8/43 Sqn
XJ692	K	FGA.9	01-02-62	01-06-64	To 8/43 Sqn
XJ692	T	FGA.9	07-08-67	01-12-67	To 8 Sqn
XK137	P	FGA.9	16-11-61	02-09-63	Category 4/R. To HSA
XL566	T	T.7	15-12-59	02-06-63	To 5 MU for refurbishment

208 Squadron

Serial	Code	Type	From	To	Comments
XE530	A	FGA.9	01–06–62	15–09–64	Re-coded 'A/GL'. To 19 MU for refurbishment
XE532	K	FGA.9	23–11–64	14–11–66	Re-coded 'A'. To 19 MU for refurbishment
XE544	L	FGA.9	28–04–60	04–11–61	To the UK for refurbishment
XE544	L	FGA.9	02–08–62	17–09–62	Category 5. Take-off abandoned; aircraft caught fire
XE546	B	FGA.9	12–10–67	16–12–67	To 19 MU for refurbishment
XE552	D	FGA.9	02–11–61	23–02–64	To 19 MU for refurbishment
XE552	M	FGA.9	18–01–68	18–02–69	To 5 MU for refurbishment
XE552		FGA.9	17–06–71	23–06–71	To 19 MU for refurbishment
XE597	G	FGA.9	07–04–60	12–10–61	To 19 MU for refurbishment
XE607	F	FGA.9	23–03–60	29–03–62	To 8 Sqn
XE609	E	FGA.9	23–06–60	14–06–62	Re-coded 'H'. To 5 MU for refurbishment
XE611	C	FGA.9	29–11–66	18–07–67	To 8/43 Sqn
XE617	K	FGA.9	nn–01–66	07–05–66	Ran out of fuel; crashed on runway at Muharraq
XE618	D	FGA.9	20–02–60	22–11–61	To 19 MU for refurbishment

One of the first two Hunters to enter service with the Middle East Air Force, T.7 XL613 arrived in September 1959 and spent the next twelve years with 8 and 208 Squadrons, and 1417 Flight. It is pictured starting up at Muharraq in December 1963, prior to flying back to Khormaksar at the end of an 8 Squadron detachment (author).

Beginning its service in the ground attack role with 43 Squadron in 1961, FGA.9 XF456 spent a further six years with 43 and 8/43 Squadrons before being return to the UK in December 1967 for reallocation to 229 OCU. The photograph was taken at Masirah in late November 1967 following the Squadron's withdrawal from Aden. Following conversion to FGA.74 standard, it was sold to the Republic of Singapore Air Force in 1971 (author's collection).

Looking rather shabby and minus its drop tanks, FGA.9 XJ692 was pictured to the rear of the pan at Muharraq on 1 January 1964. After a spell with 208 Squadron, the aircraft was sold to Hawker Siddeley in 1968 and converted to F.56A standard for the Indian Air Force (Gordon Macadie).

208 Squadron

Serial	Code	Type	From	To	Comments
XE618	L	FGA.9	02-07-65	18-07-67	To 8/43 Sqn
XE620	H	FGA.9	15-09-66	07-08-67	To 43 Sqn
XE623	C	FGA.9	23-03-60	28-08-62	Re-coded 'B'. To 19 MU for refurbishment
XE643	K	FGA.9	03-05-60	09-12-61	Aborted take-off; to HSA but Category 5
XE645	M	FGA.9	26-11-62	26-06-65	To 19 MU for refurbishment
XE647	O	FGA.9	11-05-60	12-10-61	To 19 MU for refurbishment
XE647	H	FGA.9	01-06-62	30-06-64	Collided with XK139; pilot ejected safely
XE649	S	FGA.9	06-07-67	24-06-69	Re-coded 'J'. To 19 MU for refurbishment
XE649	N	FGA.9	19-02-70	19-07-71	To 5 MU for refurbishment
XE650	A	FGA.9	18-10-70	17-06-71	To 8 Sqn
XE654	J	FGA.9	28-05-64	11-07-66	To 19 MU for refurbishment
XF376	J	FGA.9	07-04-60	31-01-61	To 8 Sqn
XF376	M	FGA.9	19-09-61	05-04-63	Re-coded 'P'. To 5 MU for refurbishment
XF376	H	FGA.9	07-08-67	21-01-69	To 19 MU for refurbishment
XF388	B	FGA.9	24-10-61	23-02-64	To 19 MU for refurbishment
XF421	H	FGA.9	07-04-60	04-11-61	To 19 MU for refurbishment
XF431	L	FGA.9	17-10-62	26-06-65	To 19 MU for refurbishment
XF431	M	FGA.9	30-05-69	07-12-71	To 5 MU for refurbishment
XF435	G	FGA.9	27-01-69	06-10-70	To 5 MU for refurbishment
XF445	O	FGA.9	28-08-62	28-02-63	To 8 Sqn
XF445		FGA.9	18-05-67	17-11-68	To 19 MU for refurbishment
XF445	A	FGA.9	28-06-69	18-05-71	To 5 MU for refurbishment
XF454	F	FGA.9	29-11-61	25-01-64	To 5 MU for refurbishment
XF462	C	FGA.9	24-10-61	23-02-64	To 5 MU for refurbishment
XF462	C	FGA.9	19-08-64	14-11-66	To 19 MU for refurbishment
XF511	F	FGA.9	07-06-66	nn-08-67	8 Sqn
XF511	H	FGA.9	nn-nn-69	nn-09-71	To 5 MU for refurbishment
XF519	C	FGA.9	nn-nn-69	nn-09-71	To UK for refurbishment
XG130	C	FGA.9	04-11-69	01-07-70	To 5 MU for refurbishment
XG134	A	FGA.9	22-03-60	11-07-61	Crashed: pilot killed
XG135	A	FGA.9	19-05-67	24-06-69	To 19 MU for refurbishment
XG154	V	FGA.9	05-05-62	28-05-62	To 19 MU for refurbishment
XG154	J	FGA.9	17-08-66	30-05-67	To 8/43 Sqn
XG154	L	FGA.9	06-08-69	19-01-71	To 19 MU for refurbishment
XG169	B	FGA.9	24-01-64	16-02-66	To 19 MU for refurbishment
XG169	K	FGA.9	29-11-66	16-01-68	To 19 MU for refurbishment
XG195	K	FGA.9	16-03-70	20-01-71	To 19 MU for refurbishment

Serial	Code	Type	From	To	Comments
XG205	K	FGA.9	20-01-68	01-04-70	Sold to HSA
XG237		FGA.9	17-06-60	09-12-61	To 19 MU for refurbishment
XG237	D	FGA.9	17-08-66	25-02-67	Category 4. Sold to HSA
XG255	E	FGA.9	02-02-65	18-05-67	To 8/43 Sqn
XG256	B	FGA.9	01-08-66	12-10-67	To 8 Sqn
XG256		FGA.9	01-12-67	08-02-68	To 8 Sqn
XG256		FGA.9	17-06-71	21-06-71	To 19 MU for refurbishment
XG261	L	FGA.9	05-07-67	21-07-69	To 19 MU for refurbishment
XG292	M	FGA.9	02-07-65	09-10-67	To 19 MU for refurbishment
XG298	E	FGA.9	29-01-64	15-09-64	To 19 MU for refurbishment
XJ632	K	FGA.9	22-03-62	31-03-64	To 5 MU for refurbishment
XJ632	B	FGA.9	21-11-67	22-09-69	Sold to HSA

The oldest F.6 converted to FGA.9 standard, XE530 was pictured at Muharraq on 26 February 1964 in 208 Squadron markings. OC Gordon Lewis's initials can be seen on the fin and a Kenya independence 'zap' covers the Sphynx on the pennant. Following accident damage sustained while in service with 8/43 Squadron, the aircraft was sold to Hawker Siddeley for rebuild and conversion to T.67 standard for the Kuwait Air Force (Gordon Macadie).

A relatively short-term resident with the RAF in the Middle East, FGA.9 XE645 and a further two MEC FGA.9s were gifted to the Royal Jordanian Air Force in 1967 to make up for losses sustained in the six-day war. In earlier times, it saw service with 208 Squadron, in whose markings it is seen at Muharraq on 26 February 1964, and with 8/43 Squadron (Gordon Macadie).

After four years with 54 Squadron in the UK, FGA.9 XG261 was reallocated in 1964 to 8/43 Squadron at Khormaksar. Two years later, following refurbishment, it was issued to 208 Squadron at Muharraq and was photographed in 1968 during an APC at Sharjah (author's collection).

208 Squadron

Serial	Code	Type	From	To	Comments
XJ636	F	FGA.9	21-09-67	20-10-69	To 19 MU for refurbishment
XJ636	K	FGA.9	15-07-71	14-09-71	To 5 MU for refurbishment
XJ643	M	FGA.9	26-04-60	22-11-61	To 19 MU for refurbishment
XJ645	A	FGA.9	03-06-66	07-08-67	To 43 Sqn
XJ687	B	FGA.9	23-03-60	26-05-62	Re-coded 'G' then to 8 Sqn
XJ687	B	FGA.9	25-11-63	09-05-66	Re-coded 'F'. To 19 MU for refurbishment
XJ687	E	FGA.9	23-11-66	17-11-68	To 19 MU for refurbishment
XJ687	J	FGA.9	28-06-69	07-06-71	To 19 MU for refurbishment
XJ688	G	FGA.9	22-03-62	26-03-65	To 19 MU for refurbishment
XJ688		FGA.9	27-09-67	06-11-67	To 8 Sqn
XJ688	E	FGA.9	06-12-68	15-05-71	To 8 Sqn
XJ691	G	FGA.9	02-02-65	27-04-67	Category 5. SOC
XK137	F	FGA.9	30-11-69	19-01-71	To 19 MU for refurbishment
XK139	J	FGA.9	27-11-61	30-06-64	Collided with XE647; pilot ejected safely
XK140	E	FGA.9	02-11-61	05-02-64	To 19 MU for refurbishment
XK140	H	FGA.9	19-08-64	02-08-66	To 19 MU for refurbishment
XK140	D	FGA.9	19-05-67	11-08-69	To 19 MU for refurbishment
XK150	B	FGA.9	20-02-64	11-07-66	To 19 MU for refurbishment
XK151	D	FGA.9	20-02-64	02-08-66	To 19 MU for refurbishment
XK151	D	FGA.9	11-09-69	17-06-71	8 Sqn
XL565	Y	T.7	01-08-64	26-03-65	To 19 MU for refurbishment
XL566	Y	T.7	29-04-67	nn-nn-67	To 19 MU for refurbishment
XL566	Z	T.7	nn-01-68	20-01-71	To 19 MU for refurbishment
XL597	N	T.7	12-12-60	25-06-63	To 1417 Flt
XL597	W	T.7	02-02-65	10-04-67	Re-coded 'Y'. To 19 MU for refurbishment
XL613	Z	T.7	01-06-60	29-11-60	To 8 Sqn
XL613	Z	T.7	30-07-66	06-12-68	To 19 MU for refurbishment

Opposite: Another long-serving member of the Middle East strike force, XJ687 was one of the first batch of FGA.9s to join 208 Squadron at Eastleigh in 1960 and, apart from a brief spell with 8 Squadron, remained with 208 Squadron until 1971. In the photograph taken at Sharjah in 1968, the dark blue stripe on the drop tank confirms that the baffle modification, to control the movement of fuel during high 'g' manoeuvres, had been applied (author's collection).

1417 Flight

Serial	Code	Type	From	To	Comments
XE589	JM	FR.10	26-04-63	26-03-64	To 5 MU for refurbishment
XE589	RC	FR.10	09-01-65	09-05-66	Category 4/R. Sold to HSA
XE599	JD	FR.10	26-04-63	01-11-63	To 19 MU for refurbishment
XE599	RJ	FR.10	03-06-64	08-09-67	Re-coded, 'GC', 'DW'. To 8 Sqn
XE614	PL	FR.10	26-04-63	22-01-65	Re-coded 'GC'. To 19 MU for refurbishment
XE614	GC	FR.10	12-08-65	08-09-67	Re-coded 'RJ'. To 8 Sqn
XF429	PN	FR.10	14-03-67	08-09-67	Prototype FR.10. Re-coded 'KS'. To 8 Sqn
XF436	SB	FR.10	26-04-63	15-07-63	Re-coded 'RP'. To 19 MU for refurbishment
XF436	JM	FR.10	17-04-64	17-02-67	Re-coded 'RP', 'PN'. To 19 MU for refurbishment
XF441	JD	FR.10	20-12-63	25-08-65	Re-coded 'FG'. To 19 MU for refurbishment
XF460	AR	FR.10	16-06-63	21-03-66	Re-coded 'GT'. To 19 MU for refurbishment
XF460	RB	FR.10	26-10-66	08-09-67	Re-coded 'DB'. To 8 Sqn
XF321	TZ	T.7	12-08-65	08-09-67	To 8 Sqn.
XL565	Y	T.7	25-06-63	01-08-64	To 208 Sqn
XL565	TX	T.7	26-04-66	08-09-67	Re-coded 'TW'. To 8 Sqn
XL566	TW	T.7	07-04-64	29-04-67	Re-coded 'TX'. To 208 Sqn
XL597	W	T.7	25-06-63	30-05-64	To the UK for refurbishment
XL612	X	T.7	20-08-63	01-05-66	Re-coded 'TX'. To the UK for refurbishment
XL612	TY	T.7	18-05-67	08-09-67	To 8 Sqn

First allocated to the A&AEE in 1958, T.7 XL566 was used for tropical trials in Bahrain before release for service with 43 Squadron, still painted in the all-over silver training livery of the period. Following refurbishment it returned to Aden in 1964 for a three-year spell with 1417 Flight. A return to Bahrain then beckoned and three more years with 208 Squadron in whose markings it is seen at Sharjah in 1968 (author's collection).

Apart from an interim period of four years with 1417 Flight, XF460 was one of four FR.10s to serve with 8 Squadron between 1961 and the type's withdrawal in September 1971. It is pictured during a detachment to Masirah in June 1965 bearing the unit's flash on the nose and pilot's initials in light blue on the fin. Following withdrawal it was sold to Hawker Siddeley and converted to FR.74B standard for the Republic of Singapore Air Force (Aviation Bookshop).

1417 Flight

Serial	Code	Type	From	To	Comments
XL613	Z	T.7	26-04-63	25-06-63	To 8 Sqn
XL613	TZ	T.7	29-10-63	28-10-65	To 19 MU for refurbishment

From 1 June 1964 until 7 August 1967, all FGA.9s allocated to 8 and 43 Squadrons were combined to form a joint unit; 8/43 Squadron. Number 8 Squadron markings were applied to a position forward of the fuselage roundels and those of 43 Squadron to the rear of the roundels. Wingtips and tailcodes were painted white.

8/43 Squadron

Serial	Code	Type	From	To	Comments
XE530	O	FGA.9	20-02-65	15-02-67	To HSA Category 4
XE546	B	FGA.9	01-06-64	23-02-65	To 19 MU for refurbishment
XE546	L	FGA.9	08-10-65	07-08-67	To 43 Sqn
XE550	C	FGA.9	01-06-64	24-05-65	To 19 MU for refurbishment
XE550	X	FGA.9	16-12-65	07-08-67	To 43 Sqn
XE552		FGA.9	08-11-64	17-02-67	To 19 MU for refurbishment
XE592	F	FGA.9	01-06-64	16-10-64	Crashed: pilot killed
XE609	A	FGA.9	01-06-64	30-06-65	To 19 MU for refurbishment
XE609	S	FGA.9	03-02-66	05-04-66	Category 5; SOC
XE611	J	FGA.9	01-06-64	29-01-66	To 19 MU for refurbishment
XE611		FGA.9	16-09-66	29-11-66	To 208 Sqn
XE611		FGA.9	18-07-67	07-08-67	To 8 Sqn
XE618	D	FGA.9	01-06-64	03-11-64	To 19 MU for refurbishment
XE618		FGA.9	18-07-67	07-08-67	To 43 Sqn
XE620	B	FGA.9	01-06-64	29-01-66	To 19 MU for refurbishment
XE620		FGA.9	15-08-66	07-08-67	To 43 Sqn
XE623	V	FGA.9	01-06-64	11-08-64	Crashed: pilot ejected safely
XE645		FGA.9	25-02-66	09-09-67	Donated to Royal Jordanian Air Force
XE649	R	FGA.9	16-12-64	25-10-66	To 19 MU for refurbishment
XE654		FGA.9	28-03-67	07-08-67	To 8 Sqn
XE655	L	FGA.9	01-06-64	11-06-66	To 19 MU for refurbishment
XE655		FGA.9	23-03-67	07-08-67	To 8 Sqn
XF376	K	FGA.9	01-06-64	31-03-66	To 19 MU for refurbishment
XF376		FGA.9	23-11-66	07-08-67	To 208 Sqn
XF388		FGA.9	08-11-64	18-07-67	To 19 MU for refurbishment
XF421	C	FGA.9	01-06-64	17-01-65	To 19 MU for refurbishment

Serial	Code	Type	From	To	Comments
XF421		FGA.9	09-10-65	23-02-67	Category 5. SOC
XF431		FGA.9	25-02-66	07-08-67	To 8 Sqn
XF435	J	FGA.9	01-06-64	21-05-65	To 19 MU for refurbishment
XF435	H	FGA.9	03-02-66	07-08-67	To 8 Sqn
XF440	L	FGA.9	01-06-64	25-08-65	To 19 MU for refurbishment
XF440		FGA.9	25-04-66	20-02-67	Crashed. Believed shot down; pilot ejected safely
XF445	Q	FGA.9	01-06-64	21-02-66	To 19 MU for refurbishment
XF445		FGA.9	26-10-66	18-05-67	To 208 Sqn
XF454		FGA.9	06-08-64	27-06-66	To 19 MU for refurbishment
XF454		FGA.9	18-03-67	07-08-67	To 8 Sqn
XF456	P	FGA.9	01-06-64	27-10-65	To 19 MU for refurbishment
XF456		FGA.9	26-04-66	07-08-67	To 43 Sqn
XG135		FGA.9	06-08-64	03-09-66	To 19 MU for refurbishment
XG154	E	FGA.9	01-06-64	16-12-65	To 19 MU for refurbishment
XG154		FGA.9	30-05-67	07-08-67	To 43 Sqn
XG169		FGA.9	16-09-66	29-11-66	To 208 Sqn
XG205		FGA.9	01-09-64	26-10-66	To 19 MU for refurbishment
XG237	M	FGA.9	01-06-64	10-12-65	To 19 MU for refurbishment
XG255		FGA.9	18-05-67	07-08-67	To 43 Sqn
XG256	H	FGA.9	01-06-64	10-12-65	To 19 MU for refurbishment
XG256		FGA.9	30-07-66	07-08-67	To 8 Sqn
XG261		FGA.9	01-09-64	02-09-66	To 19 MU for refurbishment
XG292	H	FGA.9	01-06-64	11-08-64	To 5 MU for refurbishment
XG296	A	FGA.9	01-06-64	27-05-65	To 19 MU for refurbishment
XG296	B	FGA.9	16-12-65	07-08-67	To 43 Sqn
XG298	J	FGA.9	01-06-65	07-08-67	To 43 Sqn
XJ632	C	FGA.9	14-12-64	18-04-67	To 19 MU for refurbishment
XJ645	N	FGA.9	02-02-66	07-08-67	To 43 Sqn
XJ646		FGA.9	13-10-65	07-08-67	To 8 Sqn
XJ680	F	FGA.9	01-06-64	24-02-65	To 19 MU for refurbishment
XJ680	E	FGA.9	06-11-65	07-08-67	To 43 Sqn
XJ684	D	FGA.9	01-06-64	01-11-64	To 19 MU for refurbishment
XJ684		FGA.9	01-06-65	28-07-67	To 19 MU for refurbishment
XJ687		FGA.9	23-11-66	05-08-67	To 208 Sqn
XJ688		FGA.9	06-11-65	07-08-67	To 8 Sqn
XJ689		FGA.9	09-01-65	07-08-67	To 8 Sqn
XJ692	K	FGA.9	01-06-64	06-08-64	To 19 MU for refurbishment
XJ692		FGA.9	20-02-65	07-08-67	To 43 Sqn
XK150		FGA.9	17-04-67	29-11-67	To UK. Sold to Royal Jordanian Air Force
XK151		FGA.9	17-04-67	07-08-67	To 8 Sqn

Following service with 402 WTS in Germany, T.7 XL612 was issued to 1417 Flight in Aden and photographed at Muharraq in October 1963 while on detachment with 8 Squadron. After many years subsequent service with the RAE, A&AEE and ETPS, it gained the distinction in August 2001 of being the last Hunter to operate in RAF service (Gordon Macadie).

South Arabian Air Force

Having arrived in Aden in early 1966, Squadron Leader John Severne was assigned as 'Ops 2' in HQ Middle East Command. Approximately twelve months later, he was appointed Air Adviser to the South Arabian government and instructed to form a fledgeling South Arabian Air Force (SAAF) to take over from the RAF at the time of independence. The new force would consist of a balance of transport, communications, helicopters and ground-attack aircraft, the cost not to exceed a budget of £2 million.

The MoD contracted Airwork Services Ltd to source and provide a suitable range of aircraft and to recruit suitable pilots and civilian engineers. As the DC-3 had proven ideal for rough up-country transport work for many years with Aden Airways, the Crown Agents purchased four fully-refurbished examples for £25,000 each on behalf of the British government. It was hoped to purchase Alouette helicopters from France but, as all purchases had to be in sterling, the only alternative was the Westland-Bell 47 Sioux, six of which were purchased. Another aircraft that had performed well in up-country Aden was the Army Air Corps de Havilland Canada Beaver, and six brand-new examples were purchased for the SAAF.

An initial proposal to fulfil the strike requirement was for the transfer of the four Hunter FR.10s from 8 Squadron to the SAAF at the time of the RAF's departure from Khormaksar. This was revoked as soon as it was realised that a fighter-recce element would still be needed in the Middle East. As the preferred alternative, the BAC Strikemaster, was still at the prototype stage of development, four former RAF Jet Provost T.Mk.4s (XS223/4/7/8) were acquired and converted to T.Mk.52 standard by BAC.

Squadron Leader Severne was also responsible for approving the design of the aircraft markings and uniforms for the personnel. Wing Commander Barry Atkinson MBE DFC RAF was seconded as the commanding officer and Airwork Services was contracted to maintain the aircraft. The total force of 149 personnel included thirty-three local nationals. Eighteen pilots were contracted to the South Arabian government, fifteen of them ex-RAF under the command of Squadron Leader 'Rags' Barlow, a former RAF navigator who had taken early retirement.

With serial numbers 101-104, the Jet Provosts were shipped out to Aden in crates during August 1967 and re-assembled in the following October. Flight testing commenced as and when each aircraft was ready.

On 30 November, the day after the British withdrawal, the South Arabian Federation was renamed The People's Democratic Republic of Yemen, although this was usually

Formerly T.4 XS223 with the RAF, the fuselage and wings of PDRYAF Jet Provost T.52 101 were perched on trestles for the aircraft's reassembly at Khormaksar in October 1967 (John Severne).

PDRYAF Beaver number 301, the first of a batch of six new aircraft, stands on the pan at Khormaksar in late 1967 (author's collection).

abbreviated to South Yemen. The newly-formed air force was renamed the People's Democratic Republic of Yemen Air Force (PDRYAF), the aircraft markings painted over and new ones applied.

Relations between the British contingent and the new government were poor from the start and deteriorated rapidly over the next few months. Matters came to a head when the South Yemen defence minister flew to Moscow and made a speech in which he accused British members of the PDRYAF of spying. The British government had initially instructed the South Yemen government that SAAF aircraft must not fly outside the country's borders in case they came into conflict with British pilots flying combat missions on contract for the Saudi Arabian Air Force. The South Yemen government was incensed at what it described as British interference in its internal affairs. On his return the defence minister called all British personnel to a meeting on 27 February 1968. They were informed that their services were no longer required and, under armed guard, were given an hour to collect their families and belongings and report to the airport to await the next flight out of the country.

The remaining employees under contract to Airwork were unaffected by the dismissal of British personnel. New staff were recruited to replace them, including pilots from other European countries. When the Airwork contract expired in 1970 its employees were replaced by workers from the Soviet Union and Eastern Bloc countries.

PDRYAF T.52 101 bears the special markings designed by John Severne for the new air force as it undertakes an early familiarisation flight over South Arabia (John Severne).

Glossary

AA	Anti-aircraft (artillery)		C-in-C	Commander-in-Chief
AAC	Army Air Corps		CO	Commanding Officer
AC	Army Co-operation		COC	Combat Operations Centre
ADDF	Abu Dhabi Defence Force		CRE	Central Reconnaissance
ADF	Automatic Direction Finder			Establishment
AFME	Air Force Middle East		DFCS	Day Fighter Combat School
AOC	Air Officer Commanding		DFGA	Day Fighter Ground Attack
AOG	Aircraft On Ground		DME	Distance Measuring
	(awaiting spares)			Equipment
APC	Armament Practice Camp		DZ	Drop Zone
APL	Aden Protectorate Levies		EAP	Eastern Aden Protectorate
APRF	Arabian Peninsular		ECM	Electronic Countermeasures
	Reconnaissance Flight		EO	Engineering Officer
ArDet	Argosy Detachment		FAC	Forward Air Controller
ARR	Airborne Radio Relay		FASOC	Forward Air Support
ASF	Aircraft Servicing Flight			Operations Centre
ASP	Aircraft Servicing Pan		FAW	Fighter All Weather
ASOC	Air Support Operations		FB	Fighter Bomber
	Centre		FGA	Fighter Ground Attack
BASO	Brigade Air Support Officer		FLOSY	Front for the Liberation of
BASOC	Brigade Air Support			Occupied South Yemen
	Operations Centre		FNG	Federal National Guard
BDA	Battle Damage Assessment		FOD	Foreign Object Damage
BFAP	British Forces Arabian		FR	Fighter Reconnaissance
	Peninsula		RM	Royal Marines
BFBS	British Forces Broadcasting		RN	Royal Navy
	Service		RNAS	Royal Naval Air Service
CAP	Combat Air Patrol		RNAS	Royal Naval Air Station
CAS	Chief of the Air Staff		RP	Rocket Projectile
Cat	Category		RRAF	Royal Rhodesian Air Force
CFE	Central Fighter		RSO	Range Safety Officer
	Establishment		SAA	South Arabian Army
CFS	Central Flying School		SAAF	South Arabian Air Force

SADA	Shallow Angle Dive Attack		MU	Maintenance Unit
SAP	Semi-Armour Piercing		NCO	Non-Commissioned Officer
SAR	Search and Rescue		NATO	North Atlantic Treaty
SAS	Special Air Service			Organisation
SASO	Senior Air Staff Officer		NLA	National Liberation Army
SNCO	Senior Non-Commissioned		NLF	National Liberation Front
	Officer		nm	Nautical Miles
SOAF	Sultan of Oman's Air Force		OC	Officer Commanding
SOP	Standing Operating		OCU	Operational Conversion Unit
	Procedures		ORB	Operations Record Book
FRA	Federal Regular Army		OSW	Offensive Support Wing
GCA	Ground Control Approach		PAF	Pakistan Air Force
GCI	Ground Control Interception		PAI	Pilot Attack Instructor
GGS	Gyro Gunsight		PI	Photographic Interpreter
GLO	Ground Liaison Officer		PIU	Photographic Intelligence
GOC	General Officer			Unit
	Commanding		PR	Photographic Reconnaissance
GLS	Ground Liaison Section		QFI	Qualified Flying Instructor
HAL	Hawker Aircraft Ltd		QGH	Controlled Approach
HBL	Hadramaut Bedouin Legion			Through Cloud
HMG	Her Majesty's Government		RFC	Royal Flying Corps
HQPG	Headquarters Persian Gulf		SOC	Struck off Charge
HE	High Explosive		Taceval	Tactical Evaluation
IAS	Indicated Air Speed		TacOps	Tactical Operations
IFF	Identification Friend or Foe		TacWing	Tactical Wing
IFR	Instrument Flight Rules		TOC	Tactical Operations Centre
IP	Initial Point		TOS	Trucial Oman Scouts
IRE	Instrument Rating Examiner		TOT	Time on Target
IS	Internal Security		TRS	Tactical Reconnaissance
JHQ	Joint Headquarters			Squadron
Kts	Knots		UAR	United Arab Republic
LAA	Light Anti-Aircraft (artillery)		UHF	Ultra High Frequency
LFA	Low Flying Area		USAF	United States Air Force
MEAF	Middle East Air Force		VFR	Visual Flight Rules
MEC	Middle East Command		VHF	Very High Frequency
MFPU	Mobile Field Processing Unit		VISREP	Visual Report
MISREP	Mission Report		VRET	Venom Replacement
Mod	Modification			Evaluation Trial
MR	Maritime Reconnaissance		WAP	Western Aden Protectorate

Bibliography

This section lists titles of books that were referenced while researching the history of Hunter operations in the Middle East.

Bain, Chris, *Cold War, Hot Wings*, (Pen & Sword Books Ltd, Barnsley, 2007)

Beedle, Jimmy, *43 Squadron – Fighting Cocks* (Beaumont Aviation Literature, 1985)

Haig-Thomas, Tony, *Fall out Roman Catholics and Jews* (Old Forge Publishing, 2008)

Lee, ACM Sir David, *Flight from the Middle East* (HM Stationery Office, 1980)

Pyke, Richard, *Hunter Boys* (Grub Street, 2014)

Richards, Peter, *Return to Aden* (Self published, 2004)

Severne, Sir John, *Silvered Wings* (Pen & Sword Books Ltd, Barnsley, 2007)

Walpole, Nigel, *Best of Breed* (Pen & Sword Books Ltd, Barnsley, 2006)

Williams, Graham, *Rhapsody in Blue* (Fonthill Media Ltd, 2016)

Index